The Battle of Ulundi
4 July 1879

The Battle of Ulundi
4 July 1879

And the Death of the
Zulu King Cetshwayo

Adrian Greaves

Pen & Sword
MILITARY

First published in Great Britain in 2026 by
Pen & Sword Military
An imprint of Pen & Sword Books Limited
Yorkshire – Philadelphia

ISBN 978 1 03614 179 0

A CIP catalogue record for this book is
available from the British Library.

Typeset by Mac Style
Printed in the UK by CPI Group (UK) Ltd, Croydon, CR0 4YY.

The Publisher's authorised representative in the EU for product
safety is Authorised Rep Compliance Ltd., Ground Floor,
71 Lower Baggot Street, Dublin D02 P593, Ireland.
www.arccompliance.com

For a complete list of Pen & Sword titles please contact:

PEN & SWORD BOOKS LIMITED
47 Church Street, Barnsley, South Yorkshire, S70 2AS, England
E-mail: enquiries@pen-and-sword.co.uk
Website: www.pen-and-sword.co.uk
or
PEN AND SWORD BOOKS
1950 Lawrence Road, Havertown, PA 19083, USA
E-mail: uspen-and-sword@casematepublishers.com
Website: www.penandswordbooks.com

Contents

Introduction

During the sixty-four-year reign of Queen Victoria the British Army, with its ubiquitous, red-jacketed soldiers, had fought in sixty-three campaigns throughout the British Empire. Before the first months of 1879 British military defeat was virtually unknown to the English-speaking world – until the siege in Zululand of the invading British coastal column by the Zulus at Eshowe. This ignominy was swiftly followed by a succession of disastrous and far-reaching British defeats across Zululand inflicted by the Zulus at the Battles of Isandlwana, Ntombe Drift and Hlobane. The Zulu War thereafter dominated the attention of the home government, its army, the press and public disquiet.

In a determined endeavour to salve the nation's prestige, British regiments were mobilized throughout the country and across the Empire and dispatched to Zululand to help the fight against Britain's former ally, King Cetshwayo and his most ferocious and feared Zulu army. Meanwhile, further political disaster followed with the careless death of the heir to the Napoleonic dynasty, Louis Napoleon, the Prince Imperial. The young prince had volunteered to fight with the British in Zululand, only to be killed by a Zulu scouting party. Britain had to act: her reputation of invincibility was beginning to slip away.

During June 1879 Chelmsford's reconstituted invasion columns began their approach from Durban towards the Zulu capital at Ulundi. It was a battle the British had to win.

Chapter 1

The Second Invasion of Zululand, 21 April–3 June 1879

Timescale of Main Events of the Anglo–Zulu War:

3 October 1878	The British fail in an attack against King Sekhukhune's baPedi people
22 Dec–3 Jan 1879	The British move from their Helpmekaar base to Rorke's Drift
11–12 January 1879	The British advance from Rorke's Drift to Isandlwana
16–22 January 1879	The Zulu Army advance from Ulundi
21–22 January 1879	The First Battle of Hlobane
22 January 1879	The Battle of Isandlwana
22 January 1879	Fugitives' Drift becomes the Isandlwana survivors' route
22 January 1879	Rorke's Drift
22 January 1879	The Battle of Nyezane
January 1879	The establishment of Forts Pearson and Tenedos
23 Jan–4 April 1879	Fort Eshowe and the seventy-two-day siege
28 March 1879	The Second Battle of Hlobane
29 March 1879	The Battle of Khambula
2 April 1879	The Battle of Gingindlovu and relief of Eshowe
1 June 1879	The death of the Prince Imperial of France
3 July 1879	Lord Chelmsford's advance on Ulundi
4 July 1879	The Battle of Ulundi
5 July 1879 onwards	The British withdrawal from Zululand
28 November 1879	The second British expedition against King Sekhukhune
December 1880	The Boer attack on the British column, Bronkhorstspruit
8 February 1884	The death of King Cetshwayo

2   The Battle of Ulundi, 4 July 1879

'Too many cooks spoil the pudding'.[1]

For 22 years the relationship between Britain's government in Natal and the Zulus had been friendly. That was, arguably, in no small part due to a strong friendship, spanning over a decade, between Somtseu (the name given by the Zulus to John Wesley Shepstone, Natal's Acting Secretary for Native Affairs) and King Cetshwayo, although Shepstone did treat the Zulus in a patronising manner. Moreover, Shepstone was on record for supporting the Zulus' claim to a stretch of territory on the border between the Transvaal and Zululand that had been disputed by the Boers and Zulus since Mpande, Cetshwayo's father, had reigned. However, Shepstone's support for this claim changed with the annexation of the Transvaal in 1877, part of a wider scheme to unify South Africa under British rule. Cetshwayo naively welcomed the successful British annexation of the Transvaal:

> I am glad to know the Transvaal is English ground; perhaps now there may be rest.[2]

On 11 December 1878, five large columns of well-trained and seasoned British troops invaded Zululand, a small independent country in Southern Africa whose autocratic leader, King Cetshwayo, had hitherto been no worse than indifferent towards his country's immediate neighbour, British Natal. The main invasion column, the Centre or No. 3 Column, consisted of some 4,700 men led by the British military commander in South Africa, Lord Chelmsford, an experienced and seasoned general with recent experience of suppressing local native insurrections in the Cape region.

Chelmsford and his local political master, Sir Bartle Frere, both saw the invasion of Zululand as a military adventure and an opportunity to enhance their pre-retirement reputations. They proclaimed their action was necessary to prevent an invasion of British Natal by the Zulus; but there was no such threat as the Zulus had never displayed any capability or wish to invade Natal – the British claim was a fabrication. Indeed, the Zulu king, Cetshwayo, always maintained that he never discovered the real reason for the British invasion of his peaceful country. Chelmsford's invasion force was made up of the finest British units in South Africa and was equipped with modern artillery, mounted troops and the latest Martini-Henry rifles. The invasion was expected to be swift and simple; after all, this invading force was battle-hardened and rated among the best in the British Empire, while the Zulu army's battle experience was limited to a handful of elderly chiefs. The experience of the Zulu army was based solely on two weeks' 'national service' each year, the *umKhosi*; its warriors presenting themselves for review by the king armed with nothing more than their traditional assegai stabbing spears and a limited collection of ancient muskets obtained from Arab dealers in Mozambique.

However, on 22 January 1879, and after crossing the Buffalo River border with Zululand less than two weeks later, this elite British force suffered a humiliating defeat at the Battle of Isandlwana. In less than one hour the main British camp was surrounded and attacked. Its 1,500 soldiers and civilian auxiliaries were swiftly overpowered and annihilated almost to a man by the inexperienced and ill-equipped Zulu army which had not seen action for twenty-three years. The location was a barren and desolate rocky outcrop known as Isandlwana, just ten miles into Zululand. It was an inglorious disaster which shook the British military establishment to its core, leaving Britain's world-wide reputation as a mighty military and invincible force in tatters.

On 11 February 1879 the news of the crushing defeat of British troops at Isandlwana on 22 January reached London via the Madeira cable. The unsettling report stunned the political and military establishments who, in the following weeks, rushed to formulate a suitable explanatory response. Almost immediately investigations into the disaster coupled with accusations of responsibility and blame became the main focus for the institutions of the day.

It also set into motion the journalistic establishment, which clamoured for more information to assuage the appetite for explanations for their news-hungry public into this massacre on a faraway battlefield in Zululand – which most readers had never heard of. This unexpected war was set to dominate front-page material for the foreseeable future.

Lord Chelmsford and his invasion columns had unwisely anticipated an early and easy victory over the Zulu army. His officers and most of his troops were already experienced in African warfare and Chelmsford's main fear was that the Zulus would not fight, or that his campaign would deteriorate into a series of 'hit and run' skirmishes similar to those he had recently experienced in the recent Eastern Cape Colony frontier skirmishes against the indigenous amaXhosa people.

Generally speaking, South Africa was rough fighting country, both for infantry and mounted troops. Tactics were simple and proven. The infantry would normally engage the enemy first by volley fire and then the mounted troops would charge, putting the enemy to rout. For his reinvasion Chelmsford ordered that, in the unlikely event that the Zulus would appear in any number, the troops would form a square or entrench their position to draw the Zulus into the range of their overwhelming rifle and cannon firepower. In Chelmsford's considerable experience, well-aimed rifle volley fire by calm and experienced troops supported by rockets, artillery and Gatling guns would ensure the defeat of the Zulu army. This tactic had not been used at Isandlwana as the main Zulu attack against the unprepared British camp had not been expected.

In the few months between Chelmsford's defeat at Isandlwana and final victory at Ulundi, a number of fierce battles were fought. This book focuses on the British actions following their victory at Khambula on 29 March and their rebuilding of the invasion columns to finally attack the Zulu capital on 4 July and defeat its army and king at Ulundi.

King Cetshwayo's principal royal homestead was known by the Zulus as oNdini, by the British as Ulundi, from the common root 'undi'. By modern convention, the capital and final battle is generally referred to as Ulundi. At the time the Zulus knew the battle by different names – either kwaNodwengu (from the royal homestead standing nearest the British square) or oCwecweni ('the sheet-iron fort', from a belief, inspired by the sun glinting on British bayonets, that the square was protected by corrugated iron).

Following the British victory at the Battle of Khambula, the Zulu's resolve and capacity to mount a serious offensive against the British was already fractured. At the opposite coastal end of the country, the Zulus had also been rebuffed at Gingindlovu. Their total casualties since Isandlwana now numbered over 5,000 dead with countless numbers wounded and no supporting medical facilities. All the strategic advantages that King

Cetshwayo had won at Isandlwana were irretrievably lost and the tide of war began to turn decisively against him. The king desperately tried to re-open diplomatic contacts with the British in a final attempt to discover what terms they would accept for peace, but both Chelmsford and Sir Bartle Frere needed to re-establish their damaged reputations and only a decisive military victory to avenge Isandlwana would suffice.

With his campaign in tatters after the shattering defeat at Isandlwana, Chelmsford was determined to defeat Cetshwayo without risking further humiliation. To this end he began to assemble the largest field force that Britain had sent against an enemy since the Crimean War of 1856. A total of 23,500 reinforcements of largely inexperienced British troops from England were to be pitted against the remnants of the once-invincible Zulu army, whose numbers had dwindled to below a demoralised 20,000. As Archbishop Colenso pointed out: 'the Zulus were merely an armed people, not a standing army'.[3]

During the aftermath of Isandlwana there was an impression amongst the British soldiers scattered along the Natal border that very little was being done. In fact, five days after the battle Chelmsford had sent an urgent telegram to the War Office requesting immediate reinforcements specifying at least three infantry and two cavalry regiments and another company of engineers. Significantly, he followed this telegram with a report to the Duke of Cambridge in which he clearly suggests a successor for both himself and Sir Bartle Frere:

> Might I suggest to Your Royal Highness the advisability of sending out a Major General who will be competent to succeed me not only as Commanding the Forces, but also as Lieutenant Governor & High Commissioner should anything happen to Sir B. Frere.

Once he had recovered his composure and become focused on the second invasion, Chelmsford appears to have completely forgotten the report. Conversely, and still in England, Sir Garnet Wolseley recognised the career opportunity and, eager for a field command, volunteered his services within days of learning of the Isandlwana defeat.

The result of these hasty missives was that reinforcements were rushed to South Africa and Wolseley was appointed to take over from both Chelmsford and Frere but, due to the slowness of communications and unreliable transport, the new Commander would arrive after the Battle of Ulundi and too late to deny Chelmsford his moment of glory. Chelmsford had learned much from his previous mistakes during the disastrous first invasion of January that year. Whereas his original columns were weak and failed to take proper precautions on the march, he planned for his new columns to be powerful and overwhelming. With pressure upon him, Chelmsford set about preparing for the second invasion. Meanwhile, two matters needed urgent attention: the relief of Pearson's besieged command at Eshowe and the burial of the dead at Isandlwana. The latter task also included the recovery of all serviceable wagons from the wrecked camp as there were insufficient numbers of draught animals and wagons to sustain another invasion. There was also a shortage of transport officers, and this led to another influx of special service officers, all with little or no experience in transport matters but anxious to be involved in a campaign that had the potential for career advancement.[4]

Slowly, and with some difficulty, the camps of fresh replacement regiments began to assemble in Northern Natal, together with the huge transport parks and storage depots, until all were finally in place and ready for the second march on Ulundi. Chelmsford set up his headquarters at Utrecht, while his command of 8,000 was spread between Landman's Drift, Conference Hill, the Doornberg and Dundee. He selected Dundee as his starting point in Northern Natal, even though the original route that crossed at Rorke's Drift, some thirty miles to the south, was the most direct. Chelmsford needed to avoid crossing the Isandlwana battlefield and subjecting his men to the horrors that were still much in evidence.

Chelmsford demanded the new replacement columns be much stronger than the original columns and not only protect their halts with improvised laagers each night – not done at Isandlwana – but also establish a chain of three substantial fortified posts in their wake, Forts Newdigate, Marshall and Evelyn, to guard their lines of communication. These would be garrisoned by small detachments of infantry and mounted troops; those detailed for this task would strongly resent missing the anticipated British victory at Ulundi.

For the second invasion Chelmsford planned on making two main thrusts into Zululand with two separate divisions. The First Division (Coastal) would consist of troops from Pearson's old coastal column and the Eshowe relief column and was given into the command of Major General Crealock, one of several Major Generals who had been sent to South Africa as reinforcements. Crealock was an experienced officer whose younger brother, John North Crealock, was Chelmsford's Assistant Military Secretary. Chelmsford planned that his other main thrust, the Second Division (Northern), would come from the north-west, following roughly the line of the old Centre Column. It was commanded by another new arrival, Major General Newdigate, although Chelmsford himself accompanied this column, and Newdigate, like Glyn before him, found himself with little real opportunity to exercise his authority.

Chelmsford's new columns were vastly superior to the column defeated at Isandlwana. The new Second Division now consisted of six companies each from the 2/21st, the 58th and the 94th regiments, supported by seven companies of replacements, largely inexperienced in warfare, posted from some thirteen regiments based in England to replace the lost 24th Regiment. The infantry were supported by units of engineers, artillery, the Natal Native Contingent (NNC), and service and medical units. Moving men and supplies from the coast was problematic. Newly arrived reinforcements had to march from Durban on rough tracks in mixed weather, usually baking hot, and only reached the new base at Dundee, 200 miles distant, at the end of April. The onward journey was through largely uncharted territory that needed ongoing reconnaissance, a factor that would shortly seriously embarrass Chelmsford when such a patrol, led by the French Prince Imperial, was unexpectedly attacked by a Zulu scouting party.

This was the force that Chelmsford intended would defeat the Zulu army at Ulundi. However, as Chelmsford wished to spare his men the sight of the battlefield of Isandlwana – where the dead of both sides lay unburied – he organised a new line of communication, anchored upon Dundee and crossing the Mzinyathi and Ncombe rivers upstream from nearby Rorke's Drift. This Second Division, largely composed of the inexperienced reinforcements fresh out from England, would swing down just north of Isandlwana and rejoin the old, planned line of advance near the Babanango hills.

Evelyn Wood's original column was the only one of Chelmsford's first invasion which had remained active in the field. Chelmsford was therefore reluctant to deny Wood his independent command, so he was given the local rank of Brigadier-General, and his column was re-designated the 'Flying Column'. Its orders were to affect a junction with the Second Division, and advance in tandem with it to Ulundi.

Crealock's powerful coastal First Division was formed into two brigades. The 1st Brigade, under Colonel Pearson, now a Brigadier-General, was made up of the 2/3rd Regiment, 99th Regiment and six companies of the 88th Regiment. The 2nd Brigade, under the command of Colonel Clarke, consisted of the 57th Regiment, 91st Highlanders, and six companies of the 3/60th Rifles. Both brigades were supported by a naval brigade, two battalions of the re-constructed NNC, 500 mounted scouts, and troopers supported by Royal Artillery and engineers. It began its forward progress moving from the Thukela on 21 April, the wide Tugela River being crossed at the site of the newly constructed Fort Pearson. Chelmsford did not anticipate any serious resistance from Zulus living in the coastal sector, but as a precaution Crealock's orders were to destroy two important royal homesteads that lay on his line of advance – emaNgweni and Hlalangubo (old Ulundi). He was also to establish strong posts on his line of communications. On the same date the demoralised Prince Makwendu kaMpande, one of Cetshwayo's junior brothers, had surrendered to Crealock.[5] By the beginning of July other such local dignitaries as Prince Dabulamanzi – who had commanded at Rorke's Drift – and Mavumengwana kaGodide – the joint commander at Isandlwana – had established contact with the British to discuss peace terms.

From the outset, Crealock's progress suffered from a serious lack of transport facilities, especially to maintain or transport stores. Many of the first invasion's wagons were still abandoned on the field of Isandlwana, while the delivery and accumulation of reinforcements and supplies for the new invasion created an additional demand for wagons. The Natal authorities were increasingly worried that the ordinary commercial economy of the colony would grind to a halt; wagons essential to the Colony's day-to-day existence were being sold to the army for three times their value, while civilian transport drivers abandoned their regular work for the easy pickings offered by the army. Crealock sent repeated messages to Chelmsford pleading for new wagons, oxen and mules. He received only a fraction of those he requested, and his progress became so slow that his column was dubbed 'Crealock's Crawlers' by the rest of the army. Wolseley was later to comment: 'As far as this war is concerned, this First Division might as well have been marching along the Woking and Aldershot road.[6]

The high mortality rate among the coastal column's animals worsened the situation. The coastal sector is notoriously hot and drenchingly humid, and the oppressive conditions, overwork and mismanagement led to the death of thousands of animals, most of which were simply dragged to the side of the road and left to rot. In places, the decomposing bodies of oxen could be seen every few yards along the road marking the First Division's line of advance. The pervading stench was appalling and within weeks the presence of so many dead animals began to affect the health of the troops. Outbreaks of enteric fever, typhoid and dysentery, spread by the thick clouds of flies, soon put a worryingly high proportion of Crealock's troops out of action. An *ILN* reporter with the column wrote:

> There are eight hundred men hors-de-combat from the First Division. This is a big number, out of a total force of less than six thousand. If the present rate of sickness continues there will be no field officers left at the disposal of the general. Brigadier Clarke is now laid up with fever. Yellow jaundice has lately appeared among the troops. A great deal of sickness may be ascribed to the effluvia that arises from the carcases of oxen in different stages of decomposition. These lie on the road where the troopers have to escort the convoys, at every hundred yards this horrible atmosphere has to be breathed.[7]

Nevertheless, Crealock achieved some of his objectives. He established a strong post above the AmaTigulu River, named Fort Crealock, and another, above the Nyezane River, named Fort Chelmsford. These served as staging posts for Crealock's advance, and convoys of supplies made their laborious way between them. Sadly, both of these important but unglamorous sites have, over recent years, been obliterated, with the coastal sector now being extensively and industrially farmed for sugar cane. A single stone monument near the site of Fort Chelmsford bears testimony to the number of Crealock's men who succumbed to disease. Crealock's men also pushed forward to the coast to a spot euphemistically known as Port Durnford, where contact was established with naval shipping. Port Durnford was a misnomer; the location offered nothing in the way of a natural harbour but was merely a stretch of beach where the ever-turbulent surf beat less intensely. Nevertheless, it was possible to land supplies by surfboat and it enabled the First Division to establish an important link with the wider world.[8] By the end of May, the column had assembled on the banks of the Ncome River – the border with Zululand, near Koppie Alleen – while Wood had begun to move towards it from the north. Chelmsford proposed that the second invasion of Zululand with two Divisions would commence on 3 June 1879.

On 4 June Crealock complied with his order to destroy two formidable *amakhanda*. Mounted patrols from the First Division first set fire to emaNgwani. It consisted of over 300 huts but appeared to have been deserted for some time. Two days later, the same patrols burnt Hlalangubo, which had over 600 deserted huts.

The Zulus made no attempt to distract the British from burning these two important complexes which suggests their capacity or willingness to resist was waning. Indeed, the king had experienced some reluctance on the part of his warriors to muster when he first attempted to reassemble the army at the end of May. By June they answered the summons, but it was clear that they were no longer able to fight on more than one front at a time. Many of the fighting men from the coastal districts, who had hitherto stayed in their own areas to fight the invaders, had already gone to Ulundi to be ready to fight in defence of the heartland, leaving the coastal districts occupied only by old men, women and children. Many chiefs who lived in the area had also stayed at home, and despite the fact that the nation did not consider itself beaten, some began tentative negotiations with the British. The grim truth was that while many remained loyal to the king, with their young men gone they stood little chance of resisting the huge British column that was steadily occupying their territories.

The Second Division's progress and advance towards Ulundi had been very different in character to that of Crealock's slow First Division. Still worried by the lack of transport wagons, Chelmsford had at last braved the terrible field of Isandlwana for the first major expedition to the battlefield. On 21 May, the Second Division's cavalry had ridden out to the battlefield with the intention of recovering those abandoned wagons that were still serviceable and had been ignored by the Zulus. Forty-five undamaged wagons were recovered; at the same time a token attempt was made to bury the British dead in the immediate area of the shattered camp, although those wearing red coats were left where they fell in accordance with Colonel Glyn's request that, at a future time, the 24th be allowed to bury its own dead. Reports from that day reveal a sobering sight. While many of the dead had been reduced to skeletons, and the bones scattered by scavengers, others had desiccated in the hot African sun, their features still chillingly clear. This part of the mission was initially successful, although the summer rains would undo much of their work necessitating further burials. Domestic dogs that had accompanied the first invasion to Isandlwana had been ignored by the victorious Zulus and had formed aggressive packs to compete with wild animals for food. The camp dogs had probably run off, scared by the attacking Zulus, only to return to find their masters dead. With no one to feed them, they survived by eating the carrion scattered across the battlefield. According to Lieutenant Maxwell of the NNC, their end was a sorry one:

> About half a mile from the camp I was attacked by a pack of dogs, about twenty, consisting of various breeds. Newfoundlands, pointers, setters, terriers etc., a few with collars. These were the dogs that had belonged to the camp at Isandlwana and having lost their masters, and been in the fighting, had become wild and although I tried, by calling them and whistling, could not quiet them. They followed still barking and howling some 3- or 400 yards, when they left me. These were shot at different times with very few exceptions.[9]

On 31 May Chelmsford's column crossed the Ncome and the re-invasion of Zululand commenced in earnest. Until then, Chelmsford's reputation was questionable with little more than a pattern of defeats behind him – and Zululand was still unconquered.

Almost immediately, and completely unexpectedly, tragedy struck. Because several warriors had remained at home to guard their homes and crops, the Zulus remained more active in the central districts than those near the coast. A number of Zulu scouting parties were deployed to observe and harass British progress. The main British advance could only be achieved if it continued in the face of such constant skirmishing. On 1 June the Flying Column struck camp and, having quitted the Munhla camp, moved southeast, where it halted about midday at the Umyamyene River with the mounted men, including the FLH, providing the vedettes that extended as far out as five miles. Earlier in the day, a small patrol, commanded by Lieutenant Carey of the 98th (Prince of Wales) Regiment, and accompanied by the exiled Prince Imperial of France, set out from the Second Division headquarters to select a suitable camping ground for the next stage of the advance. Despite the fact that the area had already been swept for Zulus, and the main Flying Column was only a few miles away, the small patrol was ambushed at the deserted homestead of a Zulu headman named Sobhuza, and the Prince and a number of his escort were killed. Coincidentally, Buller and Wood were both independently out on patrol to examine their onward route when they came across a horseman bolting towards them. It was Lieutenant Carey of the 98th Regiment who excitedly reported that his group had been ambushed and the Prince Imperial killed. Although stunned by the report there was little they could do. It was getting late in the day so the search for the body was postponed until the following morning. At dawn a patrol made up of the 2nd Division and the 17th (Duke of Cambridge's Own) Lancers were sent to investigate, whilst A Troop FLH, led by Captain Hutton, were also despatched along with Buller, Captain Lord Beresford and the NNH. The FLH soon came across the prince's body, wrapped it up and waited for the 17th Lancers and 1st (King's) Dragoon Guards to take charge of the body. Although the Prince's death created a political scandal, it was a minor military incident in the history of the war.

Once the Second Division had established Fort Newdigate near the Nondweni River the men could rest and supplies could safely be brought forward. A new cavalry division, consisting of the 1st (King's) Dragoon Guards and 17th Lancers, commanded by Major General Marshall, was also attached to the Second Division.

In early June Chelmsford and his staff at Fort Newdigate learned the cost of commanding and relying on so many inexperienced troops. On the morning of 5 June, Wood's Flying Column saw its first action when irregular cavalry from the Flying Column encountered a strong Zulu force on the banks of the Ntinini River (also known as the Upoko). The Zulu were positioned among boulders along the foot of a hill known as eZungeni. The Irregulars opened fire on the Zulus, but began to retreat when the Zulus unexpectedly deployed in large numbers to surround them in their classic 'horns' attack formation: realising they were in peril of being surrounded, the Irregulars rapidly retreated. The sound of firing alerted the 17th Lancers, attached to the Second Division. The Lancers had not yet seen action and were keen to display their skills against the enemy. Hearing the Irregulars had retreated, the Lancers rushed to the scene. This would be their very first engagement in Zululand and all were 'keen as mustard' to bring further honour to the regiment by routing the Zulus.[10] The Lancers did not understand Zulu tactics and deployed using the traditional and well-rehearsed European cavalry tactic of 'charging in line'. The Zulus may have been impressed as the cavalry repeatedly swept past in parade ground formation, but it was impossible for the Lancers to engage the Zulus with them randomly firing from the safety of the elevated outcrop of rocks and boulders. The rough terrain was totally unsuitable for cavalry and the Zulus held their ground while taking random pot-shots at the riders as they swept by. On one such 'pass' the regiment's adjutant, Lieutenant Frith, was shot through the body by a Zulu and killed. The 17th then retired to the Division's camp, carrying Frith's body across the saddle of a packhorse. The Zulus clearly got the best of the incident. The attempt to use regular cavalry tactics in difficult terrain had struck one cynical observer as being like 'chopping wood with a razor'.[11]

Just days later, and following a false nighttime alarm, nervous sentries fired a number of shots into the darkness which brought the whole column to an immediate state of readiness. In the mistaken belief that they were under a serious Zulu attack the infantry opened fire, which was followed by the artillery, who joined the firing with indiscriminate shelling of the surrounding area. By the time it was realized that there was no attack, eight men had been wounded, and several horses killed. The incident nearly killed a recent recipient of the Victoria Cross, Lieutenant Chard, who was on picket duty occupying a forward shelter trench with his detachment. During the confusion, rifle-fire had even been directed at Chard's position in the mistaken belief that the Zulus had taken it. Chard and his men threw themselves into the shallow trench: luckily, they survived unscathed and one can only wonder at the exchange of views once normality had been restored. Exercising patriotic restraint, those war correspondents present chose not to report the incident.

As dawn broke the two huge columns began the slow slog towards Ulundi. The daily routine was unchanging. Reveille sounded at 2am followed by breakfast, Then the slow process of collapsing tents began, packing and stowing away camp equipage on the wagons, pulling apart the laager, yoking the draught oxen and slowly setting off to the next campsite. During the day, the lines of wagons would halt for a few hours rest when they would establish a chain of fortified supply posts to guard their lines of advance. Learning from the Isandlwana experience, Chelmsford insisted a laager should be formed every night. This time-consuming exercise involved forming a huge square of wagons pushed tight together. The footsore soldiers would then have to dig a trench and build up a rampart with the spoil. Wood had used the time before the second invasion began to practice forming a wagon laager while on the march and once claimed to achieve a creditable time of thirty-five minutes.

Wood's independent command was superior in so many ways, not least his concern for the health of his men. He was insistent that they should eat a meat breakfast and have a daily supply of fresh bread. Rather cheekily, he would send any surplus from his mobile bakery back to General Newdigate and his staff.

With such a huge force to sustain, there was an almost continuous stream of supply convoys plying between the border depots and the column. To protect this vital line, Chelmsford had three forts built along the route, Forts Newdigate, Marshall and Evelyn. These were garrisoned by small detachments of infantry and mounted troops. It was a great disappointment for most of the officers who were detailed for this duty, for they were about to miss out on an almost certain British victory at Ulundi.

One of the reasons for the slow progress of the Second Division was that it was at the mercy of its irregular supply lines. Convoy duty was also unpopular: besides being unglamorous, it was frustrating and dangerous; wagons could become bogged down and lose their position with the rest of the convoy. Too often sleepless and nervous nights would be spent in a poorly formed temporary defensive position keeping an alert watch for marauding bands of Zulus.

All the while, King Cetshwayo watched helplessly as the British columns moved inexorably towards his Zulu capital. Many Zulus were now openly reluctant to gather round the king as they realised that defeat was inevitable. The initial attempt in May to regroup the Zulu army had met with partial success. Defections along the coastal regions were rumoured and some chiefs declared that they were unable to fight as their homesteads were overcrowded with wounded. King Cetshwayo called an urgent meeting of chiefs and all agreed to commence negotiations with the British – only to have them thwarted by Chelmsford.

With the column steadily approaching Ulundi, Chelmsford received news from London that Sir Garnet Wolseley had replaced him; this was the government's response to his earlier plea to be replaced. Now that Chelmsford was on the verge of victory the news came as a psychological setback, but within days he learned that all was not lost as Wolseley was being thwarted in his attempt to take command. Wolseley's intention of being landed by boat at a location only one day's ride from the column failed due to stormy weather: his wind tossed boat had to return to Durban, leaving the seasick Wolseley no option but to chase after the column on horseback. Wolseley's temporary misfortune made Chelmsford even more determined to press on with the attack on Ulundi: only then could he resign with honour. Wolseley nevertheless put Chelmsford under even greater pressure when on 30 June he telegraphed to him:

Concentrate your forces immediately, undertake no operations and flash back your moves. Astonished at not hearing from you.[12]

Aware of Wolseley's temporary inability to join the column, Chelmsford merely acknowledged receipt of the message. This made Chelmsford even more determined to press on and achieve his victory before resigning. The general advance had continued unhindered: every Zulu homestead along the route was abandoned. On 22 June a temporary base was set up, named Fort Evelyn, while the main body continued its advance. On 27 June they passed emaKhosini 'place of kings' where Zulu royal ancestors were buried. The area included a half-dozen large homesteads which were burnt to the ground, including the hut containing the Zulu symbol of the nation, the 'inkhata yezwe yacwaZulu', which dated from King Shaka. As the occupants retreated in front of the British, the troops burnt every hut and village in sight and destroyed vast amounts of mealies. This action cleared the path to the Mthonjaneni Heights overlooking the White Mfolozi River and on to Ulundi. As the British column advanced ever closer, now only 17 miles from Ulundi, they had a distant view through the haze to Ulundi itself, where intense Zulu activity could be seen on the dusty plains before Ulundi. Cetshwayo was clearly rehearsing his remaining army in a final defence of his capital.

By 28 June, a quickening of pace brought the Second Division to a strongly entrenched base camp which they named Fort Nolela, sometimes mistakenly referred to as Fort Victoria. Now only 7 miles from Ulundi, the 1st Battalion, 24 Foot Regiment (1/24th) – much to the disappointment of their commanding officer, Colonel Glyn and his two reconstituted companies of the 24th – learned that they were to be denied the opportunity of revenge for Isandlwana. That day and those following were spent preparing for the final advance on Ulundi. Cetshwayo then sent three emissaries with a herd of royal cattle, two elephant tusks and the promise of returning the two artillery guns removed from the Isandlwana battlefield as a peace offering, which was refused.

Still optimistic that he could halt the British, King Cetshwayo sent two of his royal envoys, Nkisimane and Mfunzi, to treat with Chelmsford; as a gesture they brought with them the Prince Imperial's sword taken as booty from his body on 1 June. The envoys sought terms required for a Zulu surrender; Chelmsford informed the envoys that he required the surrender of all British arms captured at Isandlwana and gave them until 3 July for the king's reply – knowing full well the king could not possibly comply with this ultimatum because the captured Martini-Henry rifles were now spread across the Zulu kingdom. Unhindered, Chelmsford continued his advance to the White Mfolozi River where he consolidated his army's position and prepared his troops for the final defeat of the Zulus. Chelmsford was under no illusion: he desperately needed the vindication for Isandlwana that this final battle would bring; only then could he return to Britain with his reputation intact – but knowing he still had to answer to Parliament, the press and the public, for his previous defeats and losses. Chelmsford was acutely aware of his predicament and wrote to the Secretary of State for War, Colonel Frederick Stanley, on this very issue:

As it is more than probable with such a large number of newspaper correspondents in camp, that many false impressions may be circulated and sent home regarding our operations … Their presence in the camp will make no difference to myself, and you may depend upon my pursuing the even tenor of my way, uninfluenced by the knowledge that I am surrounded by those who will not be sparing in their criticism if everything is not rearranged exactly to their liking.[13]

King Cetshwayo was also in a delicate position. When the envoys, Nkisimane and Mfunzi, returned to brief the king, they were prevented by the king's own advisors from personally reporting back to him. Like Chelmsford, Cetshwayo and his advisors needed this battle. Surrender to the British was not an option for the Zulu king. He knew he must suffer a military defeat in order to retain his credibility and bargaining position after the battle.

Both sides were now concentrated for battle, and it was impossible for the nervous soldiers not to be aware of the Zulus just across the White Umfolozi. Their anxiety was palpable and proportionately matched by their inexperience. During daylight, British water collecting parties came under sporadic Zulu rifle fire from the far riverbank and at night the sounds of Zulu chanting and battle preparations could clearly be heard. Late on 3 July, King Cetshwayo attempted one last call for peace. As a desperate gesture he sent a herd of his finest cattle towards Chelmsford's camp but the warriors guarding the river, the uKhandempemvu, indignantly sent them back. They wanted to fight the British invader.

Chapter 2

The Death of the Prince Imperial, 1 June 1879

*'Terrible, horrible news has fallen upon us like a thunderclap.
The Prince Imperial is dead'*

The London Times: 21 June 1879

In the first months of 1879 the Anglo-Zulu War (AZW) witnessed the British invasion of Zululand facing unparalleled defeats at Isandlwana, Ntombe and Hlobane. The embarrassing defeat at Isandlwana was only marginally offset by the heroism of the British defence that same day at Rorke's Drift. While Chelmsford and his invading army prepared for the re-invasion of Zululand, Chelmsford ignominiously suffered the result of a needless incident in a remote valley resulting in the death of three men – two troopers and the man they were escorting, Prince Louis Napoleon, the heir to the famous French Bonaparte family.

But who was this enigmatic young Prince who considered himself to be next in line to the title of Napoleon, and what was he doing in South Africa supporting a British invasion of Zululand? Curiously, his pedigree was not quite as French as France might have expected, for his family line reveals him to be half British.[1] Upon taking a brief look at Louis' pedigree, one sees his grandmother was born a Kirkpatrick, of the ancient Scottish family the Kirkpatricks of Closeburn. In her early twenties she lived with her father in Spain. He had been reduced to running something the ill-natured might have described as a wine bar. The colourful Miss Kirkpatrick gained part of her education for life 'working as a hostess learning the ways of men' in the club 'for officers and foreign visitors' run behind her father's wine shop.[2]

In 1817 the popular Miss Kirkpatrick married the insignificant one-eyed and lame Don Cipriano, Count de Teba, later to inherit the more senior title of the Count de Montijo. Fact is often stranger than fiction, and in this case the facts are even stranger than most commonly-accepted accounts of this marriage. Their relationship was one of complete opposites: the count was poor – the new countess was a spendthrift; he was a traditionalist – she was a devious dreamer. Due to her outrageous affairs, they soon drifted apart and in their later years they never saw each other.

The plot then thickens. The countess twice became pregnant and bore two daughters. It was generally noted that, curiously, the appearance of the two girls was totally different, as was their character and behaviour, and the question of the babies' father requires some consideration. The first daughter, Paca (christened Maria Francisca de Sales) was conceived and born while the hapless count was incarcerated in the grim Santiago prison where the 'liberales' were detained. Unless the countess managed a conjugal visit to her husband the identity of the child's father must be in doubt. When the second daughter, (christened Eugenia yet subsequently known as Eugénie) was conceived, society talk throughout the Second Empire suggested that her father was George Villiers, later to become the fourth Earl of Clarendon and British Foreign Secretary. While the count languished in prison, the Countess de Montijo was living with friends in Paris and records reveal that Villiers was conveniently living nearby at the same time. Villiers was known to be a special friend of the countess. Villiers' sister described the situation as 'very wicked'.

Villiers always acted *in loco parentis* to Eugénie. She lived under his protection in Bath in England for a number of years where she was known as 'Carrots' due to her auburn hair. Villiers later arranged her introduction to Napoleon III. Villiers' open affair with her mother continued into their advancing years.

Assuming the father was George Villiers, then baby Eugénie would have been totally British. This would logically indicate that her son, the Prince Imperial, fathered by Napoleon III, was half French, half British. During the years following her marriage, the new Countess de Montijo, liked to travel. A great part of her life was spent flitting, with her two daughters, from capital to capital, and from social spa to spa. She was a devious and gregarious woman, stirring, vainglorious, and an incurable romantic. She was obviously proud of her two charming daughters, whom she constantly embarrassed by praising them in public, and with her frank eagerness to marry them off to anyone with a title the moment they came of age.

She had succeeded brilliantly with Paca, the elder and best beloved daughter, who had by then become the Duchess of Alba. Eugénie had been sixteen when her sister was married, and there was much gossip about her part in the affair. She had also been in love with the duke, and she had fully expected him to propose to her. When he made an offer to her sister, Eugénie had taken poison and almost died. According to relatives, the duke had proposed to Eugénie, but understanding her sister's hope and expectation, she had persuaded him to transfer his affections. From an incoherent and frantic letter that Eugénie wrote to the duke at the time we can be sure that something happened between the three. Eugénie survived the experience and developed into a wild social beauty. She began spending time on the periphery of the French Court where her charms were much appreciated by the gentlemen.

Within a short space of time, Eugénie, a true beauty of twenty-six, was tolerably well known in French society. Perhaps she was too well known; the correct opined that a young unmarried woman had no business to have done such a lot of travelling, and also that the daughter of 'such a mother' should be avoided by men of sense. Eugénie made a point of appearing everywhere in a cloud of admirers, but it did not follow that they were after her *pour le bon motif.* She was certainly eccentric: she flirted openly; she had a reputation for having dashed through the streets of Madrid on unsaddled horses; she patronised bullfighters; she went about with a dagger stuck in her belt. And as for her formidable mother, she was more than enough to frighten off any *soupirant.*

Eugénie was rarely seen alone. There were numerous 'associations' and she had briefly been engaged to a young Spanish grandee, but had thought better of it on learning of his ongoing affair with another woman. Gossip was commonplace, so it was hardly surprising that when Napoleon III became infatuated with Eugénie, the liaison should have been looked on, not as a romance, but as a great joke. Eugénie might well have seen the Finger of Destiny pointing to her. French society saw only a clever and experienced mother and daughter pair, scheming to snare Napoleon III. He was unmarried and getting restless. He was forty-five and wanted to leave an heir. If he left it much longer, he knew he might be too late. He had already kept an English mistress, Miss Howard, and although described by many as 'having the appearance of an opium eater', he nevertheless possessed charm for women, and the number of his affairs was notorious. Napoleon failed to woo any available European lady of royal birth and made one final attempt; to engage Her Serene Royal Highness Princess Adelaide of Hohenlohe, aged 17, the daughter of Queen Victoria's half-sister, Princess Feodora of Hohenlohe–Langenburg. The proposal had to go via Queen Victoria – who was not amused, and the proposal failed then and there.

A great deal happened on 18 January 1853. Napoleon was rejected by Princess Adelaide. That same evening, he proposed to the undeniably lovely-looking Mlle. Eugénie de Montijo, ignoring all advice about her Kirkpatrick relatives. At length and quite suddenly, 'the Imperial Pamela obtained her reward' so the London *Times* put it with cheerful candour when it announced the betrothal. Lord Cowley, the British Ambassador, reported that the announcement was made to 'universal disappointment', adding that 'had Princess Adelaide accepted him, the Montijo would have been sent to the right about'.[3]

But the effect, if not manqué, could still less be described as flattering. 'We learn with some amusement,' the *Times* went on with provoking British superiority, 'that this romantic event in the annals of the French Empire has called forth the strongest opposition, and provoked the utmost irritation. The Imperial family, the Council of Ministers, and even the lower coteries of the palace or its purlieus, all affect to regard this marriage as an amazing humiliation, and they deplore the failure of the Royal marriage before on the tapis, as if they were not satisfied with the dignity and grandeur of their own Emperor, until he had cohabited with an Archduchess.'

But even her good works were 'Montijo': she was 'Montijo' in all she did or left undone. Florence Nightingale described her as 'the Empress born to be a dressmaker' – so said the critics.[4] That was all very well according to the British press; but at the root of it was the assumption that it could make no difference to Britain whom the Emperor took to be his wife, as he was in any case a 'no one'. In France people were probably less inclined to this view.

And conveniently there was news that the heir would be forth coming, possibly sometime in March. There was a report that, if a boy, he would be King of Algiers. It was hoped that Eugénie would not give birth till 20 March, the date of birth of the Roi de Rome; and, to assist the coincidence, she was heavily dosed with morphine. This increased her danger, without achieving the attended result. On the evening of the 14th her pains began. All those appointed to be present – ministers, officials, relatives – were hastily summoned. The countess was there, and the Duke of Alba, and Princess Mathilde and, of course the brother of Napoleon III, 'Plonplon': making, unless fortune favoured him, a last appearance as heir presumptive. But Plonplon's luck was out, the child was a boy. The glad news was telegraphed immediately to the Pope and then to the princes of Europe. It was boomed out by the cannon along the Invalides, a full royal salute of a hundred and one guns. Unluckily this thrilling occasion was wasted: an indifferent Paris slept.

At two days old, the baby boy received the Grand Cross of the Legion of Honour. Bounties, decorations and amnesties were showered abroad in his name. And as he lay in his cradle, all the world came to pay homage, his future subjects, the ambassadors to his father's court, the statesmen of the Peace Congress and, finally, the evil genius, the wicked fairy at the christening, the second plenipotentiary of the second Teutonic state, Count Otto von Bismarck.

The tone of the English Press had the advantage of contrast. 'The same fortune,' remarked *The Times* with judicial coolness, 'which has raised Louis Napoleon from an exile to a Sovereign has now presented him with an heir, on whom may devolve his vast acquisitions, and who will at any rate have as good a claim as any other Frenchman to the throne of the first nation of the continent'.

At birth, Louis had been enrolled as a grenadier: at eighteen months, he acquired a Lilliputian uniform and a diminutive busby; and thus habited, correct in every detail, though rather unsteady on the legs, he made his bow to the world. In his third year, he was promoted to epaulettes and began to appear in uniform at official gatherings. At military reviews he would sit perched up before the emperor, very stiff, saluting with childish gravity and importance. His formal education began, as was fitting for a young prince, in the riding-school. Even before he could walk steadily, he could ride a horse. At six months old, he had been strapped, sideways, on a minute Shetland pony, and of course photographed: in every conceivable situation, he was sure to be photographed. At eighteen months, his training began in earnest:

he was handed over to an equerry, Biarritz, who became the most important influence in his childhood.[5]

At the age of fifteen he was taken to watch his father suffer ignominious defeat by the Prussians at the Battle of Sedan. To avoid capture like his father, he and his guardians had taken a train at the next station to Maubeuge and thus, in a third-class carriage, and in the blouse of a peasant boy, he had crossed the frontier into Belgium and safety, and then on to England and the protection of Queen Victoria. (Napoleon III was later exiled to England.)

The family were welcomed enthusiastically by England, despite Queen Victoria viewing the situation as a political embarrassment, which greatly annoyed many French. With the support of the Duke of Cambridge, Louis joined the Royal Military Academy at Woolwich. He excelled in class and accepted an invitation to join the Royal Artillery at the age of eighteen. The prince had ensured that every physical feat was carried to excess; he was immediately noted for his extravagance and white-hot enthusiasm.[6] Louis had passed out seventh but, being French, he was not permitted to take a commission in the British army. His father died on 9 January 1873. Louis took the title Napoleon IV and waited for his recall to France to reclaim the family throne. However, his involvement with the British Army had been viewed by many French people as scandalous.

Meanwhile, the young Prince Imperial continued his interest in military matters and completed his education by attending the Woolwich Royal Academy where officers for the Royal Artillery and Engineers were trained. He graduated seventh out of thirty-four officer cadets in 1875. Apart from occasional military exercises, Louis then began to languish. Being a French national, he could not carry a British commission. He applied to the Emperor Franz Josef to join the Austrian Army but was refused.

When the Zulu War first broke out, not even the prince had thought it worth going to. It was hardly a war; it was a skirmish with the blacks, a punitive expedition. Then came the slaughter at Isandlwana. England's regiments had been wiped out, had fallen to the last man – and England was dumb with shock and humiliation. The affair grew 'serious' overnight. Reinforcements were hurried off – and as he was in the thick of it all, Louis' connection with Aldershot became his personal agony. His friends glowed with hope and excitement; they all expected to serve, and two of them, Bigge and Slade, were ordered out straight away. And then the third and last took leave. Wodehouse had gone; the prince was very silent and absent.

Now it was positively his duty as Heir of France to go to this war. What could he do at home? What chance had he to show he was good for anything? People were always throwing the Orleans princes in his teeth – that the Orleans princes had fought and he hadn't, and this was the perfect war for him to fight in – at the other end of the world, against savages, involving no European interest. He was not a *'homme de plaisir'*. Louis shamelessly used his mother, the Empress Eugénie, enlisting her influence with Queen Victoria – working on the Empress to such a point that she actually visited the War Office in secret to plead his cause. The young prince then applied to the Duke of Cambridge for permission to go to South Africa. Following the intervention of his mother and Queen Victoria, permission was finally granted, and the prince was allocated to Lord Chelmsford's staff, but as a civilian observer.

While the Commander-in-Chief, the Duke of Cambridge, asked Lord Chelmsford to find Louis a position on his staff, it was made clear that there could be no question of his exercising any authority within the British Army. The decision to allow Louis to travel to Zululand as an observer was undoubtedly a further burden to Lord Chelmsford, who, by April 1879, was still struggling to turn the war in his favour.

The rest, as is said, is history – the prince would leave for Zululand 'in the capacity of a spectator.[7] The South African correspondent of *Le Figaro*, Paul Deléage, neatly summed up this curious appointment:

> After all, what's the Prince supposed to be doing in this row? He'll get no credit from us, and I can't see what good it's to do him in his own country, unless he goes back a cripple – and even then! In order to calm any problems and distress with his party in France, it was emphasised the prince would have no meaningful military role.

The Duke of Cambridge wrote a letter to the already burdened Lord Chelmsford with the information pertaining to the prince's role in the army in Zululand. The final words in the letter would prove to be fatefully correct. It reads:

the Prince Imperial who is going out on his own account to see as much as he can of the coming campaign in Zululand. He is extremely anxious to go out and wanted to be employed in our army …if you show him kindness and tender him a position to see as much as he can with the columns in the Field I hope you will do so. He is a fine young fellow, full of spirit and pluck …My only anxiety on his conduct would be, that he is too plucky and go ahead.[8]

On his arrival at Chelmsford's headquarters of the Second Division he initially made himself useful in the camp by performing a variety of tasks with exaggerated enthusiasm, but the young prince quickly frustrated those charged with his care. Louis's 'plucky and go ahead' nature was illustrated early on in his campaign when, on patrol with Colonel Buller, he rode ahead to give chase to some lone Zulus in the surrounding hills without support or knowledge of the ground ahead. Despite Louis returning unharmed, Buller was outraged by the actions of the young French prince and wrote a letter of complaint to Lord Chelmsford. The commander-in-chief agreed and ordered the senior officer responsible for identifying suitable routes for transport, Colonel Harrison, to keep Louis in the camp at all times unless strong escort was provided. Louis himself saw these orders expressing concerns for his safety, but he ignored them. Although confined to camp, a serious disciplinary matter for any young officer, he was permitted to accompany several routine scouting missions locating new camp sites closer to the target of the Zulu capital. It is likely that Buller's despair and Lord Chelmsford's warnings actually encouraged Louis to maintain his seeming irresponsibility: after all, it made him the centre of attention – which he loved and desperately needed.

We may never know how much Louis' behaviour influenced the outcome of events during the fateful patrol on 1 June 1879. His background and upbringing probably ensured that 'showing off' was his norm. On the morning of 1 June, the prince had persuaded his supervisory officer, Major Harrison, to overlook the restriction on his movement and allow him to accompany a mapping patrol to reconnoitre the following day's campsite. Lieutenant Carey of the Quartermaster General's staff led the patrol of six troopers of Bettington's Horse, although for part of the journey they were accompanied by Major Grenfell, a senior staff officer, (he later became Field

Marshal Lord Grenfell). The area of the proposed campsite was the river beyond Itelezi Hill.

Militarily, the patrol lacked real purpose and made Chelmsford's position even weaker for not effectively controlling the prince. The excuse that Louis was bored with camp life and wished to make himself useful and active seems paramount. Harrison saw no danger in sending the prince out, as the area that he would visit had already been cleared of Zulus and was in sight of the main camp site with mounted men patrolling the surrounding areas. Lieutenant Carey, a French speaker who had formed a strong bond with the prince, volunteered to accompany the escort and to supervise the patrol. However, Harrison failed to appoint an officer 'in command' of the patrol and this would lead to protracted debate after the death of the prince as to who was actually in command while the patrol was away from the camp.

Accompanied by an escort of six members of Bettington's Horse, the prince and Lieutenant Carey set out from Chelmsford's headquarters to sketch the territory through which Chelmsford's second invasion would pass. A cavalry patrol had previously declared the route free of Zulus and the party was accompanied by a friendly Zulu scout, a normal procedure for a routine sketching mission. The party had intended to meet six mounted BaSotho troopers to bolster their force, but the two groups missed each other and the prince's party continued deeper into Zululand. At about midday, the group paused on a hill overlooking the valley of the Tshotshozi River. From here they spotted an apparently deserted Zulu homestead near the river and rode down with the intention of examining the Zulu huts and making coffee. The small cluster of huts was surrounded on three sides by a fully-grown mealie plantation. The question of command now arose: Carey spoke French and was used to the prince's company – Carey was the only officer in the party, but it appears that he allowed the prince to exercise a token command. Carey would have appreciated the prince's importance and the prince would doubtless have enjoyed the unofficial privilege of giving certain routine commands.

Having checked that the Zulu homestead was abandoned, the party off saddled. The homestead fire was still smouldering. Coffee was brewed and the men relaxed while the prince and Carey chatted. The safety of the group was left to a scout who was instructed to watch the surrounding area. Even though the re-invasion was well under way, Carey would certainly have known that the Zulus employed a system of fast-moving scouting parties to relay intelligence back to the Zulu commanders. One such group, from a combination of the iNgobamakhosi, uMbonambi and uNokhenke regiments that coincidentally included one of the king's personal attendants, Mnukwa, was in the area and decided to investigate the resting British patrol.

The Zulus had first seen the prince's party from a distance and, using the cover of the ground, successfully drew near to the resting soldiers. The Zulus were able to use the protection of the head-high mealie crop to close in. The Zulus realised that the British patrol was several miles from the advancing column and therefore highly vulnerable to a Zulu attack, especially as the scouting group seemed uncharacteristically relaxed and unaware of their approach. Seeing the riders taking their ease among the huts the Zulus decided to seize the opportunity and, using the cover of the ground, stealthily approached the unsuspecting party through the kraal's mealie crop until, unobserved, they were able to get to within 30 feet of the dismounted riders.

At this point, the scout reported to Carey that he had seen faces in the mealies. Unperturbed by the information and ready to depart, Carey allowed the prince to give the order for the horses to be gathered together and saddled. This took a few minutes, and it appears that no one thought the scout's information warranted any immediate action. Once the horses were saddled the prince gave the order to mount. In this critical moment the Zulus fired a close-range volley at the mounting soldiers and then charged among them: the patrol was put to flight and in the confusion every man sought to protect himself as best he could.

Amazingly, the Zulus' volley missed the soldiers, but Trooper Rogers' horse had taken fright, leaving the trooper helpless. The Zulus chased him through the huts and killed him. Trooper Abel was equally unlucky. He was spurring his horse away when a bullet struck his spine. He fell from his horse sharing the same fate as Rogers. The black scout darted away on foot but was quickly caught and killed.

As the Zulus opened fire on the patrol the prince tried to mount his horse, but something was seriously wrong. He had always been regarded as one of Europe's eminent horsemen but earlier that day he had been seen experiencing difficulties with walking and mounting his horse. Sir William

Beresford had witnessed the first occasion and initially commented that the prince's horse was too high for him but then suggested that the difficulties were solely due to the tight trousers favoured by the prince. Only a few hours later the prince had failed to perform this routine but now life-saving action.[9]

With the remainder of Carey's party mounted and galloping out of danger the prince desperately tried vaulting into the saddle but instead of grasping the saddle, he grabbed the flimsy holster strap, which gave way under the strain. He fell heavily to the ground. Dazed, he managed to regain his feet as the Zulus closed around him. Horseless, he ran towards a dried riverbed and turned to face the Zulus. He drew his revolver and fired several shots before a spear struck him in the thigh. The prince withdrew the spear to use as a weapon, but the Zulus quickly overwhelmed him before spearing him to death. The Zulus may have realised that they had killed an officer as several warriors took the opportunity to blood their spear blades in the prince's body: the seventeen stab wounds subsequently gave rise to the myth that in death, the prince had bravely 'faced his foe', just as he had prophesied. In any event, the Zulus certainly fulfilled Louis' oft-stated childhood wish to be wounded on the front of his body!

In the ensuing panic, Carey and the surviving troopers rode for their lives, fleeing ahead of the prince, only realising something was wrong when, reining in about half-a-mile from the scene the prince's riderless horse overtook them. Carey correctly presumed the prince had somehow fallen and had therefore been killed. This surmise was confirmed the following morning when his body was found. Meanwhile the Zulus disembowelled the bodies and Mnukwa took the prince's sword. There was little Carey could do. To return would mean certain death and without a doubt the prince was already dead. He decided to report the awful loss of the prince to Chelmsford and set off for camp, only to meet up with Buller who was also returning from a patrol. Carey blurted out what had happened to a shocked and incredulous Buller who ferociously responded with the words: "You deserve to be shot, and I hope you will be. I could shoot you myself". Buller was later to ameliorate his views. He knew Carey had a sound military reputation whereas the prince had wilfully disobeyed his (Buller's) orders on several occasions.

Due to the failing light and so as not to lose any more lives, it was thought advisable to wait until dawn next morning before beginning the search for the body. While the camp settled down for the night, the deeply depressed and shocked Carey wrote a letter to his wife outlining his day's ordeal. However, when the content of the letter was published, its content would embarrass him for life. He wrote:

I am a ruined man, I fear, though from my letter which will be in the papers you will see I could not do anything else. Still the loss of the Prince is a fearful thing …Our camp was bad, but then, I have been so laughed at for taking a squadron with me that I have grown reckless and would have gone with two men …As regards leaving the Prince, I am innocent …I shall be blamed but honestly between you and me, I can only be blamed for the camp ….[10]

The following day, Chelmsford sent out a recovering party to retrieve the young prince. The party found the body of the prince and the two other men badly mutilated which followed Zulu custom.[11] Chelmsford had also sent his staff surgeon, Surgeon Major Scott, to inspect the body, and the following lines are from his report at the scene. He explained:

He was lying on his back, with his left arm across him, in the position of self-defence. I counted eighteen assegai wounds all in front …There were no bullet wounds on the body …There was a patch of blood, underneath the head and the neck, which appeared to me to be caused by wounds received on the side of the neck, and also a wound through the right eyeball. The prince's body was entirely stripped.[12]

The death of the Prince Imperial came as a severe shock to Chelmsford, and the whole invasion force was stunned. The immeasurable shock waves then reverberated through both the British and French nations and across the British Empire. The news even overshadowed Chelmsford's earlier disaster at Isandlwana. Norris-Newman, the noted war correspondent for *The London Standard*, wrote at the time:

But various causes, his rank and misfortunes, his connection with the British army, the actual incidents of the fatality arising out of the duties of the expedition, and lastly, the subsequent proceedings in connection with the inquiry by court martial, all combined to invest it with a special pathos and interest, almost world-wide. Chelmsford, who had suffered so much in the campaign, 'is awfully cut up about it as he will be blamed for letting him go with so small an escort'.[13]

After that fateful Sunday, Carey tried to continue his duties, but due to the continuing pressure from his colleagues, who placed the blame on him, he requested an inquest to exonerate himself. His request was accepted. Carey was tried by general court martial. The senior military establishment immediately went on the defensive, but this time the lowly culprit was obvious. The junior officer in charge of the patrol, the French-speaking and experienced Lieutenant Carey of the 98th Regiment had inexplicably abandoned the prince to a small force of Zulus.

Nevertheless, the prince's body had to be returned cross country to Durban. Fearing that British soldiers would be less than respectful to a Frenchman, especially the grandson of Napoleon Bonaparte, the body was taken the shorter route to Port Durnford. The black-bordered Special Order laid out how the troops en route were to behave, and they were not to display any untoward disrespect or anti-French behaviour.[14]

Carey's court martial was quickly arranged. Others, though, knew of the prince's blatant irresponsibility and realised that he alone was responsible for his own demise. When the details surrounding the incident became known, Carey's brother officers softened their views. After all, the significance of the incident arose only because one of the casualties was the Prince Imperial. Had this aristocratic tourist not been present, or not exercised command of the patrol, or not been killed alongside troopers Abel and Rogers, the minor rout of an insignificant sketching party would have quickly been forgotten. As far as Chelmsford was concerned the Zululand campaign had already witnessed, on several notable occasions, the unpleasant spectacle of officers abandoning their men to the enemy. At Isandlwana two colonial officers, Lieutenants Avery and Holcroft, both disappeared from the battlefield. They were followed by Lieutenant Adendorff whose mysterious disappearance at both Isandlwana and Rorke's Drift (to which he returned the following day) preceded that of Lieutenants Coghill and Melvill, who both departed from Isandlwana under unverified circumstances. Rorke's Drift had been abandoned by Major Spalding and had then seen Captain Stevenson, his

NCOs and the NNC abandon the mission station just as the Zulus were about to attack. The case of Ntombe Drift, where Lieutenant Harward deserted his men during a Zulu attack, had yet to come to official notice. They needed an example to bring home the message that officers must remain with their men and Carey was the perfect scapegoat.

Carey's case was unique because the man he deserted was a member of the French aristocracy who had been specially authorised to join Chelmsford's force by none other than Queen Victoria. It is unlikely that more than a few of the rank and file even knew of the Prince's attachment to the army while he was still alive, yet Archibald Forbes summed up the common reaction of indignation and sentiment when he wrote 'throughout the force there was a thrill of sorrow for the poor gallant lad, a burning sense of shame that he should have been so miserably left to his fate, and a deep sympathy for the forlorn widow in England'.[15]

From the other evidence recorded, everybody mentioned that the prince was giving orders to the men. Yet Corporal Grubbs in answering the question regarding who was leading the retreat, said it was Lieutenant Carey. It mirrors a similar trait to the actions of Lieutenant Harward at Ntombe: namely, Carey, who neglected the safety of the men, was now leading the retreat. The story hardly portrays the heroics that traditionally fill the British annals. The evidence from Letocq further expressed that nothing was done to help the prince and the other two men left behind. He was asked: 'Were any orders given to stop or rally, or try to save the Prince'? He answered 'no'.[16] Due to the bad shooting from the Zulus, Carey did not believe anyone was injured and continued the retreat for some time. While it was clear from their testimonies that they believed that the prince was probably killed at the beginning, no one is critical of their own actions. It was heard from Letocq that Carey said: 'Let us make haste, and go quickly', which sums up the reality of their escape, as no attempt was made to even recover the body or show some defiant defence at a different position.[17] While it may have been useless to do something, an act of bravery may have made the situation a bit more bearable for Carey and been something the army and the public would prefer to hear.

On 5 July, *The Illustrated London News* reported details of the death of the prince, with accounts from the participants at the court-martial. The evidence was from Lieutenant Carey, Sergeant Willis, Corporal Grubb, Trooper Cochrane, and Trooper Letocq. The evidence supplied by Carey tried to shift the responsibility of command to the prince, reinforcing his earlier belief that the prince was in charge of the patrol. He maintained throughout that it was the prince's decision that shaped the patrol's movements and safety. When Carey asked the prince to wait for a stronger escort to join them, Louis had replied: 'Oh no; we are quite strong enough'.[18] In another incident, Carey suggested to the prince that the group should off saddle in a different location, but Louis chose the Zulu homestead as the area to rest. Before the attack, Carey maintained that they should saddle up and move on, but the prince ordered that they 'wait another ten minutes'.[19] Carey admitted that there were no precautions by placing a guard in the area but omitted to report that this was his duty. With the information given – that the prince gave orders to the patrol – the court may have assumed that precautions were Louis's responsibility, and that Carey did his best to prevent any danger from occurring.

In due course Carey was found guilty by court martial on a charge of misbehaviour before the enemy and was sent home to be sentenced. The findings were forwarded to London for confirmation, but Judge Advocate General O'Dowd was unable to ratify the decision, as the proceedings had been rushed – the officers of the court martial had not been sworn-in according to military regulations. He also questioned the assertion that Carey had been in charge of the patrol. Meanwhile, the British press had learned more about Chelmsford's blunders and his staff's quest for scapegoats to take the blame. The death of the Prince Imperial bore too many similarities as, yet again, a junior officer was to take the blame for the faulty decisions of senior officers. The British press protectively gathered around Carey, who duly became a *cause célèbre*. When he arrived at Southampton, still under arrest, the mayor, the city council and a large crowd spurred on by a brass band met his ship to express their support. It is possible that such a public display of public opinion persuaded the Judge Advocate General to look at Carey's case with greater care. Following a request from the Prince Imperial's mother, the Countess Eugénie, Queen Victoria intervened to bring the matter to a close.[20]

Accordingly, the decision of the court-martial was not ratified and its verdict was annulled. Carey returned to full duty with his regiment. There is no evidence that he was treated by his fellow officers in any way other than with respect and proper courtesy. When Horse Guards reviewed the court martial findings, they found that, due to technicalities, the verdict was invalid. Had Carey gathered his patrol after the attack and gone back to look for the prince, it would have resulted in their death. A letter written by the Adjutant General to the General Officer in South Africa, C. H. Ellice, shows his opinions on the situation, with blame resting more on the shoulders of Harrison for not seeking Chelmsford's permission to allow Louis out of camp and further 'his orders to Lieutenant Carey were not sufficiently explicit, and he failed to impress upon the prince the duty of deferring to the military orders of the officer who accompanied him'. Once the initial shock of the prince's death had passed, cooler minds felt that there was no charge to answer, and that had Carey gathered his patrol after the attack and gone back looking for the prince, it would have resulted in all their deaths. Carey made the sensible argument that the idea of the patrol is not to fight, but to remain alive and bring back information.[21] Carey died in 1883 while still serving in India, reportedly of peritonitis. Various historians have perpetuated the myth that he died after being kicked by his horse; there is no contemporary evidence to support this. *The Army and Navy Gazette* reported his death rather ambiguously:

> Captain J. Carey 98th Regiment, of unfortunate history in Zululand, has, we regret to hear, died under mysterious circumstances in India, a victim of much persecution.

In the military context, the prince's death amounted to little more than an embarrassing scandal. It was an insignificant incident and had no bearing on the conduct or outcome of the campaign. The prince's body was returned to England for burial, firstly at Chislehurst and then later at Farnborough Abbey in Hampshire. The death of the Prince Imperial was the highest-ranking press coverage of the year 1879, with the marriage of the Duke of Connaught to Princess Louise of Prussia in second, and in third place the defeat at Isandlwana.

Chapter 3

Buller's Pre-Battle Reconnaissance, 3 July 1879

Early on the morning of 30 June 1879, Chelmsford's combined British Second Division and Flying Column began their descent from the Mthonjaneni Heights. It was hard work, for as they came off the hills they descended into the hot and humid valley of the White Mfolozi River separating the two armies. The terrain facing the British was rough, dried grassland and thick thornbush through which they had to cut a path for their wagons. At last, they had sight of their objective which had eluded Chelmsford for six months.

King Cetshwayo was in a delicate position. With the British in sight some of his regiments appeared reluctant to take up their allocated positions but, like Chelmsford, Cetshwayo and his advisors needed this battle – surrendering to the British was not an option for the Zulu king: he knew he must suffer a military defeat in order to end the war and retain his credibility and bargaining position after the battle. From his capital at Ulundi, Cetshwayo could only watch as the three British columns moved inexorably towards his capital. Many Zulus were now openly reluctant to gather round the king as they realised that their defeat was inevitable. Cetshwayo's initial attempt in May to regroup the Zulu army had met with only partial success, perhaps due to a rumour that swept across Zululand that the British would destroy the traditional Zulu family system by taking their wives. Nevertheless, as the British advanced ever closer, greater numbers rallied to the king's call to arms. A number of Zulu chiefs had already displayed their disillusion with war and in anticipation of defeat, Prince Makwendu kaMpande, one of Cetshwayo's junior brothers, had already surrendered himself and his family to Crealock's coastal column. He was later followed by Prince Dabulamanzi, the commander at Rorke's Drift, who along with Mavumengwana kaGodide, a commander at Isandlwana, established a diplomatic relationship with Crealock. More defections along the coastal regions were rumoured and some chiefs declared that they were unable to fight as their *imizi* were overcrowded with wounded. Cetshwayo called an urgent meeting of chiefs, and all agreed to commence negotiations with the British – only to have them dismissed by a Chelmsford determined to fight the final battle.

The die was cast. As dawn broke on 2 July, the British reached their hilltop vantage point looking down on the White Umfolozi River and beyond across the Mahlabatini Plain to Ulundi, just five miles distant in the haze of the early morning. Clearly visible was the vast sprawling conglomeration of many hundreds of huts stretched between two distant ranges of hills. The plain was open and undulating, covered with long grass that was only just turning brown after the unusually protracted summer rains, with Ulundi hemmed in on all sides by the surrounding rolling hills. The great royal homesteads were scattered around them. During the morning, while preparing to resume the British advance, rumours of a Zulu attack swept across the 2nd Division, whereupon some of the troops blindly opened fire on a party of Buller's Flying Column scouts crossing the river, somehow mistaking them for Zulus. As a precaution Chelmsford ordered the troops back to the camp as the 2nd Division collapsed into chaos. Normality was only restored once it was realised that there was no Zulu attack. That evening Chelmsford established a temporary camp at the foot of the hills, remembered today as Fort Nolela, (sometimes mistakenly referred to as Fort Victoria). Chelmsford took no chances. The wagons of the two columns were deployed in mutually supportive laagers, while a stone breastwork was built as a redoubt on a commanding rise. Grass and bush were cleared around the camp, and range markers were set up. This did little to prevent yet another false alarm that night.

Ulundi was the trophy that the British had strived for through all the long vicissitudes of the campaign. The war, which had been embarked upon so enthusiastically in January, had collapsed into horror at Isandlwana. The successful defence of Rorke's Drift had offered a brief moral respite, but the Zulus had steadfastly contested each step of the British recovery. Misfortune and disaster had dogged Chelmsford at each step of the way and created in the minds of his men an impression that the Zulus were an unnaturally dangerous enemy, a view that the victories at Khambula and Gingindlovu had done little to dispel. Yet now, at least, it seemed that an end was in sight, and that victory was within their grasp. Over the previous month, the Zulus had been unable to mount a serious challenge to the renewed British advance, and their resistance had been reduced to a few dogged skirmishes. Just a few days before, British cavalry had swept through the emaKhosini valley and destroyed many of the oldest royal homesteads. Now, Ulundi itself, Cetshwayo's seat of power, lay clearly in sight before them. Even from a distance, the troops had seen large bodies of Zulu warriors rehearsing their battle positions across the plain – the king preparing his regiments for one last act of defiance.

For the inexperienced British soldiers at the temporary fort, now only five miles from the Zulu army, their anxiety was palpable. Both sides were now concentrating for battle, and it was impossible for the nervous soldiers not to be aware of the Zulus. The anxiety level was equally high among the inexperienced 2nd Division, unbloodied and fresh out of England. The far-off spectacle of the Zulus' seemingly enthusiastic preparation for battle was particularly unnerving to the young soldiers, who were all familiar with the chilling story of Isandlwana. That afternoon, British water collecting parties came under sporadic Zulu rifle fire from the far, Zulu held, Mfolozi riverbank and that night the sounds of Zulu chanting and battle preparations could be clearly heard.

Unbeknown to Chelmsford's men, serious problems beset the Zulu high command. The Zulu chiefs were anticipating their own defeat and morale was slipping away, although their army was still viewed by the British as formidable. As already noted, Cetshwayo attempted one last call for peace. In a desperate gesture he sent a herd of his finest cattle towards Chelmsford's camp but the warriors guarding the river, the uKhandempemvu, indignantly sent them back. Chelmsford was later to write of the incident: 'A large herd of white cattle was observed being driven from the King's Kraal towards us but was driven back again shortly afterwards'.[1]

At first light on 3 July Chelmsford dispatched Colonel Buller to undertake a reconnaissance of the approach to Ulundi. With a strong mounted force of some 500 mounted men from the FLH, Transvaal Rangers, Baker's Horse, Natal Light Horse and the Edendale troop of the mounted black auxiliaries. Buller crossed the river in two parties; a hundred men of Baker's Horse, commanded by Commandant Baker, had crossed at the old trader's drift directly below the British camp. This river crossing point lay under the guns of Zulu snipers who appeared not to have expected an attack there. Baker's men crossed with such dash that the snipers abandoned their position among clumps of rocks along the river and fled back towards Ulundi. Meanwhile, Buller's approaching riders had crossed at another drift a mile downstream and had swept up behind the bluffs, scattering the Zulus who were fleeing from Baker's men. While Baker regrouped, Buller's party struck out towards the centre of the plain in pursuit of their objectives: reconnoitring the proposed river crossing, choosing the ground for the coming battle and ascertaining the main Zulu dispositions. The Mahlabatini Plain, with Ulundi and its vastly sprawling conglomeration of hundreds of huts at its hub, stretched between two distant ranges of hills, and Buller was especially interested in a small rise just one mile from the king's homestead which gave a good view of the surrounding terrain. As Buller approached the grassy plain he detached sixty men of the Transvaal Rangers under Commandant Raaf to serve as a rearguard while Buller rode towards a low rise, passing the abandoned kwaNodwengu homestead on their left.

Uncharacteristically, Buller was led into a carefully prepared Zulu ambush near the Mbilane stream when a party of Zulu scouts suddenly appeared from the waist-high grass just 200 yards from Buller and then ran off towards the king's homestead. Not realizing it was a trap, Buller's men instinctively gave chase. Captain Lord William Beresford singled out one warrior and rode him down, delivering a thrust with his sword that pierced both the Zulu's shield and the man himself. Beresford announced his kill with a pig-sticking cry, popular in India: 'First spear!'

As Buller's men crested a slight rise the Zulus disappeared. As the riders advanced they saw a herd of goats being driven away in front of them. The goats then scattered, revealing a few Zulu horsemen, also riding off towards oNdini. Among the fleeing Zulus was Zibhebhu himself, one of the most skilful and respected commanders in Zululand. As many as 4,000 hidden Zulus, including Zibhebhu's own regiment, the uMxapho, had laid a trap to snare Buller's men.[2]

By now, Buller's party was descending a grassy slope on the far side of the rise at the bottom of which was the Mbilane stream. Some of Buller's command were becoming distinctly uneasy as the Zulus seemed to be leading them in one direction, and at that point Buller's Aide de Camp (ADC), Captain Sir Thomas Fermour-Hesketh, shouted that there was a large body of Zulus concealed in the grass ahead. Buller ordered his men to halt, and just in time. As he did so, a great arc of hundreds of warriors rose up around them on three sides, just 50 yards away.

Buller had unwittingly been led into a carefully prepared trap, now sprung – albeit prematurely. The Zulus had plaited and woven grass into a series of ropes specially designed to trip the horses which they rapidly pulled in to tighten. Buller's men managed to extricate themselves before the ropes could entrap them, but the flanking Zulus were already rushing to surround them. Another group of Zulus armed with captured Martini-Henry rifles then fired a volley from about 50 yards distance, which panicked several of the horses. Sergeant Fitzmaurice of the 1/24th Regiment, attached to the Mounted Infantry, fell and became trapped beneath his wounded horse. Two troopers, Pearce of the Frontier Light Horse and Peacock of the Natal Light Horse were shot and killed outright. Trooper Raubenheim of the FLH was badly wounded and fell from his horse. As the Zulus closed in, a desperate attempt was made by those still mounted to save the fallen wounded. Nearby, Lord Beresford had spotted Sergeant Fitzmaurice's predicament. The war correspondent, Melton Prior, who heard the story later that day, wrote:

In the retreat Lord William Beresford, turning round, saw the four legs of a white horse kicking in the air, and realising at once that it belonged to one of our men, rode straight for it, to discover that his surmise was quite right, the horse had been shot and the man had fallen half-stunned. 'Get up!' he said to the man, and he seemed too dazed to answer; whereupon Lord William said, 'If you don't get up at once I will jump down and punch your head', at which the man did rise, and at last Lord William succeeded in helping him onto the horse behind him, the man clutching Beresford around the waist, and so they galloped off.

All the time this was taking place the Zulus were firing all they knew from a donga close by; but I am happy to say that both got away safely. If any man ever won a V.C. Lord William certainly did on that occasion, and eventually he received it.

I remember when he came up to us that his back was one mass of blood. We all thought the man was wounded, but on close inspection we found that he had only damaged his nose in the fall from the horse.[3]

Captain D'Arcy of the Frontier Light Horse then saw Trooper Raubenheim lying on the ground. He immediately rode back to where the trooper lay. D'Arcy dismounted and, while holding the reins of his now frightened horse, helped Raubenheim to his feet. D'Arcy mounted his horse then hauled the wounded trooper up behind him. With the leading Zulus almost upon them the terrified horse managed a few yards and then threw both riders. Though severely winded by the fall, D'Arcy rapidly remounted but was forced to abandon Raubenheim to the stabbing Zulus. His body was later found cut up by the Zulus for their '*muthi*' medicine.[4]

Nearby, Lord Beresford and Sergeant O'Toole of the FLH had seen Sergeant Fitzmaurice fall and both dashed to his aid; O'Toole fired a few shots at the Zulus to keep them back, then dismounted to help Fitzmaurice into the saddle. Unable to manage this with his carbine in hand, he had, in the quaint words of his subsequent citation, 'given up his carbine'. With O'Toole dismounted and pushing Fitzmaurice onto the horse, Lord Beresford managed to get Fitzmaurice to hold onto him and galloped off to safety. O'Toole barely escaped with his life. For their gallantry, D'Arcy, Lord Beresford and O'Toole received the Victoria Cross. The bravery of Sergeant Major Simeon Kambula of the Edendale Troop, who determinedly held off a group of charging Zulus, was also recognized with the award of the Distinguished Conduct Medal.

With the Zulus in hot pursuit Buller's men were forced to ride for their lives. Near the kwaNodwengu homestead they were reinforced by Raaf's waiting men who came forward to support them pouring volleys into the pursuing Zulus. They then fell back on the river, repeatedly turning to fire volleys at the pursuing Zulus. The Zulu pursuit remained close and the 'horns' might have succeeded in cutting off the line of retreat before it reached the river had Baker's men not been waiting in support. As they drew close to the drift, the infantry and artillery on the far bank also came forward and fired on the Zulus, driving them back. For the watching soldiers in camp and about to go into battle, the level of the Zulus' spirited attack left them in no doubt that the following day was not a foregone conclusion. According to Melton Prior, 'Those who watched the brave little band return, declared that it was touch and go whether they would get across safely. However, they succeeded in doing so'.[5]

Buller's venture ended with a curious encounter. Safely across the river, Buller looked back to see a figure seemingly sketching on the Zulu riverbank. Buller shouted ordering the man to return but his command was ignored. Buller called across again, ordering him to retreat or face arrest. The figure was Charles Fripp, the renowned war correspondent from *The Graphic*. As a civilian, Fripp was indignant that he had been threatened with arrest, and demanded to know, from the first officer he met, who had shouted at him. This officer was Beresford, 'still smothered in the blood of the man whose life he had saved'. Beresford, clearly still unsettled by his recent experiences, replied 'If you don't speak more politely I'll pull you off your horse and thrash you!' Fripp promptly jumped off his horse, and to the amazement of the onlookers, put up his fists. Beresford, 'a notorious bruiser and all-round sportsman', managed to keep Fripp at arms' length until Fripp landed a kick, at which point Beresford collapsed in laughter, shouting 'Oh, he's kicked me! Take him away; I'm frightened. He's kicked me!' Fripp was eventually dragged away, unrepentant, by his fellow correspondents, Melton Prior and Archibald Forbes.[6]

As a skirmish, the Zulus had got the better of the affair. Although their ambush had been triggered prematurely, they had killed three of Buller's men and driven them from the field. Major Anstruther of the 94th Regiment noted with some satisfaction that: 'they made the beggars show themselves in number about 20,000. The cavalry killed a few, a hundred or 150'.[7] There was a distinctly uneasy feeling in the British camp at the obvious display of Zulu determination and skill.

For the soldiers about to go into battle, the level of the Zulus' spirited attack left them in no doubt that the following day was not to be a foregone conclusion. That night, the British were again kept awake by the sounds of the Zulu army's last preparations for battle: the sonorous chanting of the warriors and the shrill ululating of the women encouraging them, coupled with the piercing cries of the Zulus' war-doctors. The protective medicines they administered on this occasion were given potency by using body parts removed from the corpses of Buller's men left on the field. The grass had been trampled where Zulus had gathered around Raubenheim's body to cut off the necessary body parts. Had he been taken alive and tortured he would presumably have been taken to the royal homesteads, where the impi was doctored.

Few of Chelmsford's waiting force slept. Overall, the skirmish encouraged Chelmsford; the Zulus were clearly willing to fight and would give him the battle to win the war. Chelmsford wrote of the skirmish:

Lieutenant Colonel Buller completely succeeded in the duty entrusted him: having collected his mounted men near Indabakaombi from the thorny country near the river, he advanced rapidly towards Ulundi, passing Nodwengo on his right: he had reached the vicinity of the stream Untukuwini about three quarters of a mile from Ulundi, when he was met by a heavy fire from a considerable body of the enemy lying concealed in the long grass around the stream – wheeling about, he retreated to the high ground near Nodwengo where he commenced to retire by alternate portions of his force in a deliberate manner – the Zulus were checked, but in the meantime large bodies of the enemy were to be seen advancing from every direction, and I was enabled with my own eyes to gain the information I wished for as to the manner of advance and points from which it would be made in the event of our force advancing on Ulundi – though the Zulus advanced rapidly and endeavoured to get round his flank, Colonel Buller was able to retire his force across the river with but a few casualties ....[8]

Chelmsford later wrote of Buller's incident:

As no message had been received from Ketshwayo the following morning [3 July] and as considerable annoyance was offered to our watering parties by Zulus firing on them, I arranged for a reconnaissance to be made by Lieutenant Colonel Buller C.B. with a strong mounted force of some 500 mounted men from the 1st Squadron Mounted Infantry, the Frontier Light Horse, Transvaal Rangers, Baker's Horse, Natal Light Horse, and the Edendale troop of the mounted black auxiliaries.

Lieutenant Colonel Buller crossed the river by the lower drift to the right of our camp, and was soon in possession of the high ground on our front and the Indabakaombie Kraal. The object of Lieutenant Colonel Buller's reconnaissance was to advance towards Ulundi and report on the road and whether there was a good position where our force could make its stand if attacked.

I was also anxious if possible to cause the enemy to show his force, its points of gathering, and plan of attack.

Lieutenant Colonel Buller completely succeeded in the duty entrusted him: having collected his mounted men near Indabakaombi from the thorny country near the river, he advanced rapidly towards Ulundi, passing Nodwengo on his right: he had reached the vicinity of the stream Untukuwini about three quarters of a mile from Ulundi, when he was met by a heavy fire from a considerable body of the enemy lying concealed in the long grass around the stream – Wheeling about, he retreated to the high ground near Nodwengo where he commenced to retire by alternate portions of his force in a deliberate manner – the Zulus were checked, but in the meantime large bodies of the enemy were to be seen advancing from every direction, and I was enabled with my own eyes to gain the information I wished for as to the manner of advance and points from which it would be made in the event of our force advancing on Ulundi – though the Zulus advanced rapidly and endeavoured to get round his flank, Lieutenant Colonel Buller was able to retire his force across the river with but a few casualties.[9]

In fact, the dry tones of Chelmsford's official despatch concealed a lively exchange in which the Zulus had arguably got the better of the affair. Buller had, of course, established himself as a master of irregular warfare during the campaign, and his expertise had narrowly prevented his men from falling into a deadly trap. In due course, three V.C.s were awarded for the incident – to Beresford, D'Arcy and O'Toole – while Sergeant Major Simeon Kambula of the Edendale Troop was awarded the Silver Medal for Distinguished Conduct.

It is known that Cetshwayo departed from Ulundi just before dawn on 4 July, shedding himself of much of his cumbersome wagon train. Chelmsford then gathered his force and set off marching towards Ulundi, especially focused on the small rise advocated by Buller as the perfect site for battle and just one mile from the king's homestead. Even as the column wound slowly down from their overnight camp, Cetshwayo made one last attempt to halt the invasion. Two of the king's most trusted royal messengers came to the British camp. They were bearing the sword of the Prince Imperial, taken at his death on 1 June, as a token of the king's good faith, seeking peace terms; but Chelmsford sought nothing less than the total destruction of the Zulu nation: he needed his victory, even if Pyrrhic.

Chapter 4

The Battle of Ulundi, 4 July 1879

The burning of Ulundi means nothing in Zulu eyes.
A bloody but barren victory.[1]

It was from King Cetshwayo's dusty and sprawling capital at Ulundi that Britain's sophisticated political and military domination across South Africa had been so suddenly and seriously challenged. Situated on the Mahlabatini Plain, just 70 miles from the site of the earlier and unimaginable Zulu victory over Chelmsford's force at Isandlwana, Ulundi consisted of an estimated 1,500 huts densely spread over an area later measured to be no more than 200 acres in total, with the king's personal quarters, the *ikhanda*, located centrally. Another nine *amakhanda* were located within 2 miles of Ulundi. Movement through Ulundi was via a labyrinth of passageways radiating out from the royal household that dominated the capital. During the three weeks leading up to 4 July, the population of Ulundi was swollen by the influx of some 20,000 warriors responding to the king's urgent call to resist the British invasion. Now most of the women, children and other non-combatants had moved away towards the protection of the surrounding hills to the north and east: carrying their bundled possessions, they clogged the tracks through the bush in their desperation to escape the consequences of the forthcoming battle.

In the early hours of the morning of 4 July Cetshwayo and his escort left Ulundi. As dawn broke Chelmsford's 5,000 men camped around Fort Nolela were roused from their sleep and, without delay, set off in one all-encompassing column towards Ulundi for the final battle. It was the largest force deployed by Chelmsford for any battle during the Zulu War. The newly reconstituted and inexperienced 1/24th Regiment was held in reserve, along with the column's wagons. Two 24th companies already having been left at Fort Marshall, the remaining five were held in reserve at Fort Nolela.

The regiment's officers were displeased with not being able to avenge their regiment's defeat at Isandlwana, but Chelmsford was not prepared to take completely inexperienced soldiers into a major battle. He knew that the risk of serious casualties amongst a rebuilt battalion was too high, especially with a high proportion of inexperienced or recently arrived soldiers unfamiliar with each other or their officers. Chelmsford decided they would have to be content with watching the battle from afar.

An hour later, and unopposed by the Zulus, this cumbersome force waded across the shallow White Mfolozi River and then, in a tightly packed column, marched towards Buller's previously reconnoitred small rise in the middle of the Mahlabatini Plain. All the while Buller's riders patrolled the high ground along the route. To protect the slow-moving column, mounted men rode out to cover the column's immediate front and flanks while the 17th Lancers covered the rear. The cumbersome column enclosed Chelmsford's headquarters staff and the ammunition and entrenching-tool carts, as well as the Royal Artillery's guns, although these were positioned to enable them to come into action on each face without delay. With the sprawl of huts that was Ulundi now in full view less than two miles distant, the Zulus could be seen forming up in opposition to the advancing column; visibility over the Zulu army's position was still partially obscured by drifting smoke from a thousand Zulu campfires and from the early morning mist hanging over the Mbilane stream that wound its way between the two armies. Many thousands of Zulus could also be seen assembling on the more distant hilltops to the north. Chelmsford ordered the advancing British column to 'form square', which it did, on the move, turning slowly and menacingly to face the advancing Zulus. A few minutes later, the British gained the high ground they sought and settled down to await the expected Zulu charge.

The assembled Zulu army was to the north and east of the square, in the direction of Ulundi, with an estimated total of over 15,000 men with another 5,000 along the hills in reserve; all were formed up in regimental order. Then, as one body, they steadily began to advance for their first attack. Just as Chelmsford had anticipated, the Zulus were relying on their traditional attack formation and their 'horns' (flanks) began to encircle the square. All the Zulu regiments that had fought in the previous battles were present and command at Ulundi appears to have been shared between Chief

Mnyamana Buthelezi, Chief Ziwedu and Chief Ntshingwayo kaMahole – the victor of Isandlwana – while the vigorous Chief Zibhebhu kaMaphitha of the Mandlakazi commanded the left horn. A captured Zulu prisoner later commented:

All the army was present today. We had very sick hearts in the fight when we saw how strong the white army was, and we were startled by the number of horsemen.[2]

The Zulus' advance slowed down as it approached the now stationary square. Chelmsford presumed this indicated their reluctance to fight, so at about 8.30am Buller and his mounted troops moved out of the square and using Buller's proven tactic of provocation, rode to within one hundred yards of the massed Zulu force and raked its leading ranks with several volleys of rifle fire. This blatant and bloody taunt enraged the Zulus, who charged. Buller and his men rapidly withdrew back into the relative safety of the square, which enabled the artillery and riflemen to commence volley fire. The men forming the square were prepared for the imminent onslaught: the infantry were lined up in four ranks, two kneeling and two standing. The artillery pieces and Gatling guns were sited at the corners of the square and in the centre of the two flanks.

Battle then commenced with the mounted men on the right and left of the square becoming the first to be committed. The most determined Zulu attack came from the left horn under the command of Chief Zibhebhu. Watching the attack alongside Chelmsford's staff was the war correspondent Melton Prior, who clearly believed that the battle was not at all one-sided:

I ran down to where the 21st and 58th Regiments were heavily engaged with some Zulus, said to be 6,000 strong and 30 deep, who were charging, and it was then that I heard Lord Chelmsford say to the troops, 'Men, fire faster; can't you fire faster?' Now it is not my business to question the wisdom of this remark, but I cannot help contrasting it with Lord Wolseley's well-known order, 'Fire slow, fire slow! However, the Zulus who charged this corner did not succeed in breaking it; the terrific fire of our men made them stagger, halt, and fall back in a straggling mass, leaving a heap of dead and dying on the ground.[3]

For a period of twenty minutes the British rate of fire was so steady and accurate that the Zulus were unable to get close enough to inflict any serious damage upon the British line. Another journalist present, Charles Norris-Newman, wrote that the Zulus were:

Checked by the heavy, regular and well sustained fire from the various regiments, which swept the plateau, and gradually brought the Zulus to a stand, checked by the withering effects of that hail of bullets, which did such murderous execution as all their efforts could not prevail.[4]

Chelmsford was especially pleased with the behaviour of the infantry, until now relatively untried; the men were steady and their firing was well controlled on all sides of the square. Volley firing by sections was employed throughout the battle, although on several occasions it was necessary to wait between volleys for the volley smoke to clear. For their part, the Zulus were unable to inflict much damage on the British square, even though they possessed several hundred Martini-Henry rifles taken from Isandlwana. Their usual firearms, a collection of antiquated flintlock and percussion rifles, were never a threat to the British although Chelmsford was clearly ready for considerable casualties. He wrote:

The fire of the enemy ... was very heavy, and many casualties, I regret to say, occurred, but when it is remembered that within our comparatively small square, all the cavalry, mounted men, natives, hospital attendants, etc. were packed, it is a matter of congratulation that they were not heavier.[5]

At about 9am it became apparent to the British that the Zulus were becoming disorganised and their enthusiasm to attack the British wall of fire began to wane. They nevertheless stood their ground in the face of repeated Martin-Henry volleys, the barrage from the Royal Artillery's 7- and 9-pound guns and from the column's two Gatling guns. A number of Zulus had managed to get to within 30 yards of the British line but under such a hail of fire they could not sustain their attack. As Melton Prior recalled:

A bullet banged into one of our native allies close to us and rolled him over. By the way, it was very funny to see these men lying flat on the ground, with their shields covering their backs. Another bullet killed a horse behind us and made him jump at least three feet in the air. Then all at once there appeared to be a perfect hailstorm of bullets in our direction, and we both wriggled on our knees, until one in particular passed between us with a nasty 'phew', and my friend exclaimed, 'My God, Prior, that was close'.[6]

The attack soon began to falter, and it was evident to the British that the Zulus were beaten. Many warriors took what cover they could in the long grass and some brave individuals crawled back towards the soldiers to return fire. However, large numbers began to leave the battlefield, and this only served to weaken the resolve of those further back and previously keen to engage the British. With the Zulu attack controlled, Chelmsford again sought to inflict the maximum number of casualties upon the Zulus, and as at Khambula and Gingindlovu he ordered Buller and his mounted troops, along with the 17th Lancers, out of the square to harass the retreating Zulus. Chelmsford wrote:

The fire from the Artillery and Infantry was so effective that, within half an hour, signs of hesitation were perceivable in the movements of the enemy: I then directed Colonel Drury-Lowe to take out the 17th Lancers. Passing out by the rear face he led his regiment towards the Nodwengu Kraal, dispersing and killing those who had not time to reach the shelter of the Kraal or the bush below, then wheeling to the right charged through the Zulus who, in full flight, were endeavouring to reach the lower slopes of the mountains beyond.

Numbers of the enemy in this direction who had not taken part in the actual attack were now firing and momentarily strengthened by those fleeing were enabled to pour in a considerable fire on the advancing Lancers below them. Our cavalry did not halt however until the whole of the lower ground was swept and some 150 of the enemy killed: many of those they had passed in their speed, had collected in a ravine to their rear, these were attacked and destroyed by our mounted natives.[7]

The Lancers attacked with great enthusiasm: they were still smarting from their previous failed clash against the Zulus when they had lost their adjutant, Lieutenant Frith. This time they could charge across open country, and they fell upon the Zulus showing no mercy as they speared and hacked the fleeing and wounded warriors. The Lancers nevertheless took some casualties. The most notable was Captain the Honourable Wyatt-Edgell who was shot dead. Their commanding officer, Colonel Drury-Lowe, wrote of the pursuit with professional pride:

> The pursuit was carried out in a most determined manner by five troops of the 17th Lancers and 24 men of the King's Dragoon Guards (one troop remained inside the square unknown to me). The Zulus fled in every direction and were pursued for a distance of some three miles across the slope of the hills before mentioned, very many being killed with the lance, which proved their decided superiority to the sword in pursuit. It would, I think, be invidious to point out any particular officer or man, when all, I think, showed the same eagerness to reach the enemy, and rode with the greatest determination into the scattered Zulus, for the most time under a galling fire from the hills, where the enemy formed themselves into groups and kept up an incessant fire.[8]

Chelmsford's mounted Irregulars then joined the fray and, mindful of the massacre of their colleagues at Isandlwana, trotted among the scattering Zulus, shooting them with impunity. One of the Edendale troop was seen to shoot and wound a warrior and then set about questioning him: having got the answers he sought, the trooper shot the warrior dead. Many warriors lay down in the grass in the hope of escape, knowing that they would be out of range of the riders' swords, but once the immediate area around the square was secured the Native Contingent was released to kill any wounded or hiding Zulus. The horror of indiscriminate killing continued for another two hours and extended for several miles in all directions until the fleeing Zulus had either escaped or been killed. Major Robinson was a witness to the assegaing of wounded Zulus and asked a correspondent accompanying him not to comment on the slaughter: 'or they will think us awful brutes, as bad as we did the Bashi-bazouks'.[9] The Zulu reserves that had occupied the slopes of the surrounding hills were beyond the reach of the cavalry, so the 9-pounder guns were moved from the rear and front faces of the square to shell them.

It was immediately clear to the men forming the square that the victory had been a decisive one. For Chelmsford, it meant relief from the months of tension he had laboured under since Isandlwana. It was all the sweeter because he had been able to achieve his victory before Sir Garnet Wolseley could take command.

As soon as the last groups of Zulus had been forced back over the hills Chelmsford ordered the destruction by shellfire of Cetshwayo's royal homestead. With Chelmsford's fighting square still intact, orders were given for the column's dead to be buried and the casualties tended to. An hour later the column marched forwards for half a mile to the Mbilane stream, passing down the same grass slope where Buller's men had been ambushed the day before. After eating a midday meal, the column retraced its steps back to Fort Nolela on the far bank of the White Mfolozi River. The final battle of the Zulu war had lasted just forty minutes. *The Graphic* commented:

> Our cavalry ... galloped out in pursuit, and mowed them down on the hill-sides in every direction. It was a brilliant half-hours work, but much as we may congratulate ourselves, upon the gallant behaviour of our own men, we cannot help feeling some measure of admiration for the determined gallantry of their savage opponents.[10]

The wide-ranging patrols of Lancers began to set fire to the surrounding royal homesteads while others, including Bengough's NNC continued to track down and despatch wounded and hiding Zulus; the on-going sound of sporadic gunfire evidenced the hunt and executions. Chelmsford then gave his officers permission to ride into Ulundi itself. A race ensued and Lord Beresford was the first into the royal homestead and according to Melton Prior, was nicknamed 'Ulundi Beresford' for his daring dash. The scamper into Ulundi nevertheless resulted in further tragedy for Chelmsford when his interpreter, the Honourable William Drummond, disappeared. He was last seen riding through the vast array of huts and to the great concern of those who knew him, all attempts to find him failed. His assegaied and burned body was found several months later.

The British ransacked the king's huts and then set fire to Ulundi. Those looking for treasure were disappointed, for there was nothing of value to loot. All the while the cavalry routed the fleeing Zulus for another hour killing every warrior they could find. All mounted troops were then recalled to the square; but not before they had killed about 1,500 Zulu warriors. As was usual following a successful battle, Chelmsford addressed his gathered men and thanked them for their efforts. The entire force then about turned, and with

Ulundi now well ablaze, began to march back towards the White Mfolozi River with the band playing 'Rule Britannia' and the 'Royal Alliance March'. They passed the battlefield and its glinting rows of expended ammunition cases – later estimated to have amounted to over 35,000 rounds of Martini-Henry ammunition. By the evening, the British were all safely back in camp and Chelmsford could relax for the first time in many months. It was the victory that Chelmsford so desperately sought and, with the battle won, the British began to withdraw from Zululand.

BRITISH

Participants

The total force amounted to 4,132 white troops and 1,009 black troops.

Imperial

Lieutenant General Lord Chelmsford, with 2nd Division commanded by Major General Newdigate, commanded the column. The Flying Column (formerly the Northern Column) was commanded by Brigadier General Sir Evelyn Wood.

The 2nd Division included units from: King's Dragoon Guards; 17th (Duke of Cambridge's Own) Lancers; Royal Artillery; Royal Engineers; 2/21st Royal Scots Fusiliers; 94th Regiment; and the 58th (Rutland) Regiment.

The Flying Column included units from: Royal Artillery; Royal Engineers, 1/13th Light Infantry; 80th Regiment; 90th Light Infantry; Army Medical Department; Hospital Corps; Mounted Infantry; and Army Staff Corps.

Colonial

2nd NNC; Shepstone's Horse; Bettington's Horse; Wood's Irregulars; Natal Pioneers; Transvaal Rangers; Frontier Light Horse; Baker's Horse; Natal Light Horse; and Natal Native Horse.

On the day of the battle the newly reconstituted 1/24th Regiment was held in reserve, two companies at Fort Marshall and five companies at Fort Nolela. Chelmsford was fully aware that they were 24th Regiment in name only. They were fresh and inexperienced recruit replacements drawn from thirteen home-based regiments.

ZULU

The total Zulu force was estimated at 20,000 warriors and consisted of elements of various *amabutho* under the command of Ziwedu, Cetshwayo's brother. He was supported by three battle-experienced *indunas*, Mnyamana Buthelezi (the Zulu Prime Minister), Prince Dabulamanzi (who had commanded at Rorke's Drift) and Ntshingwayo Khoza (who had commanded at Isandlwana).

CASUALTIES

Column Two officers and ten men were killed, with one officer and sixty-nine men wounded.

Zulu casualties. Not less than 1,450 dead warriors were found around the battlefield. Most of these would have been killed during the rout.

Buller post Ulundi

Lord Chelmsford had won his victory and so denied the glory to his replacement, Garnet Wolseley. Despite the new commander's wish to retain the services of his protégé, Buller returned home virtually a mental and physical wreck. No one had seen more action or ridden greater distances than had Buller. The bloodletting had also taken its toll, and he was weary of killing. Exhausted and feverish, Buller also suffered from veldt-sores, which so crippled his hands that his writing was permanently affected.

A grateful nation was not prepared to let him convalesce quietly at his Devon home. He was promoted to colonel and ADC to the Queen and given the CMG. He was also summoned to Balmoral, where his sovereign pinned the Victoria Cross to his tunic. This was in recognition of his valour for rescuing at least four unhorsed men at Hlobane, but he could have won it many times over for other brave acts. Notably, the record for most VCs is held by the 24th Regiment, who were awarded nine campaign VC's, the second is the men of Buller's Mounted Irregulars, who received six.

Although Redvers Buller went on to higher command and a knighthood, the greatest achievement of his career was in the Zulu War, where he took command of untrained volunteers and moulded them into the most effective unit to emerge from the conflict.

Chapter 5

After Ulundi: The Beginning of the End

The death of 10,000 Zulus ... defending their hearths and homes.[1]

For Chelmsford the Zulu war was over – but at an unexpectedly high financial cost of over five million pounds. Apart from the loss to the exchequer, it cost the lives of 76 British officers and 1,007 men killed in action, plus a similar number of Natal auxiliaries. A further 17 officers and 330 men had died of disease and a further 99 officers and 1,286 men were invalided away from the campaign. Exact figures for Zulu losses are impossible to assess; they certainly lost 10,000 warriors killed in action and conservative estimates suggest a similar number probably died from their injuries.[2]

While Chelmsford's victorious column was celebrating victory at Ulundi the day after the battle, this was not the reason Major Marter was up at 3am. He was composing an embarrassing missive to Major General Frederick Marshall, commander of the Cavalry Brigade and lines of communication on the advance into Zululand. Marter had been faced with an unexpected breakdown in discipline involving members of his own detachment. Some of his men had been derelict in their duties. They had been found drunk, and others had gone absent from bivouac and sentry duty, not a pleasant occurrence for the officer in charge. Marter wrote that he was shocked by his troops' behaviour as his men had performed their duties well since crossing the Blood River into hostile Zululand on 1 June. The completed memo, after having been signed by Major Marter, was passed on the same day, 5 July 1879, to Brigade Major Captain Herbert Stewart, who added a note ordering court martial proceedings for the men drunk on duty and the commanding officers' discretion on punishment for the other offences. On 6 July, the next day, Major C. J. Bromhead (the brother of Gonville

Bromhead of Rorke's Drift fame), who was commandant of the post at Koppie Allein, also inserted an addendum indicating Marter was to escort the prisoners to Fort Newdigate for disposition. One wonders at the fate of the prisoners. Courts martial and punishments, including reduction in rank and flogging, were most likely carried out. No less than 545 British soldiers were flogged during the war: the highest number in one year for many years. The wrong doer was usually given twenty-five lashes for offences ranging from drunkenness and stealing to insubordination and desertion.

During the day after Chelmsford's victory at Ulundi, Chelmsford received a telegram from the Secretary of State for War, Lord Stanley, informing him that General Sir Garnet Wolseley had arrived at Durban to supersede him. Wolseley had swiftly countermanded Chelmsford's current operational orders in a deliberate attempt to stamp his own mark on what remained of the campaign, but bad weather had intervened and forced Wolseley to abandon his plan to get to the front line by sea, so he had had to resort to travelling overland. Chelmsford had exploited Wolseley's predicament and the delays in communication and, with certain victory so close, Chelmsford had seized the opportunity to fight his final battle of the war. The same day that the Battle of Ulundi was won, Chelmsford resigned his command. Forced to travel overland the exhausted Wolseley and his staff finally reached the hamlet of St. Paul's to be personally greeted by Chelmsford who, no doubt with a degree of smug satisfaction, surrendered his command of the remaining forces in Zululand to Wolseley, a veritable poison chalice. Wolseley made a number of references to the inconclusive nature of the Battle of Ulundi, although it could be argued that he was only trying to emphasise his role in Zululand.[3]

Chelmsford had no intention of chasing after King Cetshwayo or remaining in Africa any longer than was necessary. Capturing the king and restoring normality to Zululand would be a thankless and highly complex task, one that would fully occupy Wolseley and his staff for many weeks if not months. Chelmsford knew that before Wolseley could report anything negative, he would be back in London with his loyal staff portraying to parliament and the press the war's successful conclusion and their brilliant victory at Ulundi. Within three weeks Chelmsford was en route to London: Wolseley was welcome to a now shattered Zululand and whatever remained of the war – and worse, with King Cetshwayo nowhere in sight.

But Chelmsford had unwittingly made certain aspects of the post war situation easier for Wolseley. In the days preceding Ulundi, many Zulu chiefs, uncomfortable with the presence of Wolseley's large occupying army, had begun to negotiate their surrender. Their defeat on 4 July forced them to accept the inevitable. Within a fortnight of the battle, most of the coastal chiefs – including Prince Dabulamanzi, the commander at Rorke's Drift six months before – had officially surrendered.

Certainly, Major Philip Anstruther of the 94th noted that, after Ulundi, ordinary Zulus seemed resigned to the reality of defeat: 'There is no doubt the war is over, the Zulus come in every day bringing guns and cattle and are getting a great deal too friendly'.[4] But Chelmsford had deliberately left Wolseley with other significant problems. Wolseley regarded Chelmsford's withdrawal from Ulundi as premature, especially as the whereabouts of King Cetshwayo was still unknown, and Chelmsford had made no effort to secure the surrender of the important chiefdoms in central and northern Zululand. In the face of such uncertainty Wolseley's immediate plan was to reoccupy Ulundi, but this was amended to a position near Ulundi due to the total destruction of the Zulu capital and the profusion of Zulu corpses left rotting in the open air.

The British regular forces that had taken Ulundi promptly marched out of Zululand and left its people, particularly those whose homes had been along the invasion route, to their fate. On 6 July the column was encamped for the night when it was struck by three days of severe winter storms with hail fierce enough to kill hundreds of oxen and numerous horses. Soldiers were forced to take cover under wagons or where they could. The abnormal conditions released a plague of snake-like worms into the British entrenched position; some were over three feet long and an inch thick, which added to the troops' woe. The men were cheered with extra supplies of rum and three days later the weather cleared.[5]

With Chelmsford's army back in Natal, Wolseley immediately formed two new columns from those troops that remained. One, sent to Ulundi, was commanded by Lieutenant Colonel C. M. Clarke, and consisted of elements from the old First Division. The other, drawn from Wood's old Flying Column, commanded by Lieutenant Colonel Baker Russell, was to march north to the Hlobane area where, worryingly for Wolseley, a menacingly large force of the unvanquished abaQulusi still threatened his supply lines.

For the troops marching back into Natal it was evident that the Zulus were still a formidable force and their watching presence and numerous incidents unnerved them. Pearson's force was camped near the deserted mission station at eMvutsheni when they were joined by a number of John Dunn's followers. That evening Dunn's black scouts were manning the outer camp picket when, in the early hours of darkness, a picket of the 91st Regiment mistakenly sounded the alarm. Dunn's men scurried back to the safety of the camp, only to stumble onto a line of waiting bayonets. Mistaken for Zulus a number were seriously injured and several died of their wounds.

Chelmsford journeyed on to Cape Town, where he received an enthusiastic reception from the European population for whom Ulundi had eradicated the memories of earlier disasters. Wolseley later commented that: 'Since his (Chelmsford's) fight he is all "cock-a-hoop". Poor fellow, I can understand his feelings and am anxious to let him down easy'.[6] Chelmsford sailed home on the RMS *German* in the company of Wood and Buller, his most effective and reliable commanders. However, both had earlier confided to Wolseley that they objected strongly to Chelmsford's associating with them thereby giving the impression that they were in the same boat and going home because the war was over.

The British had destroyed Ulundi. Although the fires had long since burned out, here and there a hut had survived the flames only to slowly crumble under the effects of wind and rain, and great circles of ash marked where the homesteads once stood. At Ulundi where a dozen royal homesteads had ringed the Mahlabathini plain, with Ulundi once the most impressive sight, there was no clearing of the battlefield. Only deserted and smoke blackened villages evidenced the once thriving heart of the Zulu nation. The sight of the battlefield of Ulundi, just six weeks after the battle, was daunting: a fitting symbol of the utter destruction of King Cetshwayo's kingdom.

Dead bodies of slain Zulus remained where they had fallen, and these were left to nature's predators or to rot and wither in the sun. The British estimated that not less than 1,500 Zulus had died in the battle for Ulundi, and Buller suggested that his mounted men increased the death toll by yet another 500 during the far-ranging Zulu rout. Even after natural scavengers had done their work, skeletons and human bones littered the battlefield for many years. There were other more grisly reminders of the battle, too, as Captain Alan Fitzroy Hart later recalled when ordered to survey the area:

> The frequency with which I have come suddenly upon human skeletons in the grass has been quite forbidding. When one is not alone, the light of one's companion's presence dispels all the gloom of horrors, just as the arrival of a lamp spoils a ghost story!
>
> There is nothing so dead and harmless as a skeleton, yet when you contemplate them in solitude they appear to possess a life of their own, especially when there are so many together. Some look angry, some threatening, some foolish, some astonished, and those that are on their faces seem to be asleep.[7]

Curiously, the only attempt to clear human remains from the area occurred when an enterprising Natal trader arranged to collect cart loads of bones for onward shipment to Durban; they were then sorted for grinding into bonemeal, but the project came to a halt when the citizens of Durban realised what was happening and strongly opposed this commercial use of human remains.[8]

Wolseley had already determined that the country could not be pacified unless Cetshwayo was deposed and so, on 19 July, he summoned the chiefs living in the coastal districts to a meeting and told them that the Zulu kingdom no longer existed and that they would be informed in due course how the British intended to dispose of it. On 14 August he held a similar meeting at his new camp, pitched just two miles from the ruins of Ulundi. Among those who attended to offer their submission were Chief Mnyamana of the Buthelezi, the king's most trusted councillor, and Chief Ntshingwayo, who had commanded at Isandlwana. Surprisingly, there was no immediate attempt to pursue the king. Chelmsford, believing he had vindicated himself by bringing the war to a successful conclusion, lost no time telegraphing his resignation and prepared to leave Zululand. It was now Wolseley's task to arrange a peace settlement. Once he had established his headquarters near Ulundi at the beginning of August, Wolseley began searching for Cetshwayo. It was not easy. The local tribesmen, despite predictions to the contrary, proved stubbornly loyal. They refused, even under torture, to give the slightest hint of the king's whereabouts. For all that, there was little hope of Cetshwayo evading capture. Wolseley's patrols were scouring the country. Frustrated, Wolseley wrote in his journal:

Perhaps I am brutal, but I think it important to punish these northern tribes severely as a warning to all others in South Africa as to what they may expect should they ever be fools enough to make war upon the English. Up to the present beyond shooting and wounding some 10,000 men, we have not really punished these people as a nation, and our leniency in now allowing all the people to return to their kraals, retaining all their cattle, may possibly be mistaken for fear. I should therefore like to let loose the Swazies upon these northern tribes at once, but I have to think of the howling societies at home who have sympathy with all black men whilst they care nothing for the miseries and cruelties inflicted upon their own kith and kin who have the misfortune to be located near these interesting niggers'.[9]

On 10 August Wolseley began sending patrols north of the Black Umfolozi to try to discover the king's whereabouts and threaten the people of the Nkandla and Qudeni with force if they did not surrender. In the north the abaQulusi were still in their strongholds and fearlessly fired on passing patrols. Wolseley refused to be provoked, hoping that once Cetshwayo was captured this resistance would cease.

Wolseley's remaining and overriding priority was King Cetshwayo's capture, without which there could be no enduring peace. Wolseley was determined that Cetshwayo's capture would provide the final chapter in the whole sorry saga of the war, and from Ulundi his patrols swept through the country north of the Mfolozi River, following rumours and reports of the king's movements, many deliberately false. There had been fierce rivalry among those officers engaged in the pursuit to finally capture him. Indeed, the hunt for the king had aroused the sporting instincts of Wolseley's officers, particularly those who had arrived too late to fight at Ulundi. But the king remained elusive.

In the days following Ulundi, Cetshwayo had made his way north and accepted an offer of sanctuary from Chief Zibhebhu, whose territory still lay beyond the reach of British patrols. Leaving his family in Zibhebhu's care, he moved south to Mnyamana's homestead, north of the Black Mfolozi valley. From here he had attempted to re-open negotiations with Wolseley, but once it became clear that the British were interested only in his capture and unconditional surrender, he returned into hiding, accompanied by just a few of his most faithful attendants. But neither the surrendered chiefs nor their people seemed inclined to surrender him. 'They all want peace badly', noted Anstruther, '[they are] tired of war and want to sow next year's crops but they are very faithful brutes and can't make up their minds to give up Cetchwayo'.[10]

Three Zulu chiefs came to Wolseley with a herd of the king's cattle hoping to negotiate a peace that would secure the king's safety and his continued residence in the country. Wolseley had them detained as hostages, which confirmed Zulu suspicions. Cetshwayo moved to more inaccessible territory and was passed from homestead to homestead to avoid patrols. On 14 August Wolseley gave orders 'to burn Kraals and carry off cattle where the king is known to be and to be concealed by the inhabitants'.[11] Over the following few days, several of Cetshwayo's brothers surrendered, together with Zibhebhu kaMaphitha, chief of the powerful Mandlakazi section in the north. The chiefs were ordered to surrender all Zulu firearms and spears.

On 24 August Wolseley learned that the abaQulusi Zulus intended to resume opposing the remaining British and while he was considering this new threat, the fugitive king ordered all Zulus, including the abaQulusi, to surrender. The king knew that, otherwise, the war would have continued. Although the British presumed the war was over, they were still seriously engaged in 'mopping up' operations in the north of the country. Peace would not reach the Ntombe River area for another two months. Only then would the troops begin marching out of Zululand leaving its people to their fate.

Chapter 6

The Capture of King Cetshwayo

The British had despatched a number of patrols to run down Cetshwayo making it just a matter of time before the king in hiding was found and captured. Meanwhile, with the king still at large and to turn local Zulu people against their king, Wolseley gave orders for the searching troops to burn Zulu homesteads and carry off cattle in any area where the king was suspected to be hiding. Parties of mounted troops scoured the furthest corners of Zululand to find the king, with authority to freely engage in brutality to gain information. In one savage act, soldiers interrogated Chief Mpopha of the Hlabisa clan. He was first beaten and then questioned by soldiers using heated bayonet tips, a tactic that quickly paid off. Such brutal questioning was typically used by all the searching groups but, even at the point of imminent death, most Zulus managed to withhold information that would be useful to the searching parties.

Predictably, such methods went largely unreported by accompanying members of the press although Bishop Colenso's view became well known when he published an account in the *Cape Times* on 11 September 1879, based upon his record of notes written about the hunt for the king.[1]

We felt certain that the Zulus knew where the King was, and, if only they would give us the information, he would be caught in a few hours. We tried threats and everything else in the hours of our bivouac, until daylight next morning, but without result.

That afternoon we successfully descended a very steep hill and visited a kraal where the king had been that very morning. The chase was growing most exciting, and we immediately crossed the River Mona, and ascended a steep hill on the other side, on the crest of which was the kraal of Mbopa. Here we were thrown off the scent, and our hopes were dashed to the ground.

Having ascertained that Mbopa's son was with the King, we made Mbopa and all the people of his kraal prisoners, and carried them to the kraal of his son, which was five miles distant. We [Lord Gifford and party] then returned to the rendezvous and rejoined Major Barrow. In our absence he had brought together about forty Zulus, and we set to work to see if we could get any information from them. For a very long time we could not get anything out of them. They were as uncommunicative under threat of being shot as they were to our seductive promises. At last, however, in the controversy one of the speakers accidentally dropped the information that one of the King's own servants was amongst the group. He was instantly taken aside by Major Barrow and quietly questioned through my interpreting. We extracted from him that he had left the King that very morning, and 'after a little persuasion' he promised to put us on the following morning on to the King's trail; it was too late that day to do anything further.

At daybreak a party of us went to Mbopa's kraal and took all the people prisoners, and as they would give us no information, which we knew they possessed, we burnt the kraal and took their cattle. We then returned to the main body of Lord Gifford's party, and there a small boy told us that beer was constantly being carried to the king, and that the men must know where he was. By 'proper persuasive measures' [usually flogging] one Zulu was induced to make a confession and promised to take us to where the King had been the day before, and where he was still. The Zulu led us into the bush, but, as we had foolishly not fastened him, he gave us the slip. We scoured the bush thoroughly but never saw King, prisoner, or anybody else.

For the next two days, as the people were deceiving us, Major Barrow cleared the district of cattle. Lord Gifford went off with his party to make another effort to capture the King.

Captain Lumley rode in next. It appears he had been delayed by the kaffirs' unwillingness to deliver their cattle and 'had been obliged to use strong measures' [flogging or killing]. The party had come across a Zulu woman who instantly told them where the king had slept two nights previously. The party surrounded her kraal and returned with three brothers who, threatened with death, divulged where the King had slept the night before, some fifteen miles away. It was 11pm when Lord Gifford gave orders to saddle up and with two of the brothers as guides – the third remained as a hostage. Such systematic terrorism had eventually revealed Cetshwayo's hiding place and at dawn on the 28th the King was taken prisoner by Major Marter.

Unsurprisingly, it was not long before troops, led by Major Marter, found the king's former friend, Mnyamana, who avoided the hot bayonet treatment by warning the British that the king was hiding at a location in the Ngome Forest. On 28 August, and armed with Mnyamana's confession, the king was tracked down to a remote village by Marter. There was little the king could do, and after a short conversation, he quietly gave himself up. Marter treated his prisoner with dignity, though two of the king's servants were shot and killed when they tried to run off. A tent was provided for him and his wives, and the 60th Rifles mounted a guard over it. For two days, he remained in camp while transport was arranged. Colonel Clarke gave responsibility for interpreting between himself and the royal party to Captain Harford, brought up in Natal and a fluent Zulu speaker.

With so many bands of Zulus left wandering about the country, the potential for a resumption of conflict, albeit on a small scale, nevertheless continued to smoulder on. Indeed, neither the loss of the battle nor the burning of Ulundi was particularly significant to the Zulus, described by Bishop Colenso as 'A bloody but barren victory'. 'They all want peace badly', noted Anstruther, '[they are] tired of war and want to sow next year's crops, but they are very faithful brutes and can't make up their minds to give up Cetchwayo'.[2]

Ulundi could have been rebuilt quickly and worse, the northern abaQulusi remained bitterly opposed to any suggestion of surrender; the war could have continued. Indeed, on 24 August Wolseley learned that the abaQulusi Zulus intended to continue opposing the remaining British. While he was considering this new threat the fugitive King Cetshwayo ordered all Zulus, including the abaQulusi, to surrender. Had it not been for Cetshwayo sending a secret emissary to the abaQulusi ordering the cessation of hostilities, the war would have continued. To maintain their ascendancy the colonial elements of Wood's column were placed under the command of Lieutenant Colonel Baker Russell, 13th Hussars, with orders to quell any abaQulusi threats and pacify the northwest part of the country. Wolseley instructed that Baker Russell was to be supported by Swazi forces, but they turned out to be uncooperative, more nervous of future retribution from the Zulus than of ignoring Wolseley. British troops in the Transvaal under the command of Lieutenant Colonel Villiers were then given similar instructions with the additional task of controlling the Zulus along the Pongola River.

Captain Harford was present at the capture of the king. An extract from his recently discovered diaries clarifies the sequence of events:

In my spare time I went over the battlefield of Ulundi and picked up one or two relics in the shape of shields, assegais, etc. A few days after we arrived, Jim came to me to say that he knew the spot where Cetewayo's 'Somtseu' were buried and asked if he might go and make a search. I told him certainly, but I would like to go with him, but he said that he would rather go at first by himself and if he found that they had not been taken away he would go with me to get them. However, it turned out that they had been removed, and squatting down, snapping his fingers to emphasise matters, he declared that it had only been done that very day, as the earth from the hole was quite fresh. I should much like to have gone with him afterwards, to have a look at the spot, but I never got the chance.

Several small expeditions consisting of officers and men acting independently were traversing the country in the hope of capturing Cetewayo, and as it seemed likely that our Column would be at Ulundi for some little time, Captain Stewart, 3rd Dragoon Guards, who had joined us on special service, came to my tent one afternoon and told me that if he could get Sir Garnet Wolseley's sanction he proposed to start an expedition of his own, consisting of officers only, to hunt for Cetewayo, and asked if I would come as interpreter. Needless to say, I said that I should be only too delighted, if Colonel Clarke would allow it, and I also begged that my co-Adjutant, Towers-Clarke, might be one of the party; to which he agreed. Happily, both Sir Garnet Wolseley and Colonel Mansfield Clarke quite fell in with Stewart's venture, and the following officers formed the expedition: Captain Stewart, the Chief; myself, Interpreter; Lieutenants Hutton, Smith and (name forgotten) 3/60th; Lieutenant Shepherd, 80th; and Towers-Clarke, 57th Regiment.

We took no food of any sort with us, intending to live on what we could get or find at the Kaffir kraals, but Stewart carried a flask of brandy in case of accidents. Our transport consisted of a mule and my Helpmekaar pony to carry cooking utensils, blankets, etc. The mule had to be led, and all except Stewart and I took their turn at this, and a nice lot of trouble he gave us on many occasions. My pony either followed like a dog or was driven along with a whip. Our time was limited to three weeks, when the Column would be on the move again. On the day of our departure, Major McCalmont, 7th Hussars, and I think it was Lieutenant Creagh, R.A., two of Sir Garnet's ADCs, turned up and said that they were coming with us. But the first night out, with only boiled pumpkin for dinner and nothing but boiled mealies to look forward to the next day, so damped their ardour that when we continued our journey at daybreak they decided to return to camp – and were considerably well chaffed on their sudden change of mind.

First of all we headed towards St. Lucia Bay, travelling over some beautiful country and coming across lots of game, buck, zebra, buffalo, etc. We had a rifle and a few rounds of ammunition with us, our only armament, but reserved it for use only if we got hard up for food, otherwise had we been on a shooting expedition we could have had some splendid sport. Being still at war, nearly all the kraals we visited in the hope of learning something of Cetewayo's whereabouts were denuded of men, none but the very old and the women and children remained, and from these neither information or supplies of any sort could be obtained. When we asked for milk, etc., the invariable reply was, "How are we to get milk when our men are all away fighting?" However, we always got as much food in the shape of mealies and Kaffir corn as we required, by opening the pits in the centre of the cattle kraals (where they always store their crops) and by picking up an odd pumpkin now and again in the fields, all of which we paid for to avoid trouble of any sort.

The Column worked its way along in accordance with the reports received from various quarters by the intelligence department, until one morning a Kaffir arrived at our bivouac and informed the Brigadier that he knew the place in the Ngome bush where Cetewayo was hiding, and could show him the way to the kraal. Young Oftebro, our interpreter, who was the son of a missionary and who had lived among the Zulus all his life, knew the country well and was also a personal friend of Cetewayo's, so without any delay Colonel Mansfield Clarke sent him off to accompany a squadron of the King's Dragoon Guards under Major Marter and a company of NNC under Captain Barton, Royal Fusiliers, to effect the King's capture. When the party had started, I shall never forget the kind way in which Colonel Clarke said to me, "You know, Harford, I would have sent you, but Oftebro knows every inch of the country as well as the King himself, and his thorough knowledge of the language is most important", (or words to that effect).

The king was led into camp in triumph on the last day of August 1879. The fact of Major Marter's party capturing Cetewayo was a great blow to Lord Gifford's expedition, which had run him to earth and were on the point of bagging him, but not knowing the lie of the country had got to a place where they couldn't move without being seen by day and were holding on till it got dark. Marter's party, being led by experts, took a route completely concealing their movements, almost under Gifford's nose, and rapidly surrounding the kraal captured him. In telling me the story afterwards, Oftebro said that as soon as the kraal had been surrounded and our troops were closing in on it, one or two shots were fired, but Cetewayo saw that the game was up. He himself then went up to the hut that the King was in, and spoke to him from outside, and directly Cetewayo heard his voice he said, "Is that you?" …(calling him by his Zulu name), and after a few minutes' conversation, quietly gave himself up.

At dawn, almost at the first streak of light the following morning, a Kaffir messenger from Major Marter appeared with a note fastened in the slit of a small stick. The Brigadier, Towers-Clarke and I were sleeping under our wagon. The Brigadier lay between us, I being on the outside. On handing me the stick, the bearer whispered, very quietly, "He is caught!" and I woke the Brigadier, handing him the stick without a word. "Marter's got him", he said, as he jumped up, and went off to tell the news to Captain Hart, and in a very few minutes it was known throughout the camp. A cart had also been asked for, for the conveyance of the King and his wives, which was immediately sent off under the guidance of the messenger. On the way in, I believe, some of the followers gave a lot of trouble and had to be fastened to the troopers' horses, but eventually all arrived safely.[3]

On arrival in camp, the sight of so many soldiers alarmed them considerably, and Cetewayo looked the picture of fright as they drove up. After alighting from the cart, the King (with his wives hanging on to him as if they thought he was doomed to immediate execution, and absolutely terrified), strode in with the aid of his long stick, with a proud and dignified air and grace, looking a magnificent specimen of his race and every inch a warrior in his grand *umutcha* of leopard skin and tails, with lion's teeth and claw charms round his neck. Well over six feet, fat but not corpulent, with a stern, severe and cruel countenance, he looked what he was, a savage ruler.

A tent was provided for him and his wives, and a guard mounted over it of the 60th Rifles, and for the two days he remained in camp Colonel Clarke very kindly paid me the compliment of giving them [the royal party] over into my charge. For Cetewayo there was only exile. He was taken across country, to the beach at Port Durnford on a mule wagon in charge of Lieutenant Poole, R.A., with a mounted escort. Along the way he pointed out to his captors the bush where his uncle, King Shaka, used to sit when judging cowards in his army. On 4 September he boarded the steamer *Natal*, destined for the Cape. A fortnight later, he and his faithful retainers were securely lodged in quarters at the old Dutch castle in Cape Town.

Lieutenant H. A. Amyatt-Burney's report concurred with Harford's account:

As we were about to move off again, a Zulu appeared coming towards us. Major Marter entered into conversation with him through an interpreter, and just as he was going away the Zulu said to the interpreter, 'Which way is the inkos ['headman' or 'chief'] going?' Major Marter said, 'I am going over that hill in front'. The native said, 'I think you had better go round that way (pointing to the right), as the wind blows from there today. I have had my say.' He then turned round and walked off. The hint was promptly taken, and everyone became very keen, as Major Marter told the officers that he thought there was a very good chance of their capturing the King. We then worked due east around the hill, and after a steep climb came to a kraal three miles on. We halted a little distance off, and the Major with the interpreter rode up to the kraal, which by the way belonged to Umnyamane, who had surrendered some days before. Major Marter asked for two guides, and two young men got up immediately, and led the way to another kraal about two miles off, situated on the top of a plateau looking down into the valley of the Ngome Forest. The aspect of the country had now changed altogether. Hitherto it had been very monotonous, nothing but a succession of undulating hills covered with rough grass, a good deal of which had been burnt; now the country was green and dotted here and there with clumps of trees, the Ngome Forest forming the background.

On our approaching this kraal, the guides signed to Major Marter to halt his men close under the edge of the forest, and they then beckoned to him to follow them, and leading the way through a strip of wood, they pointed to a thick bush overhanging the valley about fifty yards on, signing for the Major to go on to it. This he did and perceived a kraal of twelve huts surrounded by a wattle fence, in the valley below. On his return he ordered all the men to draw their swords and leave their scabbards behind with the led horses and mules. This was to prevent the clanking of the swords giving any warning. He also told our natives to strip, so as to appear as much as possible like Zulus, and he left a Sergeant and eight men in charge of everything. This done he told the men that from all he could gather the king was in the kraal below in the valley, and that his capture depended on their obeying silently and quickly any order they might receive; that they would have to lead their horses down the side of the mountain, through the forest; and that when they arrived at the edge of the bush they would have to ride about a quarter of a mile.

The right troop under Lieutenant Alexander was to extend on the right side; the left troop under command of Captain Godson to extend to the left, and come up on the left of the kraal – the squadron being under the command of Captain Gibbings. The natives were sent round by a circuitous route to the left, to cut off all chance of escape down the valley. When these preparations were completed, Major Marter told the guides to show the way, which proved a very rough one, being simply a Kaffir path. We all dismounted and advanced by single files, leading our horses down a very steep incline, strewn with rocks and stones; here and there a huge trunk of a tree barred the path; at another place there was a drop of some feet off a rock with a nasty landing; in fact to men in cold blood it would have appeared almost impossible to have got horses down at all. Eventually all reached the bottom of the hill in safety, and, though several horses slipped up, none were much damaged. The forest extended to within four hundred yards of the kraal, and there was a most convenient knoll between it and us, so that the inhabitants were unable to see anyone approaching from our side until we were quite close.

Directly everyone was clear of the forest, Major Marter gave the word to mount, and he then waited for the guides, who had crawled through the long grass to see if all was right. On their return they appeared greatly excited, signing the Major to go on; and he accordingly gave the order to advance at a walk as long as we were hidden by the knoll. On arriving at the top he gave the word to gallop, and led the way himself. The ground between the forest and the kraal was rough and stony. One man came to grief through his horse putting his foot in a hole and rolling over him. As the cavalry appeared in sight of the kraal, our natives showed themselves in the very nick of time on the other side. One shot was fired, but it is uncertain from which side. Carrying out Major Marter's instructions we rapidly and completely surrounded the kraal. The inhabitants, who numbered twenty-three, were standing at the very narrow entrance to the enclosure and armed, some with assegais, some rifles. Major Marter dismounted and went inside the enclosure with the interpreter. Umkoosana, an induna of the Unodwengo regiment, who had stuck to Cetewayo throughout his flight from Ulundi, was told by the interpreter to show Major Marter in which hut the king was. This he did (it was the third hut to the right of the entrance) and was then told to request his majesty to step outside and show himself. The king at first refused to do so, saying he was afraid that directly he put his head out of the hut he would immediately be shot. When assured that his life was safe, he coolly asked 'What rank does the officer hold to whom I am to surrender?' Major Marter replied that he was the representative of the Commander-in-Chief. Mr Oftebro, the interpreter, and son of the Missionary at Ekowe, who had known Cetshwayo since he was a boy, then spoke to him. Cetshwayo immediately recognised his voice, and called out to him by name, asking if it was safe for him to come out.

On being assured in the affirmative he appeared crawling out of the hut in the usual Kaffir fashion, on his hands and knees. He wore a moncha made of otter-skins, and had a ringkop on his head. The upper part of his body was covered with a large red tablecloth, embroidered with green flowers, fastened from the neck in front, and hanging over his shoulders. Directly he stood up, all doubts as to his being the king were set at rest, as at a glance we could see his superiority both in appearance and carriage to all other Zulus. He looked round on everyone with the greatest scorn and stalked majestically into the middle of the kraal. Six Dragoons were immediately dismounted and told off as his guard, with loaded carbines. Cetshwayo was informed that if he attempted to escape he would be immediately shot, and he was then marched outside the enclosure, while the huts were searched. Amongst the articles found were several Martini-Henry Rifles, nearly all of which belonged to the 1st 24th, a battered bugle, and a private's glengarry cap, a few very fine assegais, including two barbed ones which belonged to the king himself, and which were found in his hut, and a double-barrelled central fire gun, which Major Marter eventually appropriated to himself, to the very great disgust of the officer who found it ....[4]

Following his capture the king was placed under guard at a temporary encampment on the Black Umfolozi before being placed in a wagon sent to convey the royal prisoner to Sir Garnet Wolseley's headquarters at Ulundi. He did not, however, choose to ride much in the wagon as he complained of its shaking him, and preferred to walk. The soldiers were not permitted to approach within 30 yards of the king. The party arrived at Wolseley's camp overlooking the scarred remains of Ulundi on the morning of 31 Aug, having slept the night before about four miles from the overnight White Umfolozi camp. Three wives, a female servant, and a daughter were with him, besides one chief, Umkosana, and three other men, five of his servants having escaped, or having been shot in attempting to escape.

Arrogant as ever, Wolseley declined to meet with the king, merely sending him a message that he would remain a captive of the British – at that the king's resolve left him and he was seen to dejectedly crumple. An *ILN* correspondent described the King's arrival at Ulundi:

In front of the King's escort came some of the Dragoons and the men of Lonsdale's Horse who were present at the capture, clearing a broad path of eighty yards wide, along the centre of which marched first some Dragoons, between whom walked Cetshwayo, very upright and dignified, glancing keenly from side to side, but expressing neither astonishment nor fear at his humiliating position; indeed, the constant expression of his face seems one of quiet and kindly repose, and there is certainly nothing cruel or even harsh in the expression of his features.

He was wearing a bright-coloured damask table-cloth and the usual head ring worn by all married Zulus. Directly following him came another Dragoon, then some of the Native Contingent, followed by some 60th men. He was conducted straight to a tent, which he occupied by himself, while the women and the men occupied respectively two others. Orders had previously been given that an escort was to be ready at 2pm to accompany the King to Pietermaritzburg.

Cetewayo, having had some food and a rest, undisturbed, was placed together with the four women, in one of the ambulances with Umkosana, who rode on the hind seat, while his followers were placed on another mule-wagon, which came immediately behind the ambulance. It must have been a pretty tight squeeze, as the women, like their liege, were decidedly not of a slender make. However, Cetewayo took his seat very quietly, and at ten minutes past two the party started, under the command of Captain Poole R.A. staff officer; the escort consisting of twenty men of the Natal Horse and twenty of Lonsdale's under Captain de Burgh, of the Natal Horse.[5]

They had proceeded no further than Fort Victoria – about ten miles from Ulundi – when an officer overtook them with orders to proceed as quickly as possible to Port Durnford, where the *Natal* would be in readiness to convey Cetshwayo to Cape Town. The king was then escorted to Port Durnford on the coast and taken aboard the steamer *Natal*. Here he posed for some rather pained photographs – only the second ever photo-session he had agreed to. On 4 September and accompanied by his *induna*, EmaKhosini kaZangqana, some attendants and *isigodlo* girls, he was taken by sea from nearby Port Durnford to Cape Town and lodged in apartments in the old Cape Castle. His kingdom had already been divided up among British appointees.

On 2 November the young British nurse from the army hospital at Utrecht, Sister Janet Wells, arrived at Cape Town en route home to England. While awaiting passage, there was sufficient time for her to be received by King Cetshwayo, who was being held a prisoner at the Castle. The Zulu king had become something of a tourist attraction for officers returning home and he rather enjoyed the respectful attention he received. Janet was very surprised to learn from the king that he had already heard of her kind treatment of Zulu warriors at Utrecht and was pleased to meet her. Talking to Captain Ruscombe Poole, the officer commanding his guard, she learned something of his lifestyle. The king was a grossly obese man with a large belly who took very little exercise, his royal authority being based on strategy and diplomacy. He was still an imposing looking man and in his youth he had been a remarkable athlete and an outstanding warrior. His diet, in view of his regal position, was mainly meat. He had numerous wives who visited him at his command. His first wife, however, stayed at his side most of the time. Janet, like a true Victorian lady, drew a veil over the king's, to her mind, unconventional domestic arrangements. When Janet met the king he was clearly suffering from an uncomfortable stomach complaint and, through the king's interpreter, Henry Longcast, the young nurse proposed a solution and was duly given permission to relieve the king. The king agreed.

The combination of a diet with little fruit and fibre and a lack of exercise were not conducive to a good digestive transit. Without further ado, and knowing exactly what to do, the nurse collected some soap, rubber tubing, funnel and a bucket, and after mixing a large hot mixture of soapy water soon relieved the King of his discomfort. With the mission accomplished, she left him with a large bottle of castor oil to ensure the royal colon did not get blocked again. As a mark of gratitude for this, and in recognition of Janet's work with the wounded Zulus at Utrecht, Cetshwayo presented her with his matching necklaces and bracelets, which survive to this day.

Once the remaining groups of Zulus heard their king had been captured, most sought to make peace. Most of the lingering resistance in Zululand evaporated once the news of the king's capture circulated. Only in the north, in the troubled areas around Luneburg, did the survivors of the raiding bands of the chiefs Mbilini and Manyanyoba hold out, until at last the British lost all patience with them.

The remnants under Chief Manyanyoba also sought to give themselves up but their attempt to surrender unfortunately coincided with an order from Wolseley that troops should 'clear Manyanyoba out'. On 1 September the commander of the troops on the Transvaal border, Colonel Villiers, ordered troops under Colonel Black to march out to Manyanyoba's stronghold overlooking the Ntombe River where groups of warriors promptly surrendered. The troops then advanced towards a number of caves where the remaining warriors, women, children and animals were hiding. Unfortunately, one of the warriors in a cave inadvertently discharged his rifle whereupon the warriors who had just surrendered were immediately slaughtered by their guards who suspected a trap. The surrender of Manyanyoba and his people came to a halt and the troops marched back to camp. Colonel Anstruther of the 94th wrote:

The day before yesterday we hustled the tribe (Chief Manyobo) who did the mischief. They are outcasts, not proper Zulus or Swazies, and live in caves in the surrounding hills which they won't come out of so they were told to send their women and children away and give themselves up. They did the former but not the latter. The women and children came in good quantities to our fort in Luneburg, five miles off where four companies of the 4th are so the day before yesterday some of us and the 4th from the Fort went up the hills and set to work to blow up the caves with gun cotton. There were a great many tremendous explosions but, I am afraid, very little damage was done. We got two prisoners and blew in the entrance of a lot of caves and the 4th unfortunately lost two men, their sergeant major and a corporal who went into one of the caves and were shot immediately. It was very stupid. We got all their goats and cattle and I fancy they will give one of the prisoners to Manyobo's head man and the other to his son. They are a very small insignificant tribe but have been doing a lot of mischief. An expedition has gone out against them today and they will be harried til they give in.[6]

The British troops returned to deal with Manyanyoba on 5 September and attempted to smoke the Zulus from their caves, without success. On 8 September the troops returned and destroyed the caves with dynamite, notwithstanding that they were still sheltering many Zulus. On 22 September Manyanyoba, unprepared to take further losses, surrendered to the British. He and his surviving followers were escorted to the Batshe Valley near Rorke's Drift where they sought to settle.

And on that inglorious note, the war came to an end. The British troops marched on, either to pursue a different quarrel against King Sekhukhune in the north-eastern Transvaal, or to depart for distant garrisons around the Empire. For the Zulus, the repercussions of the invasion had scarcely begun. For Wolseley, the king's capture sealed the end of the conflict. Now he had to plan the future of Zululand. At home the Disraeli government had fallen, to be replaced by Gladstone's Liberals, and no one had any interest in annexing Zululand. Wolseley's instructions were succinct. Having exiled Cetshwayo he would impose a settlement and depart, leaving the Zulus to make the best of their defeat. Wolseley divided Zululand into thirteen independent kingdoms, each with an appointed chief with a proven interest in supporting the British and opposed to the traditional house of Shaka.

At home the British nation cheered. Starved of good news and needing a lift, the public welcomed home the worn-out regiments that had suffered greatly during the mismanaged campaign. Chelmsford underwent a period of severe depression in the aftermath of Isandlwana and requested that he be replaced.[7] Colonel Glyn suffered a breakdown at Rorke's Drift but eventually recovered sufficiently to take a limited part in the second invasion of Zululand. Colonel Hassard, Officer Commanding Royal Engineers, had such a severe nervous breakdown that he was replaced. Colonel Pearson, the defender of Eshowe, was invalided home suffering from mental and physical exhaustion. By the end of September 1879, the last detachments of the British Army had left Zululand with their baggage. Durban became chock-a-block, with the bars doing a roaring trade. In the general confusion one event put the finishing touch to the war. Lieutenant General Sir William Butler wrote that just before one crowded transport was due to sail for England the captain received an order to delay sailing. Six soldiers found to be insane during the course of the war (including Rorke's Drift defender Private Wall) were about to be embarked under escort for consignment to a home lunatic asylum. Once on board the escort mistakenly returned to shore. In the ensuing confusion the lunatics were hidden by other soldiers and apart from Private Wall, the lunatics were never found.[8]

There were plenty of heroes to fête, and their names became known in every household. After years of refusing to involve herself in the nation's affairs, Queen Victoria was pleased to pin decorations and orders on the fresh tunics of her brave soldiers. For several weeks, the country enjoyed being proud of its army – until memories faded and fresh news replaced the old. As Kipling perceptively wrote:

> It's Tommy this, and Tommy that,
> And chuck 'im out, the brute!
> But it's Saviour of 'is Country,
> When the guns begin to shoot ….

Meanwhile, public opinion at home had polarised against the war. Disraeli refused to receive Chelmsford who had cost the country so much and brought discredit to the British Government. Some newspapers continued to pillory Chelmsford. Popular songs mocked him and even some of his fellow peers were critical. But it was those who really mattered, the Horse

Guards and Queen Victoria, who rallied to his support. Chelmsford was showered with honours. His rank of lieutenant general was confirmed and the Queen used her influence to have him appointed Lieutenant of the Tower. He later became a full general and Colonel of the Sherwood Foresters and then of the 2nd Life Guards. After his retirement, honours still came Chelmsford's way. Queen Victoria appointed him Gold Stick, an honour that was carried over when her son, Edward, succeeded her. He also made the ageing general a Knight Grand Cross of the Royal Victorian Order. On 9 April 1905, at the age of 78, Lord Chelmsford had a seizure and died while playing billiards at the United Services Club. So died a man with many admirable attributes but who was thrust into a position for which he was not intellectually equipped. Instead of being a long-forgotten Victorian general, his name is still remembered as the man ultimately responsible for the Victorian Army's greatest military defeat.

There was to be no redemption for Sir Bartle Frere either; he was recalled home, his credibility ruined forever, though he defended his position to the bitter end. On his deathbed his last words echoed his belief that he was right: 'Oh, if only they would read *The Further Correspondence* they must understand', referring to his official justification for the war.[9] He died of influenza the next day, 29 May 1884. Although he was buried in St. Paul's Cathedral, no politician was invited to accompany the procession. His coffin was led into the cathedral by two dukes, one field marshal and three major generals. Queen Victoria was represented along with an array of lords, knights and ordinary soldiers. Later, a statue of Frere was erected on the Thames embankment, paid for by public subscription.

At Ulundi there was no clearing of the battlefield. For many months only deserted and soot blackened villages evidenced the once thriving heart of the Zulu nation. The dead bodies of slain Zulus remained where they had fallen, and these were left to the predators or to rot and shrivel in the sun. The British roughly estimated that not less than 1,500 Zulus had died in the battle for Ulundi while Buller suggested that his mounted men increased the death toll by yet another 500 during the far-ranging Zulu rout.

And on that inglorious note, the war came to an end. For the weary British troops there were fresh battles to be fought, either to pursue a different quarrel against King Sekhukhune in the north-eastern Transvaal, or to depart for distant garrisons around the Empire. For the Zulus, the repercussions of the invasion had scarcely begun.

King Cetshwayo in London.

In the aftermath of the Zulu defeat, the captive king had been held, in some comfort, in the old Dutch Castle in Cape Town. Once the initial shock of defeat and exile wore off, Cetshwayo found himself not without influence in Zulu affairs. His celebrity was such that he received a string of visitors to his apartments, mostly passing British gentry, many of whom became sympathetic to his plight and were in a position to influence official attitudes. With the stability of Zululand collapsing, Cetshwayo began increasingly to lobby to be allowed to return to his country, under British authority, to restore order.

His personal circumstances improved when he was moved from the castle to a nearby farm, Oude Moulen, on the Cape flats. Once he had recovered from the ignominy of defeat and exile, he had begun campaigning to be allowed a voice in Zulu affairs. The king's plight attracted the attention of a number of well-connected tourists to the Cape, whose itinerary included a visit to the King. There was no lack of visitors to Oude Moulen, especially for English travellers calling at the Cape. Everyone was only too anxious to catch a glimpse of the 'ignorant and bloodthirsty despot' who had defeated and then defied the British army. Expecting Frere's 'monster' they were completely disarmed by Cetshwayo's calm, jovial good nature. The king, for his part, never missed an opportunity to plead his cause. Among his more important visitors were the two sons of the Prince of Wales, Prince Eddy and Prince George (later King George V) who were touring the world in HMS *Bacchante*. After exchanging photographs with the young princes, Cetshwayo urged them to bring his plight to the notice of their grandmother, Queen Victoria. The result of this meeting is uncertain, but a visit from another of Queen Victoria's relations, Prince Louis of Battenberg, undoubtedly proved helpful. When Prince Louis called on the king at the beginning of 1881, he was accompanied by a young woman, Lady Florence Dixie, who was immediately captivated by the royal prisoner. Next to the ever-faithful Colenso women, Lady Florence was to become Cetshwayo's most convinced and passionate champion. Her support did much to publicise Cetshwayo's misfortunes.

Cetshwayo repeatedly asked to be allowed to visit London to put his case in person and each time he was refused, even as the post-war settlement imposed on Zululand slid the country into anarchy. Under the determined guidance of Bishop Colenso, Cetshwayo formally requested permission to meet Queen Victoria in order to outline his claim for reinstatement as King of Zululand. On 14 September 1881 permission for the visit was telegraphed to Sir Hercules Robinson, the High Commissioner in South Africa, but the King's visit was deliberately delayed by British officials in South Africa who were worried by the implications of his return to authority in Zululand.

The king was finally granted permission to visit London in 1882. He left Cape Town for London on 12 July, accompanied by three of his *izinDuna* who had accompanied him in exile, as well as an interpreter, Robert Dunn, and – to keep a close eye on him – Henrique Shepstone, a member of the powerful dynasty who largely shaped colonial Natal's policies. The king arrived off Plymouth on 5 August and was greeted by a throng of journalists, all keen to interview the man who had humbled British troops at Isandlwana and Hlobane. Throughout his trip, Cetshwayo played the role of an experienced diplomat, receiving visitors with quiet dignity, always publicly regretting the war and apparently marvelling at the power and benevolence of his hosts.

From Plymouth he was taken to a comfortable house in Melbury Road, London. News soon spread of his arrival, and curious crowds gathered outside in the hope of catching a glimpse of him. Cetshwayo was obliged to make frequent appearances at the window. He was nervous; at first, uncertain of his reaction, but when his appearance was greeted with enthusiastic cheers he accepted the obligation with good humour. Crowds, indeed, soon dogged his every move as Londoners became enchanted by the man whom they found very different in person to the scowling savage portrayed by the illustrated press in 1879. Although a large man, the king cut a considerable dash in a smart outfit of European clothes and carried himself with considerable majesty. When Cetshwayo and his attendants were photographed by the fashionable society photographers, Bassanos, such a crowd gathered outside that one young boy was heard to comment: 'He ain't Ceta-wayo, for he can't get-awayO!' Shown a statue of Achilles in Hyde Park, the king observed quietly, 'You see, it was not so long ago that they fought as we do – without clothes.'[10] Taken to the Royal Arsenal at Woolwich, he was impressed – as his hosts intended – by the display of Imperial might. 'I feel that I have grown up, so to speak, in a day; that from the childhood of understanding I have suddenly sprung to manhood.' Wherever he went he was enthusiastically received by crowds of curious Londoners.

On 14 August Cetshwayo was taken from London, by special train and yacht, for a brief audience with Queen Victoria at Osborne House on the Isle of Wight. According to the press, a 'large crowd assembled to witness the departure' and the king and his attendants 'were greeted with hearty cheering.' In the event, the royal audience lasted scarcely fifteen minutes and was apparently cool – the Queen was, after all, one of Lord Chelmsford's most loyal supporters – but polite enough. The Queen presented Cetshwayo with a silver cup as a souvenir, now displayed in the KwaZulu Cultural Museum at Ulundi. Later, the Queen urged her government to facilitate King Cetshwayo's repatriation and commissioned her portrait painter, Carl Sohn, to paint his portrait.

Diplomatically, the mission was only a partial success. Cetshwayo came increasingly to be seen as a viable solution to an increasingly volatile problem. The Government in London began to consider an extraordinary *volte-face* in policy – the restoration of a man whom British troops had waged a six-month war to depose. It was argued that Cetshwayo was the only man with sufficient authority to impose order in Zululand and that, since he would be entirely dependent on the British for his return, he would no longer be a threat to British interests. It is more likely that the three interviews he had with Lord Kimberley, Secretary of State for the Colonies, were more important. His return to Zululand was secured on certain conditions. He must disband the Zulu army, agree to a British Resident acting as his advisor, observe boundaries laid down by the British authorities, and agree to a portion of his country to be defined later, being allocated to those Zulus who did not wish to live under his rule. Apart from the last, the King agreed. When he protested that part of his country would be taken from him, Kimberley advised him to wait and see how much was lopped off before refusing to agree to the condition. Cetshwayo reluctantly accepted this advice.

The Colonial Office agreed that the king might be restored to Zululand, but only to part of his old kingdom. Large tracts of the country were to be set aside for those Zulu chiefs who had ruled in his absence – and who would be unlikely to welcome his return. More importantly, the king had several meetings at the Colonial Office to discuss his political future. It was finally agreed that he would be restored to Zululand – although the full and restrictive conditions to limit his authority were kept from him until after his return to the Cape.

Diplomatically, the mission was of limited partial success. The Natal authorities did everything they could to delay the king's return, citing diseases in Zululand, but the reality was that they needed more time to reduce the area over which the King would have control. Further, his return was kept from his countrymen. When the permission finally came it was tempered by news that shocked the king: two large swathes of Zululand had been disposed of. One was an area to be known as the Zulu Native Reserve under the control of John Dunn and Chief Hlubi. The other area had been allocated to Chief Zibhebhu, a former rival of the King who would have control of Zululand north of the White Umfolozi River. This was contrary to the terms he had been advised to accept in London. Cetshwayo reluctantly signed the agreement and the following January he was granted permission to return to Ulundi with a view to reuniting his shattered nation.

The king and his entourage left England at the end of the month. For Cetshwayo the mission had been a huge political and diplomatic success and, indeed, the impression Cetshwayo had created in the minds of the British public did much to alter their opinion of the Zulu people. In the years since the invasion many had become uneasy about the justice of the war, and the king's apparent dignity in defeat helped to modify the public's image of the Zulus as ruthless savages to noble warriors.

On 10 January 1883, after an absence of almost four years, Cetshwayo arrived back on Zulu soil. He landed from HMS *Briton* at Port Durnford with just a few Zulus waiting to greet him. He was escorted to his old capital by Sir Theophilus Shepstone – who had 'crowned' him just a decade earlier, and who had come out of retirement for the occasion. Once news of his return spread, his old supporters, *amakhosi*, *izinduna* and commoners alike flocked to renew their allegiance. Cetshwayo set about rebuilding a new version of

Ulundi, not far from the complex destroyed in 1879. It was a smaller affair – perhaps just a thousand huts – but still an impressive statement of his authority. He was, however, supervised by a British Resident, and he found his country deeply divided by several years of friction between his supporters and the new appointees set up by the British.

He was re-installed at Emtonjaneni, where even more conditions were put upon him; many thought these additional conditions were clearly a deliberate trap to cause his downfall. Meanwhile Zululand was in turmoil and with Cetshwayo sandwiched between his enemies and Natal, and with the northern Abaqulusi rising in his support by laying waste to their enemies, he was freshly required by the terms of his restoration to maintain peace across Zululand. The king sought help from the Natal authorities, but this was refused. Amidst the confusion of Zulu clans raiding other Zulu clans a bewildering chaos began to ferment.

His rebuilding of Ulundi was the trigger to unleash a period of fierce factional fighting. The bitterness that had built up across the country during his exile immediately became apparent. His own followers, the Usuthu, now sought to settle a number of old scores. His followers bitterly resented the oppression they had suffered at the hands of his former general, *inkosi* Zibhebhu kaMaphitha, and they were keen to take revenge on him. There was nothing the king could do to restrain them. With little authority and no army his power to control events was minimal. The king's enemies were more or less given a free hand. Zibhebhu, the main target for Usuthu hostility, seized his opportunity to prepare for war. The crisis was reached in March 1883. Probably without King Cetshwayo's knowledge – and certainly without his sanction – a number of royalist supporters assembled an army to attack Zibhebhu. Zibhebhu anticipated the Usuthu attack, massed his own supporters, and on 30 March 1883 he routed the royalists in the forested Msebe Valley and shattered their alliance.

News of the attack caused consternation in Ulundi. Cetshwayo assembled his military advisers to discuss the crisis, and, despite the British ban, summoned those who still recognised their old allegiances. But again Zibhebhu struck first. At dawn on 21 July 1883, while the Ulundi women were collecting water from a stream, they saw a rapidly advancing phalanx of warriors silhouetted against the dim sky and raced back into Ulundi with the news. Zibhebhu had made a daring night march with 3,000 warriors and was advancing to attack Ulundi itself. As soon as word spread, the royalist warriors hurried out of their huts, but their commanders were still in agitated discussion with the king when Zibhebhu fell upon them. Panic set in. Urged to flee, Cetshwayo replied, 'Am I to run away from my dog?'[11] The royalist stand soon collapsed in confusion, and flight was the only option. The Mandhlakazi routed Cetshwayo's force and destroyed the king's *amakhanda*; the royalists were heavily defeated with over 500 warriors killed.

Most of the king's young warriors were fit enough to run away, but many of the king's elderly councillors were swiftly overtaken and captured. Over sixty of the most important chiefs loyal to King Cetshwayo were driven into a cattle kraal where, penned together and regardless of their stature, they were then systematically slaughtered without mercy. Those slain included Ntshingwayo, who had commanded at Isandlwana and Khambula and Sihayo of Fugitives' Drift whose sons had precipitated the British ultimatum. Apart from firing the royal *amakhanda*, the king's property, including presents from Queen Victoria and his flamboyant uniforms and trinkets, were seized and removed by Zibhebhu's men.

Meanwhile the king had been led away on horseback by his bodyguards, but not far from Ulundi, the horse collapsed. Taking refuge in a small thicket of scrub, he was spotted by two young warriors from Zibhebhu's army, who hurled spears at him, striking him in the thigh. Even under such circumstances he maintained his composure. 'Do you stab me, Halijana son of Sumfula?' he asked, recognising one of his assailants. 'I am your king!'[12] Awestruck, the young warriors assisted him in dressing his wounds and helped him on his way. Having escaped the slaughter Cetshwayo then discovered his new homestead burnt to the ground. He continued on to the territory of *inkosi* Sigananda kaSokufa, head of the Cube people, a staunch loyalist who lived in the rugged country above the Tugela River. Here he hid for a while in a cave at the head of the Mome stream until, in October, exhausted and fearful for his life, he surrendered himself to the British authorities in Eshowe where he sought protection from the British Resident Commissioner. The *Daily Telegraph* reported:

The termination of that extraordinary contest, in a military point of view, though its political results are by no means clear, has been formally announced by Sir Garnet Wolseley in despatches to her Majesty's Government. Our memory may now be turned for a brief space to the remarkable situation and character of the fallen native sovereign, who now finds himself (to compare small affairs with great) in a position similar to that of Napoleon III [exiled to England].

With the conclusion of the war Cetshwayo was a beaten man and undoubtedly suffering stress and depression.

He was not alone. (see Appendix 3)

Chapter 7

The British Attack against King Sekhukhune at Tsate, 28 November 1879

Having defeated the Zulus, Wolseley marched out of Zululand. Ever ready to embrace his next challenge, he headed north to Pretoria, capital of the old Transvaal Republic, to quell an upsurge in republican sentiment amongst Boers not reconciled to the British annexation of 1877. Wolseley was convinced their agitation would melt away when faced with the sight of British troops fresh from their successes in Zululand. En route was Sekhukhuneland.

Although the British had defeated the Zulus, the same tensions that had provoked the war in Zululand were still bearing down upon the Pedi nation, ruled by King Sekhukhune. Their formidable power-base lay in a corner of the Transvaal just 120 miles east of Pretoria and north-west of the Swazi kingdom. Sekhukhune had proved to be an able and determined ruler who was fiercely opposed to further European settlement. As recently as 1878 his warriors had seen off a full-scale British expedition against them led by Colonel Rowlands VC.

But now Wolseley was in charge. Still nurturing his resentment for having missed the opportunity of defeating the Zulus at Ulundi, the equally glittering prize of defeating King Sekhukhune was still his for the taking, especially as Chelmsford had earlier failed to subjugate him. Unaffected by the Zulu campaign, Sekhukhune was still at large and earlier British attempts to subdue him and his Pedi people had already cost the British government too much. Wolseley led the expedition, delighting in the knowledge that Chelmsford had previously failed. He wrote: 'If the Govt. at home wants me to fight, I am only too glad to meet their wishes as fighting in any shape is the greatest and most enjoyable of pleasures in life to me.'[1] On 18 October Wolseley reached Standerton. He wrote: 'The news from Sikekhuni's country is very serious, Sikekhuni will fight'. Adding, no doubt tongue-in-cheek: 'This is a great bore for me'. Wolseley had hoped the utter humiliation vented upon Cetshwayo might have reduced King Sekhukhune into submission. Instead, the Pedi were preparing for a last-ditch stand for fear the Zulus' fate might befall them.

By the middle of October, Wolseley concentrated all available troops in the Transvaal and moved his headquarters to Middleburg. Wolseley's principal attack column was placed under Lieutenant Colonel Baker Russell; all had recent battle experience in the Zulu campaign and most had been present at the Battle of Ulundi. Among his mounted irregular troops was the even more experienced Frontier Light Horse. While the NNC had been disbanded at the end of the Zulu campaign, Wolseley set about raising new native auxiliary forces from the various African groups in the Transvaal. The Swazis also offered 10,000 magnificently attired warriors in return for the promise they could keep any Pedi cattle they could plunder and share whatever fine was levied against the Pedi people. A few Swazis had rifles, but the majority of the warriors were armed with assegais. They marched over 150 miles from the Swazi king's royal homestead and drilled on the way.

Wolseley and his staff approached the new campaign with typical energy and efficiency, arriving at Fort Webber on 28 October to find that, owing to transport difficulties, supplies were behind schedule and inadequate. With great energy Wolseley personally set about rectifying this state of affairs and then reconnoitred the area ahead to get some idea of the nature of the objective and any terrain problems. The plan was to advance up the course of the Oliphants River and swing round north of the Pedi base at Tsate. Then, following a valley that ran southwards along the eastern edge of the Leolu Mountains, he planned to advance directly towards his objective of Tsate. The Swazis, meanwhile, would advance directly from Swaziland, to the south-east, and mount a direct attack on Tsate in the rear.

On 23 November Wolseley advanced. He was not opposed, but King Sekhukhune had meanwhile gathered his fighting men ready to make a determined stand in front of his capital. There are few accurate assessments of their numbers but there were probably less than 10,000 warriors. They were, however, heavily armed with obsolete but poor-quality weapons which represented the profits of their involvement from working in the diamond industry. Their position was a strong one. Tsate was a large settlement of about 3,000 huts nestled at the foot of a horse-shoe of rocky hills and protected by an isolated outcrop known to the Boers as the 'fighting koppie' after their earlier failed campaign. This unusual feature lay between the township and the valley beyond, directly in the line of Wolseley's advance. It is a jumble of volcanic rock, no more than 300 feet long, 200 feet across and 150 feet high, but it was a natural fortress with deep fissures, crevices and caves hidden among the piled-up boulders that the Pedi had carefully reinforced with rows of stone walls.

As was invariably the case with campaigning in Africa, the terrain was difficult, made worse by violent rainstorms and hail which harassed the advancing column until the narrow old Boer track, overgrown with dense bush, became almost impassable. The wagons stuck and the cracking of the whips overlaid by the thunder and lightning must have reminded many of the advance on Isandlwana or the withdrawal from Ulundi. Men of the 21st and the 94th Regiments who had been marching under arms for 24 hours arrived, soaked and dispirited, as they stumbled into the new camp site in the early hours of 27 November. Everything was now in place for the final assault on Sekhukhune's fortress base.

After viewing the kopje from a safe distance, Wolseley selected a suitable camp site and a position for the guns. His plan of attack was to first strike the mountain with the Irregulars and auxiliaries, who would advance past the kopje on either side to attack the Tsate township. This frontal attack was largely a feint, for Wolseley had instructed the Swazis to approach over the hills from behind the township and to storm it, hopefully taking the defenders in their rear and by surprise. Meanwhile the kopje would be shelled and contained by the regular troops. Once the township defenders had been destroyed or driven off, the isolated rock fortress would then be assaulted from all sides. But unbeknownst to the attackers, there were numerous deep caves above the township to which the Pedi were prepared to move if driven from their defensive positions. The British were also unaware that Sekhukhune and his retinue had already retreated to one of these caves in order to watch and control the battle.

Well before dawn on the morning of 28 November, the men were silently roused, the tents were struck and, without any loud orders, the men formed up in front of the camp. The column then moved forward swiftly across the valley with sufficient moonlight to enable them to see the mountain. Wolseley and his staff seated themselves under a tree to watch the attack and, at the first glimmer of dawn, a shell was fired into the 'fighting koppie' which instantly became alive with the defenders firing and yelling to alert the sleeping Pedi in the town and on the hillside.

While the infantry in the centre did no more than line up in support of the guns, the Irregulars and auxiliaries began their attack on the town from both flanks. To the left they were met at first by strong resistance from Pedi defenders concealed in rifle-pits, an unheard-of tactic for natives and one which took the advancing British troops by surprise. The Pedi were also positioned behind walls in front of the huts, but these were soon outflanked and the defenders rapidly retired to the slopes above the settlement. On both sides the fighting became a sporadic struggle to clear these slopes, while the artillery continued to shell the isolated 'fighting koppie'.

Once they realised the British were in earnest, the Swazi regiments moved quickly up the heights behind the town and at about 6am the first line of their distinctive shields appeared across the summit in the early-morning light. They then swept down the hillside towards the battle inflicting a great massacre on the fleeing Pedi. The Volunteers and the Swazis met halfway up the mountain, where the Pedi dead lay in profusion.

Clumps of warriors were still concealed among the rocks on the upper slopes and there were stiff flurries of hand-to-hand fighting as the Swazis cleared the boulders. Many Pedi women and children were still hiding in the caves and a great crowd of them was soon driven out, running towards the town, which added to the chaos. By about 9.30am a great cloud of smoke began to billow up as the town's huts were set alight; Tsate was in the hands of the invaders. The loss of life among the Pedi, both fighting men and non-combatants, had been heavy.

Only the 'fighting koppie' resisted. With the town taken, the troops were now able to surround the kopje on all sides and Wolseley gave the order for it to be taken by storm. The regulars, unused to this type of warfare, were clumsy and vulnerable but it was a type of fighting at which the Swazi excelled. They jumped casually from boulder to boulder spearing any Pedi they found hiding. By about 10.30am the attackers had completely overrun the kopje.

But there remained a serious problem: hundreds of Pedi men, women and children refused to surrender and were still hidden among the caves, firing on anyone who approached them. Wolseley ordered parties of Royal Engineers to blow up some of the caves with guncotton, a tactic which had earlier worked well at Ntombe. But the Pedi were familiar with the concept of explosives from their diamond mining days; they would run forward and cut the fuses before the charges could explode.

Then an impressive thunderstorm developed. Clouds blotted out the sky so that an inky blackness descended over the battlefield, only to be rent with sudden lightning flashes and deafening peals of thunder. The Pedi warriors still trapped on the kopje spotted their chance. The soldiers being deployed as a cordon were clearly disorientated and distracted by the storm so hundreds of Pedi made a rush at the nearest part of the line, bounding over the boulders and in some cases leaping clear over the heads of the crouching soldiers. Despite the breakout, there were still hundreds of men and women hiding among the crevices. When they refused to surrender, the troops and Swazis were all withdrawn and a cordon of men was placed in a trench around the kopje with the object of starving them out. The remainder of the force retired to camp at about 1p.m.

Altogether, three officers and ten Europeans had been killed and another thirty wounded. The dead were buried close to the camp. The loss among the African auxiliaries was not properly recorded, although some assumed that the Pedi losses ran to thousands. The survivors of the 'fighting koppie' then began to surrender. The hill was covered with unburied dead from the fighting and a heavy stench of death soon hung in the air. Many Pedi, weakened by wounds and lack of water or food, never emerged from their hiding places and, after the last surrenders, the Royal Engineers were again ordered to dynamite the most conspicuous of the caves.

A party of Irregulars and Swazis was sent out to hunt for King Sekhukhune, and on the morning of 2 December he was discovered hiding in a cave. The Swazis laid siege to the entrance, but the king refused to come out until a party of Ferreira's Horse arrived. They dismissed the Swazis and assured the king that he would be safe. When, at last, the king emerged he was taken under guard to Wolseley's camp, and for the second time in a few short months Wolseley witnessed the sight of a once proud and powerful African monarch brought before him as a prisoner.

With the king's powerbase now destroyed, Wolseley dismissed his troops. The Swazi were sent home, driving before them herds of Pedi cattle as a reward for their decisive role in the attack. A few of the Irregulars were left to hold forts around Sekhukhuneland. The regular 94th Regiment returned to their base at Lydenburg, while the rest, with Wolseley and his staff, set off for Pretoria, arriving there on 9 December to find a large crowd turned out to watch the captured king arrive in town aboard a wagon.

At the end of March, Wolseley left the Transvaal, his job there done, and at the beginning of April he embarked at Durban for home. Eight months later, the Boers in the Transvaal rose in deadly revolt.

The British casualties figures for the attack against King Sekhukhune are as follows:

Killed at the Stad and 'fighting koppie' and buried at the camp on the plain:
Captain W. G. Lawrell 4th Hussars, Wolseley's Staff
Captain J. E. Macaulay 12th Lancers – in command of Transvaal Mounted Rifles
Corporal P. MacNally 2nd Bn, 21st Regiment
Private H. Donahoe 2nd Bn, 21st Regiment
Private W. Weston 2nd Bn, 21st Regiment
Private Chipps 94th Regiment
Corporal E. Mitchell Border Horse

Killed on the mountain or at the Stad, but buried at Fort Victoria at the top of the mountain:
Lieutenant Alister Campbell, RN Swazi Native Contingent
Sergeant Major R. Wilson Ferreira's Horse
Private W. Reston 2nd Bn, 21st Regiment QMS
Trooper N. McLeod Border Horse
Trooper Mackay Border Horse
Trooper P. Matibe Transvaal Mounted Rifles.

The remains of these thirteen men were reinterred at the northern end of the 'fighting koppie' by Mr. B. P. Margetson and a party of the Northern Transvaal Soldiers' Graves Association on 25 December 1961.

Joseph Lehmann records that three officers were killed and seven wounded; other ranks, seven killed and forty-three wounded.

Smith records that three officers were killed and five wounded; other ranks, ten killed and about thirty wounded. Insofar as deaths are concerned, the latter figures appear to be correct.

Chapter 8

The Battle of Bronkhorstspruit, 20 December 1880

The Boers … have all the cunning and cruelty of the Kaffir [sic] without his honesty or courage … they could not stand up against our troops for an hour'.[1]

Before engaging in war against the Zulus, and aware of smouldering Boer resentment against the British, Sir Bartle Frere and Lord Chelmsford knew that once they had become fully engaged against the Zulus there was a probability of a Boer uprising in the north – behind British lines. To discourage the Boers from rebelling, the Number 4 Northern Column under Colonel Rowlands VC was held back on the Boer border, while the remaining four columns invaded Zululand. Rowland's brief, wisely, was to observe the Boers and make such observations of them obvious.

Following the Battle of Ulundi, and while waiting to return to England, the 94th Regiment was brought to battle by the Boers as a direct consequence of the Zulu War. With surplus troops in Zululand, Wolseley decided to take the opportunity to finally deal with King Sekhukhune. This second Sekhukhuni campaign – the first was in 1878 – was conducted to boost Wolseley's image at home. But both campaigns showed British vulnerability and severely weakened any restraint the Boers still felt that might have precluded them from risking military action against the British. Although not a battle of the Zulu War, the engagement at Bronkhorstspruit was fought by the 94th Regiment who had earlier fought against the Zulus at Ulundi and then, without pause, were ordered to take part in operations against King Sekhukhune's stronghold in the Transvaal.

Coinciding with the end of British hostilities against the Zulus and Pedi, Boer resentment moved from passive to potentially active; all it needed was an excuse. On cessation of hostilities against King Sekhukhune, the 94th Regiment left Zululand and marched across the old border into the

Attack on Fighting Koppie.

Fighting Koppie and Tsate Town.

Bronkhorstspruit Boer memorial.

British graves and memorial at Bronkhorstspruit.

Wolseley cheering on the attack at Tsate.

King Sekhukhune.

British soldier collecting
polluted drinking water.

Beards on campaign.

Route to the Ulundi White Umfolozi River.

Prince Dinizulu, aged 18.

Clearing the caves at Ntombe, 'at the war's end'.

Drawing of 18 Melbury Road taken from *The Daily Telegraph*. In 1882 the house was the home of King Cetshwayo and his entourage during his brief but highly significant visit to London.

18 Melbury Road today. (*Spudgun67 via Wiki Commons/CC BY-SA 4.0*)

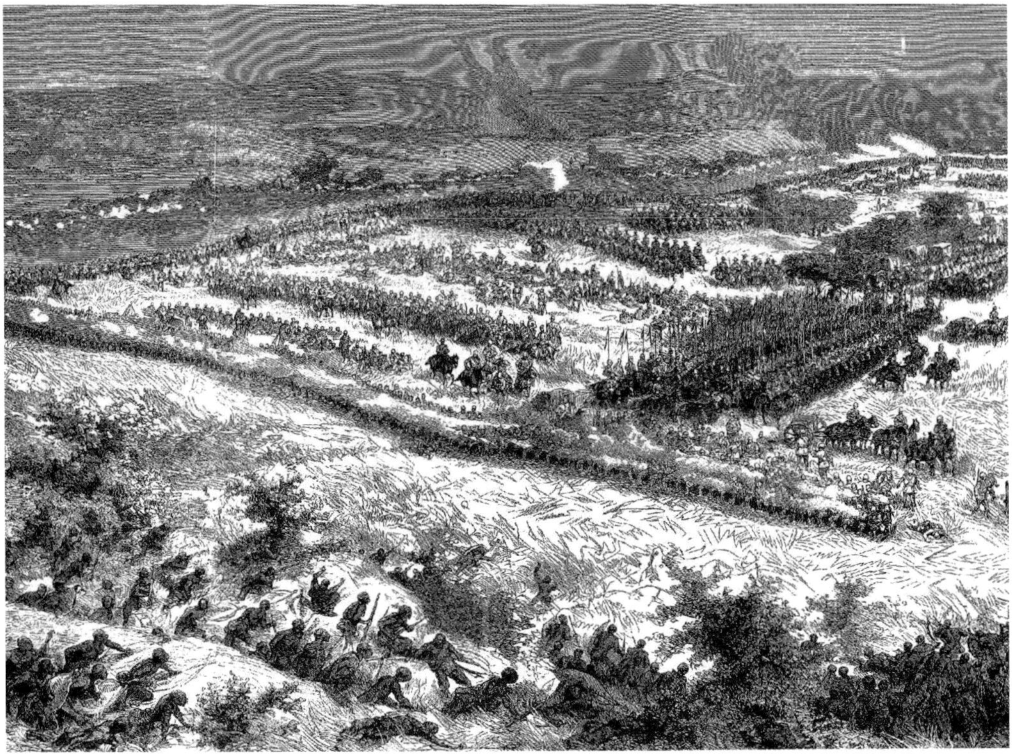

The Battle of Ulundi.

Prisoner King Cetshwayo in London.

Transvaal to take over their new garrison role of watching the Boers. Without replacement uniforms and clad in tattered rags, they were proud of their achievements, for which they would be granted a new honour for their colours. The 94th were then widely distributed throughout the Transvaal: E and G companies were sent to Pretoria; A and F companies were posted to Lydenburg; C company was ordered to Wakkerstroom; B company to Marabastad; H company to Standerton; and D company to Newcastle in northern Natal. After having fought in the Anglo-Zulu War of 1879, followed by a series of engagements against Sekhukhune, and then experiencing 'tedious periods of garrison duty in isolated posts', the 94th Regiment was low in morale, and facing increasing levels of desertion. Indeed, one of the lessons learned from the Zulu War by Britain's enemies was that the British army was not invincible.

The British woes and defeats suffered during the war had been closely observed, which encouraged the Boers to plot and plan to seize the day and stand against the British. But Boer dissention was nothing new. The Transvaal Boers had been antagonistic towards the British ever since the Great Trek of 1838 when, in large numbers, they had abandoned the Cape in protest against British rule and high taxation in order to seek self-government in the unknown lands to the north – later named the Transvaal (rough translation 'across the Vaal River'). The Boers had long memories, and many were still smarting from the annexation of the Transvaal by Britain in 1877. The Boers refused to participate in action against the Zulus, with minor exceptions, even though Britain partly went to war against the Zulus to facilitate Boer farming expansion into Zululand.

On 11 November 1880 a public meeting of Boers took place at Potchefstroom to express anger at a fine levied by British officials against a local Boer farmer, Pieter Bezuidenhout. The farmer had refused to pay a fine and the British decided to confiscate his wagon in lieu of payment of £27 5s 0d. After the wagon was removed it was immediately offered for sale, whereupon a crowd of Boer protesters seized the wagon and drove it off. The British Administrator in the Transvaal saw this as an act of aggression which he felt required a firm hand. He sent a military detachment to Potchefstroom which inflamed growing Boer resentment.

Meanwhile, on 5 December, two companies of the 94th, together with medical, commissariat staff and families, set off to march to Pretoria, the regiment's new posting. The total strength of the column was 262, under the command of Colonel Anstruther.

Secret meetings of Boers were then held across the Transvaal, and, on 13 December, the leading Boers proclaimed the Transvaal a South African Republic. They decided to take immediate military action and despatched three commandos. One was to intercept the 94th Regiment marching from its base at Lydenburg to strengthen the British garrison at Pretoria where local Boer disaffection was growing. Another went to Potchefstroom, and the third to the border to discourage any British attempt to send reinforcements from Natal. A lack of transport wagons had already delayed Colonel Anstruther's advance from Lydenburg for a week while extra wagons were hired from local Boer farmers. Because there were few available wagons, exorbitant rates were demanded which Anstruther reckoned would cost £1,000 in total. Once the column had obtained the requisite wagons, the column could set off. Their progress was limited to about 8 miles each day due to the poor condition of the rutted track and numerous streams that had to be negotiated. On 15 December news reached the column that all companies of the regiment would be concentrating at Pretoria. Anstruther wrote that the whole move was due to the Boers agitating, although he noted that the Boer families along the route were 'friendly and civil' – even if a regular comment was 'if you don't give us back the Transvaal we'll fight like cats', which Anstruther took as friendly banter, commenting:

> They have, I am sure, no intention of fighting though if we are firm with them, as I hope we will be, there might be one or two little disturbances.[2]

By 19 December the column was wet and weary having had to cross the flooded Oliphants River. The following morning they paused at a Boer farm to purchase fresh provisions and make amends after some of the soldiers had stolen fruit from the farmer's orchard. Little was made of the incident and the stolen fruit was paid for with an apology. At the time, Anstruther noticed an unaccountable number of horses corralled around the farm, all saddled and ready to depart. He took no action. On the day following the battle, he recalled that he had overlooked the significance of the horses. Unbeknown to Anstruther, the farm was the rendezvous for the Boers detailed to intercept the column, but taken by surprise by the approaching British column, the Boers had hidden themselves in a nearby barn but had no option but to leave their horses in full view of the British. At about 10am, the column continued on its way with the intention of stopping for the night at a crossing point at the Bronkhorst stream just a few miles distant. The whole column of marching men and thirty-four wagons extended nearly one mile and blissfully continued on its way with the band playing.

The column was about two miles from the intended camp site when a Boer rider approached the leading wagons showing a white flag of truce. The British were unsure what was happening, but Anstruther had the presence of mind to give the order to halt and close ranks. The order was passed down the column and the band stopped playing. The rider approached Anstruther and handed him a document, an ultimatum signed by a Boer leader, Piet Joubert and countersigned by Paul Kruger. The order instructed Anstruther not to continue across the river until certain diplomatic negotiations between the British and Boers were resolved. It warned that if the troops advanced beyond the stream the Boers would construe the movement as an act of war.

The rider added that two minutes would be allowed for the column commander to decide his course of action. While Anstruther was considering his predicament and the two-minute ultimatum ticked away, the Boer commando, under the protection of the white flag, approached the column to within 200 yards of the wagons and positioned themselves behind rocks and trees. According to witnesses Anstruther replied:

I have orders to proceed with all possible dispatch to Pretoria and to Pretoria I am going, but tell the Commandant I have no wish to meet him in hostile spirit.[3]

As Anstruther made his comment of non-cooperation, the rider holding the white flag turned his horse and made a signal to the Boers who immediately opened fire on the helpless and unsuspecting column. The unprotected wagons and watching soldiers, many of whom had placed their rifles in the column's wagons, were mostly unarmed and consequently sitting targets for the Boer marksmen. Within minutes, Anstruther was shot six times.

The officers and most of the NCOs were killed or wounded, along with more than half the soldiers. To save the lives of the remainder, the seriously wounded Anstruther gave the order to cease firing and to hoist something white to signify their surrender. This done, firing ceased on both sides and the Boers closed in. They ordered the surviving soldiers to lay down their weapons, which they did. The Boers then collected up all available weapons and drove off the wagons containing arms and ammunition, and anything else they considered of use or value. The column conductor, Mr. Egerton, received permission to ride to Pretoria to get medical assistance. Leaving the column under a Boer guard to fend for itself as best they could, the survivors began tending the wounded and burying their dead. The following day the fit survivors were marched off by the Boers to Heidelberg and the less serious casualties escorted to Pretoria. Boer losses were kept secret; British survivors' reports of Boer casualties ranged from two to thirty killed.[4]

As with a number of earlier engagements during the Zulu War, of which Anstruther had been an experienced commander, it is surprising that Anstruther blatantly ignored accurate intelligence of Boer unrest and warnings that something was amiss. On 16 December, Anstruther had received a written warning that British relationships with the Boers were disintegrating and warned him to be fully on his guard and to deploy patrols before advancing his column. Anstruther seems to have ignored the warning as his scouting was casual, with only one man sent in advance of the column to observe the route and one scout to scan the surrounding hills. Only thirty rounds of ammunition were carried by each soldier instead of the usual seventy and reserve ammunition boxes remained sealed on the wagons, so it was clear that no one in the column was expecting to be attacked. From Boer reports, it is evident the Boers had tracked the column for several days. A makeshift British hospital was constructed at Bronkhorstspruit and it remained there for three further months before the remaining more seriously wounded were allowed to travel to Pretoria. Bronkhorstspruit was the opening clash of the First Boer War, more commonly known to South Africans as 'The Transvaal Rebellion'.

The Boer attack on the unsuspecting column was premeditated and shocking in its sudden and wilful execution. The objective was to cause the most serious damage as swiftly as possible in order to send a shock message to the procrastinating British to resolve Boer claims for independence. British losses were in the ratio of 37:1 and it must be acknowledged that had Anstruther not disobeyed orders to expect resistance from the Boers and had he not been careless in the extreme by permitting only thirty rounds per soldier, his column might have fared better. Likewise, he had not considered it prudent to issue weapons or ammunition held in the column's wagons, leaving many soldiers momentarily unarmed.

The 94th lost one officer (Lieutenant Harrison) and seventy-three men in the carnage of the attack. Another four officers and ninety men received wounds, of which three officers – Anstruther, Captain Nairne and Captain MacSwiney – and eighteen men later died. One officer and 105 men became prisoners of the Boers. The other six companies of the regiments spent the war besieged by the Boers: C, D and H at Standerton, E and G at Pretoria, B in Marabastad, and a small detachment of fifty men at Lydenburg.

At the conclusion of the war the 94th Regiment remained in the Transvaal until the final ratification of the peace convention with the Boers and then, on 5 November 1881, they commenced their march back to Natal. After almost three eventful years, the end of the regiment's service in southern Africa was in sight. Having encountered not only the Zulus, Pedi and Boers on the fields of battle, they had faced the ravages of disease, the extremes of weather, the boredom of garrison duty and endured the claustrophobia of siege life – it was time to return home. On 24 March 1882, seven companies embarked on the *Dublin Castle* and sailed for Queenstown, Cork where they arrived on 20 April.

At home, there were celebrations and campaign medals for the survivors. At Bronkhorstspruit, Colour Sergeant Maistre had been one of two NCOs carrying the Regimental Colours when the column was attacked by the Boers. To prevent the capture of the Colours, Maistre hid them in the bedding of another NCO's severely wounded wife. The next day the Boers permitted two volunteers to walk to Pretoria to seek medical help. Maistre wrapped the colours around his body and smuggled them out to safety. For his actions in saving the Colours, Maistre was awarded the Distinguished Conduct Medal.

The 94th Regiment was entitled to the honour 'South Africa 1879', but when the awards were announced in 1882 the 94th had already amalgamated with the 88th Regiment and become the 2nd Battalion Connaught Rangers.

Due to the previous service of the 88th in the Cape Frontier, the honour was awarded as 'South Africa 1877-78-79'. No battle honour, medal, clasp or bar was issued for the campaign against Sekhukhune in 1878 or for service against the Boers in 1881.

Evaluation

Bronkhorstspruit was another disaster for the British army, especially in terms of the unnecessary loss of life construed at the time as cold-blooded murder by the Boers. Yet, with all the disasters of the Zulu War still fresh in British commanders' memories, Colonel Anstruther adopted the identical tactic of 'it won't happen to me'. He failed to obey his orders relating to the size of the column and insisted on hiring extra wagons from the Boers, who deliberately procrastinated in order to allow their approaching troops to close with the column. He was then warned that relationships with the Boers were rapidly deteriorating and to make haste with his progress to Pretoria, which he did not. He was further advised that the Boers might take aggressive action against his column, which he ignored, and failed to issue his men with sufficient ammunition, and in the case of the band, no weapons. When he came face-to-face with an unaccountable number of Boers' saddled horses at the farm stop-over, he failed to realise their significance. He was certainly 'taken in' when allowing the heavily armed Boers to approach his wagons after the Boer messenger rode up to the column under the white flag of truce, which the Boers then disregarded by opening fire on the defenceless column.

Subsequently, there was considerable anger in the British press at the Boers' disregard of their own flag of truce but, by the time the regiment returned home, the first Boer conflict was over and Bronkhorstspruit was rarely mentioned. Once again, the incident was widely considered to have been unnecessary and any investigation into the battle would have highlighted Anstruther's many failings. For the Boers, their situation was identical to that of the Zulus a year earlier. They were the dominant population controlled by a minor governing authority, the British, and, denied their right to run their own country, they rebelled. As for the public at home, it all seemed to be an extension of the string of embarrassments following on from the Zulu War – and best forgotten.

And like many of the battlefields of the Zulu War, the location of the ambush at Bronkhorstspruit has long since become overgrown. The roadway where Anstruther's column was ambushed has disappeared. The original track ran on an east-west line and has subsequently been reclaimed by nature. The new road cuts across where the ambush occurred, near where the monuments are, and runs north-south. The British gravestones are still there to be found, but they were moved at some point, being set flat in the ground, therefore making them difficult to find.

Neither side could be proud of the Boer rebellion. The British would not treat with the Boers, who became militant and, at Bronkhorstspruit, the Boers should have honoured the flag of truce and did not. There could be no pride attached to what had happened and both sides needed to move on.

Bronkhorstspruit was the opening military action of the First Boer War, and although it was a morale-boosting victory for the Boers, it was soon forgotten. In contrast, for the British, who had been dismissive of the military effectiveness of the Boers before the battle, it was a humbling experience. To deflect from the scale of the loss, senior British officers criticised the Boers for advancing on the British column under a white flag and placed blame on Anstruther, citing his 'neglect' and 'absence of caution'. Despite this, Major General Sir George Pomeroy Colley, the British Army's commander-in-chief in Transvaal and Natal, acknowledged in a despatch to the British government that: 'This will materially alter our situation, as encouraging Boers, who will now also feel themselves committed'.[5] The Boers besieged several towns over the next month, and engaged in three significant battles during January and February 1881; at Laing's Nek, Schuinshoogte (Ingogo) and Majuba Hill. The Boers won each one, and after the death of Colley while commanding the British in the last battle, the British government signed the Pretoria Convention, granting Transvaal self-government under British suzerainty, effectively reinstating the South African Republic.

Tensions between the British and the Boers never faded and, in 1899, conflict broke out again with the start of the Second Boer War.

Chapter 9

Going Home and the Death of King Cetshwayo, Long Live the King

As detailed earlier, the king and his entourage left England at the end of December 1882. The mission to meet Queen Victoria had been a huge political and diplomatic success and the impression Cetshwayo had created in the minds of the British public did much to alter their opinion of the Zulu people. In the years since the 1879 British invasion many had become uneasy about the justice of the war, and the king's apparent dignity in defeat helped to change the image of the Zulus from one of ruthless savages to noble warriors – a view that has continued to colour popular perception to thisday.

Behind the scenes, diplomatically, the mission was only a partial success. The Colonial Office agreed that the king could be restored to Zululand but only to part of his old kingdom. Large tracts of the country were to be set aside for those Zulus who had ruled in his absence – and who could not be expected to welcome his return – and he would not be allowed to re-establish the Zulu's traditional royal *amabutho* system.

Meanwhile. Zululand was in turmoil. The Natal authorities had done everything they could to delay the king's return, even to falsely citing diseases in Zululand, but the reality was that they needed more time to reduce the area over which he would have control. When the permission came it was tempered by news that shocked the king; two large swathes of Zululand had been disposed of. One was an area to be known as the Zulu Native Reserve under the control of John Dunn and Chief Hlubi while the other area had been allocated to Chief Zibhebhu, a former rival of the king who would have control of Zululand north of the White Umfolozi River. This was contrary to the terms Cetshwayo had reluctantly accepted in London.

Nor was his return announced to his countrymen: when on 10 January 1883 he finally arrived back on Zulu soil he found only a few Zulus waiting to greet him. He was escorted to his old capital by Sir Theophilus Shepstone – who had 'crowned' him just a decade before, and who had come out of retirement for the occasion. Once news of the king's return spread, his old loyal supporters, chiefs and commoners alike, all flocked to renew their allegiance.

He was re-installed at Emtonjaneni where even more conditions were put upon him. Many thought these additional conditions were a deliberate trap to cause his downfall.[1] Meanwhile Zululand was in turmoil and with Cetshwayo sandwiched between his enemies and Natal, and with the northern Abaqulusi rising in his support by laying waste to their enemies, he was required by the terms of his restoration to maintain peace across Zululand. The king sought help from the Natal authorities, but this was refused. Amidst the confusion of Zulu clans raiding other Zulu clans, chaos began to ferment.

King Cetshwayo set about rebuilding a new version of Ulundi, not far from the complex destroyed in 1879. It was a smaller undertaking, a thousand huts, but still an impressive statement of his position and authority. As a precaution, he was supervised by a British Resident but he found his country deeply divided by several years of friction between his supporters and the appointees set up by the British. In particular, his followers bitterly resented the oppression they had experienced during the king's exile at the hands of his erstwhile general, Chief Zibhebhu kaMaphitha, and they were keen to take revenge upon him. Probably without King Cetshwayo's knowledge, and certainly without his sanction, a number of royalist supporters assembled an army in March to attack Zibhebhu.

Before Cetshwayo could react, Zibhebhu struck first. At dawn on 21 July 1883, the women serving at oNdini were gathering water from a stream when they noticed a column of warriors silhouetted against the shadowy sky, advancing rapidly. Zibhebhu had made a daring night march with 3,000 warriors and was advancing to attack Ulundi itself. The women fled with the news and as word spread, the royalist warriors hurried out of their huts, but their commanders were still in agitated discussion with the king when Zibhebhu fell upon them. The attack caused consternation. Cetshwayo had assembled many of his most prominent advisers and those who still recognised their old allegiances to discuss the crisis. Urged to flee, Cetshwayo replied,

'Am I to run away from my dog?' Yet the royalist stand collapsed in confusion, and flight was the only option. The Mandhlakazi routed Cetyshwayo's force and set about destroying the king's *amakhanda*: the royalists were heavily defeated with over 500 experienced warriors killed.

Most of the king's young warriors were fit enough to run away, but many of the king's more elderly councillors were swiftly overtaken and killed. Over sixty of Cetshwayo most loyal and important chiefs, stripped of their assegais, were driven into a cattle kraal where, regardless of their stature, they were systematically slaughtered. Those killed included Ntshingwayo, who had commanded at Isandlwana and Khambula and Sihayo, whose sons had precipitated the British ultimatum. Apart from firing the royal *amakhanda*, all King Cetshwayo's property, including presents from Queen Victoria, flamboyant uniforms and trinkets, was seized and removed by Zibhebhu's men. The surviving Usuthu women and children were rounded up to be absorbed into the Mandhlakazi.

Cetshwayo had been rushed away on horseback by his bodyguards, but not far from Ulundi the horse stumbled and fell due to his weight Taking refuge in a small thicket, he was spotted by two warriors from Zibhebhu's army and without realizing who he was, they hurled their spears at him, one striking him in the thigh. Even under such circumstances he maintained his composure: 'Do you stab me, Halijana son of Sumfula?' he asked, recognising one of his assailants; 'I am your king!'[2] Awestruck, the young warriors assisted him in dressing his wound and helped him on his way. Having escaped the slaughter Cetshwayo then discover his new homestead burnt to the ground. He continued on to the territory of *inkosi* Sigananda kaSokufa, head of the Cube people, a staunch loyalist who lived in the rugged country above the Thukela River. Here he hid for a while in a cave at the head of the Mome stream.

Rumours soon began to spread across the Zulu nation that the king had been killed at Ulundi. Cetshwayo sought assistance from the British, who ignored his plight. Fearful of being captured by the Mandhlakazi search parties, Cetshwayo was forced to flee to Eshowe, where, on 17 October 1883, exhausted and fearful for his life, he surrendered himself to the British authorities where, a beaten man, he sought protection from the British Resident Commissioner.[3]

Without doubt, the 21 July routing at Ulundi of King Cetshwayo by previously loyal Zulus marked the final stages of the demise of the Zulu nation. In essence, a Zulu chief, Zibhebhu, achieved everything that Lord Chelmsford had failed to achieve when he invaded Zululand in 1879.

King Cetshwayo died following a meal on 8 February 1884, probably poisoned by assassins among his own people. He had earlier been seen on a walk and appeared fit and well. Zulus were familiar with numerous forms of poison that could be administered in beer or snuff, both of which were to the king's liking. Curiously, the king's staff on the day failed to raise the alarm for four hours. When the British doctor eventually examined the body, he requested a post mortem, which was refused by the Zulu officials present – and there the matter closed.[4] To prevent his grave from becoming a future rallying point for Zulu dissenters, the king was buried in an isolated and beautiful part of the Nkandla Forest at Nkunzana, near the Mome Gorge.

Francis Colenso wrote to her brother:

They have just tortured him to death as they did his father [Bishop Colenso] seven months ago. He said, when he heard of his [Bishop Colenso's] death, that it was his own death warrant; then came Ulundi and since then blow after blow, indignity after indignity, has been heaped upon him – it is difficult not to say with the intention to break his heart.[5]

Several months later, a letter was published from a British doctor who had examined the king during his captivity:

As ex-King Cetshwayo is stated to have died suddenly of fatty degeneration of the heart, it may interest readers to know what was the state of his heart in August 1882. In auscultation the heart sounds were absolutely normal and the appended sphymographic tracing will show the healthy state of the arterial system.[6]

Without doubt, the death of King Cetshwayo marked the final stages of the demise of the Zulu nation. The king's supporters were determined to lay his body to rest away from the malicious influence of both the British and anti-royalists. After the necessary rites his body was traditionally wrapped in a fresh bull's hide and smothered in blankets to be allowed to desiccate in the heat of a closed hut. Later, his remains were taken by wagon back to Chief Sigananda's territory and buried in isolation not far from the Mome Gorge. The wagon was left on the spot and allowed to decay; its remains can now be seen in the Zulu Cultural Museum at Ulundi.

Ironically, after his death, which had resulted from powerful divisions within the country unleashed by the British invasion, Cetshwayo's image came increasingly to be viewed as unifying. He was seen by many tribes suffering under the reality of colonial rule as the representative of a golden age of power and independence. In 1906, African discontent again turned to violence over the issue of a newly implemented poll tax. The 'rebels' sought to draw on the mystique of Cetshwayo's name to unify their movement. The king's grave was used as a rallying point for the rebellion, and, in a final bitter irony, it was nearby, in the Mome Gorge, that colonial forces inflicted a crushing defeat on one of the last traditionalist armies raised in Zululand. Conquered but not defeated.

The Zulus depicted King Cetshwayo as a great bird protecting its young and ensuring the fertility of its eggs without regard for individual self-interest. When the great bird died in 1884, the eggs were abandoned and left to rot.[7]

Footnote: In 1897 Zululand was formally incorporated into Natal. During the following years much of the land was officially appropriated and given over to white settlement.

Chapter 10

Prince Dinizulu

On 21 May 1883, fearing for the safety of the adolescent Prince Dinizulu, the successor to King Cetshwayo, the Boers brought him to safety in the Transvaal and pronounced him King of the Zulus. When King Cetshwayo died, and with British encouragement, the two main Zulu chiefs in the northern part of Zululand, the hated Chief Zibhebhu of the Mandlakazi and Chief Hamu of the Ngenetsheni, set about trying to finally destroy their historical enemy, the loyalist Usutho whose strong allegiance was traditionally with their king. They commenced a series of vicious attacks, and, on 30 March 1884, the two armies met in a full-scale battle. The disorganised Usutho were utterly defeated, and worse, they lost their leading ranks, slaughtered to a man.

Even with the battle won, Zibhebhu never achieved total victory over the Usutho as the greater proportion of the tribe were able to retreat ahead of Zibhebhu's warriors to the safety of their caves but were then subjected to siege tactics by Zibhebhu and a group of well-armed white bounty hunters and adventurers. Natal was unaffected by the human tragedy unfurling, as it was conveniently distant; the Usutho were soon starving. The disinterested British watched but did nothing to prevent the situation worsening. With the Zulu nation in deepest chaos, Natal and Boer settlers looked acquisitively at Zululand for its fertile farmland and abundant labour force. Not only had the old Zulu order finally collapsed, but Zululand was also now open to some serious plunder. With the Boers and British still acting malevolently towards them, the remaining Zulus were now trapped between two aggressive white powers.

On 21 May 1884 the Boers crowned Dinizulu in exchange for three million acres of northern Zululand. Sporadic violence continued for four more years, during which Dinuzulu secured Boer help to defeat Zibhebhu, but this cost the lives of a number of the prominent supporters of the old order.

Following a contrived scuffle in 1886, the Boers murdered Prince Dabulamanzi, the Zulu chief who had commanded at the Battle of Rorke's Drift. Negotiations between the British and the Boers began and in 1887 the Cape Government took full control of Zululand and its affairs by annexing the whole country. One probable reason was British concern that Boer expansion towards the Indian Ocean would give the Boers a seaport that, in turn, could threaten British interests in Natal. The proclamation was read to the Zulus at Eshowe. King Dinizulu and his chiefs were horrified and astonished by the proclamation's requirements. Dinizulu had never accepted the invasion of 1879 as an absolute defeat because, following Ulundi, the British had abandoned Zululand and its people to their fate. He now found that, not only had the British and the Boers stolen his country from under him, but the British – who now proclaimed jurisdiction over him – refused to accept his rightful status as Cetshwayo's heir. They preferred to lend their support to rival groups within the Zulu kingdom with the sole intention of undermining the residual influence of the Zulu royal house. In November 1887, the British allowed Prince Zibhebhu and his followers to return to northern Zululand from their exile in the Eshowe district in what can only be seen as a deliberate attempt to counterbalance support for Dinizulu.

Either by accident or design, Zibhebhu's homestead at Bangonomo was not far from Dinuzulu's own settlement at Nongomo. Dinuzulu was understandably furious at finding himself living so close to the man he considered responsible for the death of his father. Dinuzulu began assembling a large force of warriors at the stronghold of Ceza Mountain and, when the British sent armed police to order him to disperse, he chased them off. In fear of Dinuzulu's army, Zibhebhu moved his own followers close to a British outpost at iVuna Hill, but on 23 June 1888 Dinuzulu attacked them. Riding ahead of his men on horseback, Dinuzulu, still only twenty years old, led a ferocious charge that scattered the Mandlakazi, all within sight of the British fort. Zibhebhu and the survivors fled. In an attempt to restore some order, the British immediately hurried troops into Zululand to confront the victorious Dinuzulu but then commenced suppressing him.

The ongoing policy of 'divide and rule' had fatally damaged Dinuzulu's ability to resist, and where once the kingdom had presented a united front against the invasion of 1879, many influential Zulu figures now chose neutrality or sided with the British. Although the fighting spluttered on for several months, Dinizulu was never in a position to inflict defeats upon the British comparable to his father's victories at Isandlwana and Hlobane, and after the dispersal of a royalist force at Hlopekhulu Mountain, near Ulundi, on 2 July 1888, Dinizulu and his uncles, Ndabuko and Shingana, fled to the Transvaal Republic. Worried the British might take retributive action against them, the Boers denied them sanctuary and instead the weary fugitives crossed back into Natal and surrendered to the British colonial authorities.

Prince Dinizulu was detained on the grounds of causing 'public violence' and charges of high treason were eventually brought against him for allegedly supporting armed resistance against the British. Although no evidence was produced, Dinizulu was charged with 'determined resistance and attacks against Her Majesty's Forces, led in person by Dinizulu'. Dinuzulu and his two uncles were tried for high treason, found guilty, and all three were sentenced to varying periods of exile on the island of St Helena, which served as a British political prison. The royal party was allowed to take several wives with them; Dinizulu took with him two wives, Silomo and Zihlazile, and the British Government allowed a stipend for their maintenance. For the first time, apart from King Cetshwayo's brief time in England, members of the Zulu royal family were exposed to British culture, and Dinuzulu in particular was still young enough to enjoy the experience. He learned to speak and write English, to wear Western clothes, and to play the piano. Queen Silomo bore him two sons on the island, Prince Solomon Nkayishana Maphumuza and Prince Arthur Edward Mshiyeni, while Queen Zihlazile bore him two sons, David Nyawana and Samuel Bhekelendaba, and a daughter, Victoria Mphaphu.

For the second time in ten years, a Zulu king had to endure the humiliation of capture and exile. Meanwhile, unrest among the Zulu people stirred. They remained fully exposed to the consequences of conquest. The worst excesses suffered were a complete lack of influence in their own administrative affairs, the denigration of their customs and beliefs, the expropriation of their lands and their enforced involvement at the lowest levels in the burgeoning settler industrial economy.

Again, but too late, the British tried to control the unrest spreading from Zululand. The native population across Natal was becoming increasingly unsettled so the authorities reacted by imposing another hut tax of fourteen shillings or cattle in lieu. The Usutho let it be known that they would refuse to pay, and furthermore, severed the remaining ties with the British Resident Administrator of Zululand, Melmoth Osborn. When the dispirited Usutho began cattle-raiding those clans subservient to Osborn, he responded by despatching British and local units of Natal police. The result was a stalemate as the troops were unable to penetrate the thick bush country occupied by the Usutho and a truce resulted. The British responded by putting a track through the forest to prevent a reoccurrence of the Usutho protests and then strengthened their control by conducting retributive public hangings and savage thrashings, worsened by carrying out the thrashings in instalments.[1] Under such harsh British domination, the Zulu social structure virtually collapsed. Disease and a six-year famine severely damaged their ability to feed or re-establish themselves and by 1889 the forceful collection of the hated hut tax had left young men with no option but to take up six-month work contracts in the growing towns and cities of Natal, with a powerful negative effect on Zulu social life. This ongoing crisis was followed in 1897 by the Rinderpest Epidemic, a fatal cattle disease that had spread from Cape farms virtually destroying the Zulus' remaining cattle. And then, just as they began the long process of restocking, the deadly East Coast Fever obliterated their fledgling herds. To compound Zulu woes, Natal's new governor, Sir Arthur Havelock, established a fresh committee to consider the opening up of Zululand to white settlers. They collectively agreed that nearly half of Zululand was to be taken from the Zulus. At the same time, a £1 tax was levied on all migrant workers who had previously evaded the hated hut tax.

The colonial government then brought in the *Code of Native Law*, which governed all Zulus both in Natal and Zululand. Offences were itemized along with fixed penalties, and *lobola* (marriage) rates were standardised. But in trying to control the Zulus, the authorities had overstretched their patience. Talk of rebellion began to fan through the people. For the rural Zulus unaffected by the war, little changed; they maintained their traditional homesteads and customs and continued to respect their local chiefs. The following year Dinizulu was tried and banished to St Helena. In January 1898 Dinizulu, still widely accepted by the people as the Zulu king, returned to

Zululand in an attempt to restore stability, but without any official standing. The British bluntly refused to acknowledge his claim to the throne. To suppress his authority further, the British appointed him to the position of regional advisor. This gave him a reasonable salary but subjected him to official control. Dinizulu built himself a new homestead, oSuthu – a name associated with his father's followers since the 1850s – at Nongoma in northern Zululand.

At the same time, the Anglo-Boer War broke out. Although some of the fiercest fighting of the war took place in Natal, both sides were keen to maintain the fiction that it was a 'white man's war' and were nervous of inflaming any lingering Zulu hostilities. Nevertheless, the British were acutely aware that Zululand represented a back-door route into Natal by way of Vryheid, and indeed, in late 1899 and early 1900, the Boers made sorties as far as Nquthu and Nkandla. With limited forces available to repel them, the British unofficially – and ironically – pressurized Dinizulu into tacitly supporting them by patrolling the borders and collecting intelligence. A number of Zulu chiefs, including both Mehlokazulu and Zibhebhu, were allowed to arm their followers and, following the withdrawal of Boer forces at the end of 1900, they were given permission to further harass the Boers by raiding deserted farms in the old New Republic. By this time the larger Boer concentrations had been broken up, but small guerrilla bands continued to raid into Zululand, looting Zulu livestock and attacking small British outposts.

In 1902, the authorities, probably due to the rise in warnings of a widespread Zulu rebellion in protest at so many public measures, created a land commission that divided Zululand into tracts of land. About half the country, nearly 4 million acres, was nominated specifically as reserves for use by the Zulus, but this half was the most infertile, unproductive and susceptible to cattle disease. The remaining 3 million acres were productive farmland and nominated for white use only. Much of this was then given over to recently introduced sugar cane plantations.

The authorities swiftly moved the Zulu population into the more unproductive areas but many resisted. Such people were classified as squatters and were duly evicted to the reserves. The Secretary of Native Affairs declared, rather flippantly, that the authorities could congratulate themselves as their natives were 'the best mannered and the best behaved, and the most law-abiding in South Africa'.[2] Giving the best land to the white settlers seriously stunned the whole Zulu nation; the first murmurings of a peasant revolt began to spread. Rebellion was in the air.

In 1905, the authorities levied and enforced a new and prohibitive 'poll tax' on the native population across Zululand and Natal. The tax coincided with a total crop failure, caused by swarms of aphids, which was followed by a violent and destructive hailstorm. Zulu folklore recalls that these events were 'signs' that action must be taken against the white people's laws. The Zulus resisted paying the tax in increasing numbers until the authorities became alarmed. Matters came to a head on 7 February, when men of the Fuze clan demonstrated against tax collectors and killed two officials. The authorities reacted immediately by proclaiming martial law and despatched a column under Colonel Duncan McKenzie to quell the disturbance with permission to use whatever force he deemed necessary. McKenzie's men raided the Fuze homestead, killed a number of Zulus deemed to be 'resisting' and captured another thirty. Following their trial, Whitehall confirmed the sentences. Twelve were shot by firing squad and three were hanged. McKenzie then toured northern Natal and middle and southern Zululand, raiding and destroying any *umutzi* suspected of supporting the rebels. His subordinate, Colonel Lechers, ordered the surrender of hundreds of men who had earlier demonstrated. When the surrendering process stalled, Lechers ordered their homestead be shelled, an action for which he was later to receive a knighthood.

The feared rebellion now took hold north of the Tugela River. The Zondi clan under their chief, Bambatha kaMancinza, attacked a police post at Kate's Drift, leaving four police dead, including their sergeant. Many hundreds of Zulus flocked to support Bambatha. They wore their tribal war accoutrements and more than a thousand warriors gathered in full war regalia, something the British has presumed was now a memory. Surrounding chiefs rallied to Bambatha's call and, using their local knowledge and King Cetshwayo's grave as a rallying point, began attacking McKenzie's force. In a fit of pique, McKenzie ordered Cetshwayo's grave to be disturbed and burnt along with a number of neighbouring homesteads. McKenzie had numerous spies 'loyal' to the administration who reported that Bambatha would shortly be moving his force through the remote and densely wooded gorge at Mome. The gorge is several miles long, overlooked by rolling hills and, even today, thick with dense vegetation. As such, it could hide a number of *impis*. McKenzie closed in on the unsuspecting Bambatha and positioned his artillery so that it could fire directly into the gorge. On McKenzie's order, the artillery opened fire causing huge casualties among the Zulus. Many tried to flee but ran into the prepared positions where they were shot down in their hundreds. McKenzie's men had been deliberately issued with dum-dum bullets, which caused horrendous injuries to the fleeing Zulus, of which a total of 1,500 were killed, including Bambatha. A body was presented to the authorities as that of Bambatha, although folklore holds that he duped McKenzie's men and escaped. The British medical officer removed the head, which was shown to a number of chiefs, who readily confirmed it was that of Bambatha. The head was then buried with the body.

The fire of rebellion spread, and more chiefs rallied to the protest. On instructions, McKenzie and his men undertook a murderous campaign killing anyone they chose, rebel or otherwise and, in a final bitter irony, it was nearby, in the Mome Gorge, that colonial forces inflicted a crushing defeat on one of the last traditionalist armies raised in Zululand.

The campaign lasted nearly six months and involved 20,000 soldiers and men from police and militia units. By the end of the action, some 2,500 Zulus had been killed, with another 5,000 put in prison; the authorities lost twenty-five of their men. This time, no death sentences were issued, but the alleged ringleaders were banished to St Helena. The remainder were given short sentences, which included flogging or mutilation. Dinizulu had been powerless and inactive throughout the rebellion. Although viewed by the Zulus as their king, to the British he was a mere *inDuna* and therefore insignificant. The authorities arrested him anyway and charged him with high treason – for allegedly harbouring the fugitive Bambatha – which carried the death sentence. His trial took place in November 1908 at Greytown, where most of the evidence against him came from Bambatha's wife, who admitted she had lived near Dinizulu. He was found 'not guilty' of the more serious charges but convicted of harbouring Bambatha during the rebellion, which he strenuously denied. He was taken to Pietermaritzburg Prison to serve a four-year term. In 1909, Louis Botha, a former Boer general, became

Prime Minister of the new Union of South Africa, and in 1910, the colony of Natal became a province. Botha ordered Dinizulu's release. On leaving prison Dinizulu built himself the new homestead at uSuthu. Supplied with copious amounts of alcohol, he died in 1913.

Chapter 11

Conclusion and Aftermath of the Zulu War

Zululand, having been conquered by us, according to Zulu law, really belongs to Her Majesty the Queen.[1]

Chapter timeline

1879

4 July	Chelmsford and British forces defeat Zulus at Ulundi.
15 July	Lieutenant General Sir Wolseley supersedes Chelmsford
28 August	King Cetshwayo captured in Ngome Forest.
1 September	Wolseley partitions Zululand.
28 November	King Sekhukhune defeated at Tsate

1883

10 January	King Cetshwayo returns to Zululand.
30 March	Zibhebhu routs King Cetshwayo's Usuthu in northern Zululand.
21 July	Cetshwayo defeated at Ulundi by rival chiefs, Zibhebhu and Hamu.

1884

8 February	King Cetshwayo dies.
30 December	Zululand annexed by the British and becomes a province of Natal. All of Zululand brought under control of Natal authorities.

With the defeat of the Zulu army at Ulundi the British invasion of Zululand was, theoretically, successfully achieved. From the British perspective, King Cetshwayo's army had needed to be defeated and neutralised in order to protect the European population of Natal against the threat of an imminent Zulu invasion. Natal's European population had certainly believed that the Zulus had been preparing for war. The invasion of Zululand also served to redress the grievances of the flow into Natal of Zulu refugees, fleeing from what Reverend Hepburn branded 'a godless despot'. From Britain's standpoint the invasion of Zululand could, therefore, be considered morally righteous.[2] A Dutch merchant, by the name of Vijn Cornelius, who happened to be parley to Cetshwayo's military preparations prior to the formal declaration of war, wrote of a general expectation of war. He tells of how: 'The men and young men of Zululand have all been called up to the king for some reason or other – although in Natal it was widely believed they were coming to attack the whites'.[3]

At this point it is worth remembering that, pre-war, King Cetshwayo had a fearful reputation among Natalians, black and white. During the year leading up to the war the Natal population had been regularly reminded by Chelmsford and Frere that Natal faced the distinct possibility of a Zulu invasion – with all that that involved. Historically, Cetshwayo was never the benevolent king. If roused to anger his ruthlessness knew no bounds. The most demonstrable example of Cetshwayo's untempered aggression is shown in his alleged slaughter of any female members of the inGuge tribe if they were found living with a man less than forty years of age. His supplementary order demanded that the family of any such woman who fled to either Natal or the Transvaal would also forfeit their cattle.[4] In 1876 Cetshwayo had ordered the indiscriminate slaughter of dissidents in the Tonga tribe, as well as the sacking of numerous Christian ministries in Zululand which had been 'befriended during his father's lifetime'.[5]

With the aforesaid in mind, it remains difficult to identify any legitimate reason for Britain going to war with the Zulus.[6] It is therefore not surprising that by March 1881, nearly two years after the war, the defeated Zulu king continued to struggle to find any justification for the war.[7] While held prisoner at the Cape he dictated a letter to the Governor, Sir Hercules Robinson, in an attempt to understand recent events. In his inimitable way King Cetshwayo poignantly wrote: 'Mpande did you no wrong, I have done you no wrong, therefore you must have some other object in view in invading my land'.[8] That 'other object' continues to elude the majority of historians who study the Zulu War and who still rely heavily or exclusively on the Zulu refusal to comply with the British ultimatum of December 1878 as the justification for war. Many historians' sources are based on contemporary accounts that were highly subjective purely because it was inevitable that they were written by surviving senior British officers with important reputations to preserve. Regarding the unexpected defeats, sufficient scapegoats abounded, some obligingly now dead from loyally following their commanders' orders. Apart from private letters and reports from those involved, official military accounts of the day tended to rely on the official *Narrative of Field Operation*, but that narrative refrained from any allusion to controversy. Perhaps the most honest explanation can be credited to Laband and Thompson in their *Field Guide to the War in Zululand* in which they state: 'There is still no general agreement on the causes of the Anglo-Zulu War', although the sustained Boer migration into Zululand was clearly the precipitating cause of the war.[9] In reality, Frere's reasons for the Zulu War were widely accepted by the white population of Natal. The overriding and terrifying assumption that a bloodthirsty Zulu invasion of Natal was imminent can today be seen as little more than an official excuse for war.

Understandably, Natal's European settlers took their pre-war cue from the British who directly influenced the Natal newspapers to regard the war as inevitable, although there is evidence that few actually considered it desirable. However, once the war began, support for the official Frere line strengthened immeasurably. Frere's propaganda had been successful. The white population believed they had been spared an appalling fate at the hands of invading Zulu *impis*. More importantly, they had seriously profited with small fortunes made from supplying Chelmsford's army at exorbitant prices.

There were many who resolutely believed that the war had been an unnecessary evil. The Bishop of Natal, John William Colenso, known to the Zulus as '*Sobantu*' – 'Father of the People' – preached that the Zulu nation under Cetshwayo had presented no real threat to Natal. Nevertheless, the High Commissioner, Sir Bartle Frere, and the Secretary of State for Native Affairs in Natal, Sir Theophilus Shepstone, had deliberately provoked the conflict to further their wider ambitions for South African confederation. There can be little doubt that Colenso was right in his damning assessment and that Isandlwana and all the other defiant battles were nothing more sinister than brave acts of self-defence by the Zulu king and his army.

Tragedies abound in any war. Perhaps the most obvious in this war was the absence of any intention by the British to pursue their policy of confederation once the war was won; instead, they withdrew then abandoned Zululand. Not satisfied with victory, their invasion force deliberately wasted the land along their lines of withdrawal. They then exiled the Zulu monarch to remove any form of national leadership and departed from Zululand leaving the impoverished Zulus to their fate.

The reason for this lack of purpose was clear; circumstances had changed since the first invasion six months earlier. Disraeli's government was on the verge of collapse as a direct consequence of the war and with it went Britain's political enthusiasm for further colonial development or military adventure in southern Africa. Worse still, the setbacks experienced by Britain in the Zulu War sent a clear message to her brooding adversaries, especially to the Boers in the Transvaal and Orange Free State; if the British lion could be seriously mauled by a force of inexperienced part-time warriors, they reasoned that a well-prepared European force would undoubtedly fare even better.

Defeating the Zulus in set battles was one thing – holding them down subsequently was going to be another matter. Following the battle of Ulundi, Sir Henry Bulwer suggested to Wolseley that Zululand should be divided into four independent chiefdoms, later increased to thirteen, and the whole country placed under the supervision of a British adviser. A number of influential people with vested interests, including traders, missionaries and local officials, were all eager to advise Wolseley on the method of control. During Wolseley's stay in Zululand while awaiting the capture of King Cetshwayo (an exercise referred to as 'Catchewayo' by the troops) he sought advice from anyone who professed detailed knowledge of the Zulus and in typical Wolseley style, he pitted one against the other. He wrote:

> I worked them all separately as far as possible in obtaining news for me & [I] then compare their statements: I have a horror of being in the hands of any one man especially if that one be not an English officer.[10]

Whether or not that was a reference to John Dunn is not clear but there can be little doubt that Dunn, traitor to his former friend King Cetshwayo, was looking after his own interests and was slowly but surely managing to have increasing influence upon Wolseley. Dunn had earlier been forced to flee from Zululand following the outbreak of war and had then joined Chelmsford's Intelligence Department. Wolseley liked Dunn and he accepted that Dunn knew more about the Zulus and Zululand than anyone from whom Wolseley sought advice. Dunn appeared to be the archetypal Englishman. He wore expensive European clothes, spoke as eloquently as any senior officer and he had the ability to mix socially at the highest level, notwithstanding his proclivity to having numerous Zulu wives and concubines. Needing his counsel but clearly perplexed by Dunn, Wolseley wrote:

> He is a power in Zululand and I intend making as much use of him as possible. My idea is to increase his powers by making him paramount Chief over the District of Zululand lying along the Tegula [Thukela] & Buffalo rivers frontiers of Natal. I shall thus secure the civilizing influence of a white man over the district of Zululand nearest to us, and he and his people will be a buffer between us and the barbarous districts of Zululand beyond. He is at heart more a Zulu than an Englishman, but he has none of the bloodthirsty and conquering instincts of the Zulu people.

He went on:

> I have never met a man who was more of a puzzle to me than Dunn. He has never been in England and most of his life has passed in Zululand without any English or civilised society, and yet in his manners he is every way the Gentleman. He is quiet, self-possessed and respectful without any servility whatever, and his voice is soft and pleasant. He is much more of the English Gentleman than any of the self-opinionated and stuck up people who profess to be 'our leading citizens' in Natal. He leads a curiously solitary life, but he says he enjoys it thoroughly, being in every way his own King, without any policeman in his dominions to serve him with a writ or lay rough hands on him for taking the law into his own hands. He has as many wives & concubines as he wishes to keep and he has a clan about him who are all ready to obey his slightest nod. He pays periodical visits to Natal and has his books, letters and newspapers sent to him regularly. I wish I dared make [him] King of

> Zululand, for he [would] make an admirable ruler: however I am giving him
> the largest District in the country, an arrangement that I believe will be the
> small end of the wedge [of] civilisation inserted into it.[11]

John Shepstone, Acting Secretary for Native Affairs in Natal, also strongly influenced Wolseley, despite Wolseley privately despising Shepstone. Due to Shepstone's extensive knowledge of all the senior Zulus, he prepared a list of Zulu chiefs whom he considered fit for appointment as the thirteen new regional chiefs. Theophilus Shepstone, brother of the Acting Secretary, was certainly instrumental in the preparation of his brother's list. The majority of those selected were prepared to accept the Zulu royal house as nothing more than the total cause of their nation's downfall. On this subject, Wolseley wrote:

> Such breaking up of the cohesion of the country will, I firmly believe, preclude
> for the future all, or almost all, possibility of any reunion of its inhabitants
> under one rule.[12]

Having considered all the advice, Wolseley prepared to enforce a strict settlement on the defeated Zulus. On a very hot 1 September 1879, two hundred of the most senior Zulu dignitaries and chiefs were summoned to the newly established British headquarters at Ulundi where Wolseley addressed them concerning the fate of Zululand. Through his interpreter, John Shepstone, the gathered assembly was brusquely informed that their captured king was being sent into exile at the Cape and would never be permitted to return to Zululand. They were then informed that Zululand was to be divided into thirteen independent chiefdoms, each ruled by a Zulu chief selected and appointed by the British, each chief to have command under the overall supervision of a British administrator. There was not to be the remotest possibility that any one individual, of royal birth or otherwise, could rise in the image of King Shaka to re-unite the Zulus. As expected, John Dunn was awarded the largest and most influential chieftainship in Zululand, along the border with Natal, in return for his loyal services to the British during the campaign.

It is generally accepted that the British invasion of Zululand quickly and severely disrupted the Zulus' economic structure and caused massive loss of life. The Zulus' military defeat and the capture of their king would now ensure the destruction of their political system. Wolseley knew only too well that over several decades the royal house had inextricably penetrated all aspects of Zulu social life to the extent that King Cetshwayo, through his previously loyal chiefs, exercised total control over the Zulu people. Power in the hands of one king, in the mould of Shaka or Cetshwayo, was now to be made impossible.

Without exception, the thirteen new chiefs were men who had either fought for the British or had deserted King Cetshwayo prior to his capture; none could exercise much control over their people. Chiefs were appointed with the deliberate intention of creating political disharmony and rivalry. One of the appointed chiefs was a complete outsider. In recognition of his service to the British by providing mercenaries for the Natal government, a Sotho Chief, Faku, was appointed chief of the district near Rorke's Drift, previously dominated by Chief Sihayo. On appointment, Faku ordered Sihayo to leave his district, together with his son Mehlokazulu. Chief Mnyamana, Cetshwayo's chief councillor, was likewise offered a remote territory but refused to accept it. Various interpretations are given for this. Many Zulus assert it was out of loyalty to the exiled king. His own explanation to the Boundary Commission was that:

> I honestly considered that I was going to be given a tract of country which, though amply large enough for my extensive following, yet, it did not include one-third of the land where my kraals were situated.[13]

Mnyamana knew that part of his own northern area, the land of the abaQulusi, was to be allocated to Chief Hamu. This settlement was Hamu's reward for defecting to Colonel Wood's northern column during the campaign. For these reasons, Mnyamana refused to sign the paper as he did not see his way to govern a people that were unlikely to respect him as their chief. The remainder of Mnyamana's chiefdom was therefore given to Ntshingwayo, and as a consequence the second most powerful man in Zululand (after King Cetshwayo) was excluded from the settlement. Ntshingwayo in turn was reluctant to accept the district because it contained so many Buthelezi and Mdlalose people, as well as another chief's (Sekethwayo's) personal homestead. Sekethwayo was appointed a district further to the west.

Only four of these thirteen carefully selected chiefs were present at the meeting where the agreement was signed. Amongst the stipulations was the obligation to respect their new boundaries, to abolish the Zulu military system and ensure the right of the people to seek employment beyond Zululand. This latter requirement was especially destructive to Zulu society as it encouraged a migration of male Zulus to areas of strong British commercial interest, especially farms in Natal and the more distant diamond fields located to the north near present day Johannesburg. The Zulus were also forbidden to import firearms or become involved in any form of trade that did not have its origin in British controlled Natal or the Transvaal, a stipulation of immense financial value to Chief Dunn. Capital punishment without trial was forbidden; land could not be sold, traded or purchased without British permission and the chiefs were to keep the peace and apply the law according to the 'ancient laws and customs' of their people, so long as these laws did not offend the sensitivities of the British administrator, although, for some weeks, no one could be found to accept this poison chalice. In October a Mr Wheelwright was appointed to the civilian position of British Resident in Zululand, a post that attracted an annual salary of £600 plus an expense account of £100. He was tasked with the role of being the 'eyes and ears' for the British government and monitoring the thirteen chiefs. He had no voice or power: the position lacked any credibility and this thankless task soon proved impossible – he resigned.

Melmoth Osborn, formerly a senior Natal official and close friend of Theophilus Shepstone who had served in the Transvaal, was persuaded to consider the task; he accepted and was duly appointed as the British Resident Administrator of Zululand. He was soon to discover that the position lacked any real authority other than to offer advice to the new chiefs and to oversee them if it appeared that they were acting beyond the terms of their appointments. Wolseley clarified the situation when he wrote:

> I have been careful to make it clear that we intend to exercise no administrative authority over the country, and that we wish to disturb the existing conditions of life and government only where, as in the cases of the military system and

the barbarous practices of witchcraft, these conditions were irreconcilable with the safety of British subjects in South Africa, or with the peace and prosperity of the country itself.[14]

The inevitable result of Wolseley's deliberately unreasonable settlement quickly plunged Zululand into chaos. The country lacked leadership, control and supplies. Within weeks, Zulu fought against Zulu as the new borders of the country and individual chiefdoms indiscriminately cut across both the social and political groupings that had developed during the previous fifty years.

Wolseley further instructed that King Cetshwayo's relatives must abandon their homes and move into Chief Dunn's territory along the border with Natal, an order that was simply ignored as Dunn was considered to be a traitor for supporting the British against his former friend and ally, the king. Wolseley also instructed the appointed chiefs to collect all royal cattle and firearms and deliver them to the British Resident. Of all Wolseley's diktats, this most irritated the Zulus; after all, cattle were virtually the currency of the Zulu economy. King Cetshwayo owned most of Zululand's cattle, which made him the most powerful man in the kingdom. The royal herds were easily recognized by their whiteness, indicating that they belonged to the King. Due to their large number, they were distributed through many royal households and represented the livelihood and sustenance of many ordinary people who tended the herds. Wolseley's instructions merely gave those newly appointed chiefs who felt sufficiently confident the legal opportunity to seize the King's cattle and plunder from those Zulus who had previously been loyal to King Cetshwayo. This disruption quickly developed into a crippling and very destructive civil war. More Zulus died during the immediate period following the Zulu War than in the war itself.

To give his draconian plan the cloak of official respectability, Wolseley appointed a second Boundary Commission to demarcate both the new external border of Zululand and the thirteen internal boundaries. The Commission was instructed to ignore his earlier assurances that the Zulus would be left in full possession of their land. The northern limit of the kingdom was to be moved southwards to the Phongolo River to exclude the abaQulusi and Emagazini people, together with most of Hamu and

Mnyamana's people. In the north-east the new boundary would follow the Lubombo Mountains and the former territory; land that was now excluded from the new Zululand would be given back to the Tongas.

Wolseley's determination and confidence had increased further once King Cetshwayo was captured then imprisoned in Cape Town. The new boundary commission was given instructions to lay down the borders of the chiefdoms following, where possible, natural physical features. As soon as the plans were finalised, Wolseley invited the commission to inform the chiefs of Zululand that:

> Having been conquered by us, according to Zulu law, (Zululand) really belongs to Her Majesty the Queen, but as Her Majesty has no wish to increase her dominions in South Africa, as an act of grace to the Zulu people, she has now parcelled out the country into independent chieftainships. It is, therefore, for her officers, on her behalf, to decide the extent of territory that is by her favour to be allotted to each Chief. This was a right freely exercised by Cetshwayo, as well as by his predecessors, and it is a right which devolves upon the Great Queen by right of conquest, and that must not be disputed.[15]

Wolseley deliberately ignored the findings of the earlier 1878 Boundary Commission and additionally reduced the Zulus' western boundary, to the benefit of the Transvaal.

When the Boundary Commissioners informed Wolseley that some of the appointed chiefs were unsuitable, he typically suppressed their report. In due course, a number of settlement errors became obvious, but Wolseley merely commented that the fault lay with the Zulus' unwillingness to comply with the settlement's terms. In reality, the new borders of the country and the boundaries of the chiefdoms ensured that established clan groups were now placed under different clan chiefs and long-standing rival groups came under the same appointed chief. Many Zulus found themselves under appointed chiefs who they considered to be inferior or disinterested in their responsibilities. Many of these disaffected Zulus then responded by ignoring or resisting the new chiefs.

When the matter of growing unrest was brought to Wolseley's attention, he instructed the Boundary Commission to inform the growing number of disaffected Zulus that they were free to move to another chief's territory but the Zulu people were not like any other people; they were bonded historically to the districts where they had been born or which their ancestors had won by farming or warring. The Zulu people were only to be moved from their districts as a last resort. They were not prepared to move merely to satisfy white attempts at political or economic manipulation.

King Cetshwayo's relatives were treated even more harshly. In retaliation for the war, Wolseley gave instructions that members of the royal house should abandon their homes and move into Dunn's territory. It was an order that was simply ignored. Wolseley had very effectively subjugated the Zulu nation, and his hurried and hard-headed settlement satisfied the immediate needs of the home government in a moment of crisis but, in less than two years, the overall situation in Zululand was doomed to deteriorate to such an extent that the Colonial Office would have to abandon the arrangement. The growing unrest would become so serious that uncontrollable violence on a wide scale would threaten British interests as well as the very structure of Natal. With the conjunction of these elements, the inevitable spectre of rebellion began to fester throughout the nation. It would soon erupt into a decade of violence and civil war that would more effectively destroy the basis of Zulu royal power than the British invasion. British officials claimed that the ordinary people had retained possession of most of their land but by losing their king and their ability to raise an army, they lost the means to defend Zululand. Natal and Boer settlers now greedily looked at Zululand for its fertile farmland and abundant labour force. The old Zulu order had finally collapsed.

Meanwhile, disease and a six-year famine severely damaged the Zulus' ability to feed or re-establish themselves. This ongoing crisis was followed in 1897 by the Rinderpest epidemic, which virtually destroyed their remaining cattle, and then, just as they began the long process of re-stocking their herds, the deadly East Coast Fever obliterated their fledgling herds. Under British domination, the Zulu social structure had virtually collapsed. The young men became migrant labourers and headed from Zululand towards the growing towns and cities. Then, in 1904, the authorities created black reserves and moved the Zulu population into the most unproductive areas.

Those who resisted were classified as squatters and were duly evicted to the reserves – leaving the best land to the white settlers.

The traditions of the Zulu *amabutho* continued to shape the defiant attitudes of the Zulus towards colonial authority into the early twentieth century. The authorities levied and sought to enforce a prohibitive 'hut tax' on the population. Many Zulus living in Natal took up arms to protest at the harsh levels of taxation imposed upon them. One of the few Zulu chiefs to openly support them was Mehlokazulu kaSihayo. Mehlokazulu had served throughout the Zulu War as an officer in the iNgobamakhosi regiment, and in 1906 he joined forces with the rebel leader Bambatha. But the balance of power had swung even more in favour of the Europeans, and the rebel army was crushed at the Battle of Mome Gorge where both Bambatha and Mehlokazulu were killed. Zululand's turmoil resulted in a ferocious civil war, from which it never properly recovered.

*   *   *

Today, the battlefields of Zululand have remained largely untouched since 1879. Once the war was over the Swedish Mission Society at Rorke's Drift reoccupied its property and demolished the ruins of the old buildings. However, two of the present-day buildings, which stand on the site, are built on their original foundations and replicate Witt's house and storeroom. The coastal site of Gingindlovu has long been covered in sugar cane, introduced by European settlers in the early part of the twentieth century. Nevertheless, the remains of Pearson's entrenchments are still visible at Eshowe and the hills around Nyezane are unchanged, while in the northern sector the lonely battlefields of Hlobane, Khambula and Ntombe remain as they were. The clay hut floors of King Cetshwayo's royal Ulundi settlements have survived, baked to brick when the British razed the complex; the king's private quarter has since been carefully reconstructed. It is a phoenix risen from the ashes and today the site is a fitting memorial to the pride of the old Zulu kingdom. Recent research into the Zulu War of 1879 has radically altered perceptions of the conflict and broader threads of South African history have begun to develop, encouraging occasional visitors to many historical locations.

To the British at the time, the war seemed to be a triumph of European civilisation over African savagery. Today, the war can be seen within the context of the systematic reduction of independent African groups in South Africa in the face of expanding power of the developing settler economy. (See Appendix 4 for press reaction at home)

Modern writers' interpretations of the war have reflected these changes. The shock felt by the British at the Zulu victory at Isandlwana created a particular image of the Zulu people in British folklore. It is only in the last twenty years that scholars have come to understand something of the Zulu perspective of the events of 1879. Today's histories of the Zulu War present a more even-handed view of the conflict. Many issues remain unresolved and historians remain divided. Isandlwana attracts particular controversy. It retains an aura of mystery, mainly because of the magnitude of the battle and because surviving accounts, reports and maps are often conflicting as a result of some accounts being written by authors yet to visit Zululand or explore the battlefields.

The first feature film about the Zulu War, *Symbol of Sacrifice*, was made in 1918 and recreated many of the events of 1879 in a way designed to arouse a patriotic response from its audiences. The film was unusual for its time in that its plots included both British and Zulu characters. In 1964 the popular feature film *Zulu*, based on the events at Rorke's Drift, was released. In 1979 *Zulu Dawn* expanded on this view, presenting the battle of Isandlwana as a classic example of British Imperial folly, but the film lacked the power and conviction of its predecessor. It was not until the 1980s that *Shaka Zulu* again portrayed Zulu characters at the centre of their own history.

The Zulu War, although not the starting point, can be seen as the turning point for Late Victorian Imperialism. In the years that followed, the legacy of the Zulu War permeated the culture of an expanding British Empire to such an extent that it has vigorously accompanied both Zulu and British culture well into the twenty-first century. In 2005 Prince Mangosuthu Buthelezi wrote:

> The facts reveal that those colonial officials within South Africa who engineered this war committed grave injustices against the Zulu people and their King, the effects and legacy of which are still with us to this day.[16]

At the turn of the nineteenth century most Zulus continued to wear traditional native dress, to live in their scattered homesteads and to maintain their herds of cattle – which were their currency. But things were slowly changing. By 1904 some 18,000 Zulus were working in Natal, no longer for their homesteads but as migrant labourers in Natal's towns and cities.

For the Zulus who remained in their homesteads, nature played some nasty hands with a series of devastating natural disasters: locusts; several years of droughts: the devastating and highly contagious cattle disease, Rinderpest; and then East Coast Fever which killed most of the remaining cattle herds. As if this wasn't sufficient to depress the Zulu leaders, they had to contend with extensive land seizure by the Natal authorities, forcing Zulu farmers to become land tenants or squatters. Forty-two per cent of the best land was given over to white farming.

But the will of the people was resilient; the result was a strengthening of the Zulu belief and support of their royal house. Following decades of despair and adversity the Zulu monarchy was constitutionally recognized in the new post-apartheid South Africa.[17]

After the Zulu war, a steady stream of visitors made their way to the two battlefields of Rorke's Drift and Isandlwana. That stream continues to this day. Most of the early visitors were disturbed to discover the battlefield of Isandlwana was still littered with debris from the battle – smashed boxes, derelict wagons, rotting clothing and, most distressing, scattered bleached human bones. Following a number of protests from visitors, the Governor General of Natal instructed Alfred Boast to organise the cleaning of the site. The task took one month and was completed on 9 March 1883. Boast listed no less than 298 cairns marking graves, each containing upwards of four bodies. He even removed the skeletons of the artillery horses killed in the ravine during the flight along the Fugitives' Trail – some cairns have since been found to contain the bodies of both men and horses.[18] The bodies of Captain Anstey and Durnford were re-buried by their families, Anstey at Woking and Durnford at Pietermaritzburg. Over the years, a number of regimental and family memorials were erected at Isandlwana. In March 1914, a memorial to the 24th Regiment was erected by the regiment. It was not until 2001 that a memorial to the Zulus was built at Isandlwana.

It has to be a total triumph of mankind that today, of all the visitors to Zululand, it is the British who are the most numerous and popular with the local people. After everything the Zulu people have endured in the name of Christianity, modernisation, socialization and progress, the majority of Zulus continue to live in their timeless way, yet hold the British in high regard – one warrior nation respecting another.

Footnote: On Monday, 30 October 2006, English Heritage fixed one of its famous blue plaques – which mark the residence of a significant historical figure – to the imposing front of a Victorian townhouse at 18 Melbury Road, Kensington, London. The plaque commemorates the fact that, for two weeks in August 1882, the house was the home of the Zulu king, Cetshwayo kaMpande, and his entourage during his brief but highly significant visit to London.

The prime mover behind the efforts to secure a blue plaque to recognise the king's visit to London was archaeologist Dr Tony Pollard, who in 2000 directed the official battlefield survey at Isandlwana. He said:

> While in Africa I was told a story by a Zulu about the king's meeting with Queen Victoria in England, about how his magic was greater than hers. It struck me that if these events are still talked about in Zululand today, we should certainly be remembering them here in Britain. People tend to think of events like the Zulu War taking place in some exotic, far-off place but they also had an incredible impact in Britain and this plaque will hopefully remind people of that.

Each blue plaque is unique. King Cetshwayo was a man defeated in war by the British, schemed against and vilified by British politicians, yet he was cheered through the streets of London before, on Queen Victoria's order, being returned to Zululand. He died a broken man, his kingdom having been divided into thirteen lesser parts, each with an independent ruler.

See Appendix 5 for decorations and medal awards; Appendix 6 for the 'Welsh' subject; and Appendix 8 for Sister Janet's Obituary.

Appendix 1

Lieutenant Henry Curling RA – An Independent View of the War's End

Apart from a dearth of pens and paper while on campaign, many soldiers lacked the writing skills needed to make writing letters home a significant pastime. Letters home were occasional, usually written after events and, not infrequently, subject to memory failure or embellishment – especially when the press paid generously for lurid accounts.

Of all the letters so far discovered, the collection of letters from Lieutenant Henry Curling RA are especially significant. He was erudite and a prolific writer of letters to his mother – which have all survived in three ledgers. As an artillery officer he was more independent from the influences of the army high command than his other officer colleagues. His independence allowed his profusion of letters to be equally objective and subjective; objective in detail and subjective to reflect his personal feelings and impressions.

In 1999 Curling's original and unknown letters, unpublished, were donated to the *AZWHS* by a descendant of Curling for research and publication. Curling was the Royal Artillery officer who tried to save the artillery guns at Isandlwana – and survived. His incisive letters home record his many first-hand experiences, including the approach to Ulundi.[1]

The day after the second invasion got underway, yet another disaster occurred. Lord Chelmsford's painstaking preparations and precautions had not taken into consideration the vanity and recklessness of the heir to the French throne, Louis Napoleon, the Prince Imperial. Like Curling, the Prince had graduated to a commission as an artillery officer, although he was not eligible to serve in the British Army. Anxious to test his courage, he badgered the War Office until he was allowed to travel to South Africa and join a reluctant Chelmsford as an extra aide. There had been episodes when the prince had galloped off alone after Zulus when attached to Buller's command. The latter refused to take responsibility for the prince, which had resulted in Louis being confined to camp duties.

Thinking that he would be in no danger, Chelmsford's staff allowed the prince to ride out with a six-man escort and another officer, named Lieutenant Carey, to look for a suitable campsite for the following day. At the prince's insistence, they had descended into a wide valley and stopped for a rest by an abandoned kraal. Just as they prepared to mount up and resume their patrol, a Zulu scouting party that had approached through the long grass attacked them. It happened so quickly that there was no time to offer any resistance, and it was every man for himself as they pulled themselves onto their horses and spurred away. Two troopers were quickly shot and killed before they could mount. Louis' horse was panicked by the commotion and took off with the prince desperately clinging on to the holster attached to his saddle. After 150 yards, the strap broke and Louis went sprawling. In an instant, the Zulus were upon the prince and stabbed him to death.

The next morning a search party retrieved his body. A service was read in the camp, and the body was placed on Curling's gun carriage and carried around the assembled parade. The pallbearers were Captains R. Alexander and F. Vibart, and Lieutenants J. Wodehouse, E. H. Elliot, S. B. Parsons and Henry Curling. The next morning, the body was taken back to the base camp at Landsman's Drift and from there it was conveyed by relays until it was returned by sea to England. The Prince Imperial's death provoked an enormous amount of press coverage and the impact on the British public was even greater than that of Isandlwana. The main reason was that the special correspondents were in camp and the story received great attention, which was out of proportion to its importance.

Lieutenant Henry Curling was a prolific letter writer, and his letters home reveal a calm and independent oversight of events.

7 June 1879 With Lord Chelmsford's Column, Ityotzozi River, Zululand. To Mama

We are now well into Zululand and far farther in than any of the Columns have been before. I only hope that we shall have a fight soon before we get farther into the country.

We get more careless everyday and one trembles to think of what would happen should we be attacked at night. Our arrangements on the march are pretty good and the worst that could happen would be to lose a part of our baggage but at night we are shut up in a huge entrenchment half a mile long, far too large for us to defend properly. The natives retreat before us, fighting us as they go.

You have heard, of course, all about the poor little Prince Imperial's death and yesterday, the Adjutant of the 17th Lancers (Lieutenant John Cokayne Frith) was killed in a skirmish in which I believe the enemy suffered no loss.

I was one of the pall bearers at the Prince's funeral: poor little fellow, everyone feels so sorry for him and ashamed that he should meet his death in such a way.

No one knows where the Zulu Army is and until it has been defeated we are in a very ticklish position. I wish I could tell you all I think about it but don't like to do so in a letter … We do not seem to profit from our experience, Our baggage columns are larger than ever and we carry tents, camp-beds etc., just the same as before. None of the troops from England believe in the enemy and we old stagers are called alarmists.

You would hardly believe it possible but we do not know the road and are wandering on with the greatest uncertainty as to where we shall go.

…Colonel Wood's Column marches a few miles ahead of us. It is a pity we are not organised like him but we consist of Generals with large staffs: too many cooks spoil the pudding and we have no less than five generals (including two brigadiers) with us. We are having lovely weather and are making the most of the short season before all the grass is burnt.

Whether we shall finish the war remains to be seen but there can be no real peace until the Zulus have been thoroughly beaten and their cattle taken. The conditions of peace are very mild and there is some little chance of the Zulu King giving in to save himself. We cannot be certain that his chiefs will agree with him and everything will remain in a most dangerous state. I am wonderfully strong now, can sleep anywhere, at any time and eat anything.

I had no end of trouble about that letter that was put into the *Standard* and have been freely abused in the local papers for the remarks about the Volunteers. After all, letters are dangerous things to write freely as one is not certain who may see them. There was nothing untrue in my letter and yet what trouble it has got me in.

Arthur Harness also commented on the top-heavy nature of the Staff:

There is also a tremendous staff: all Lord Chelmsford's and General Newdigate's. Indeed, the whole thing has taken such large proportions that it makes one rather sad and wish for the old days when two or at most three tents formed the headquarters camp; now it is as large as a regiment.

Curling had written in his letter dated 2 February:

Most of those who escaped were volunteers and native contingent officers who tell any number of lies. Curling's parents had allowed the letter describing their son's escape to be published in the '*Standard*' on 27 March which included the above offending sentence. Once this became known back in Natal, it sparked a minor diplomatic incident, which involved Curling's commanding officer, Colonel Harness.

Harness wrote a letter to his sister Caroline from Landman's Drift Camp, dated 24 May:

I think I told you of one of my subaltern's letters to his mother being published in *The Standard* some time ago. His letter, which comments most unwarrantedly on the conduct of the volunteer officers and officers of native contingents, calling them all 'liars' etc., has been copied into the colonial papers and the result is that I have had to advise him to write an apology. I do not see what else he could do. Is it not too stupid of his people to put such a thing in print?[2]

Shepstone, who commands the volunteers, came to me and said his men thought it the unkindest cut of all that my battery, which had been such friends, and that all had liked so much, should abuse them in that way. I could only say that what a man writes to his wife or mother, he could hardly dream would be in print and that it was written under excitement etc, etc, and that he was very sorry etc.[3]

Once again, Curling seems to have incurred Harness's displeasure and promotion seemed ever distant. It may have been this incident that prompted Harness to leave Curling at Fort Marshall, one of the strong points built to guard the route to Ulundi.

30 June 1879 Fort Marshall, Zululand To Mama
We are quite out of it here from any news of what is going on and never get any letters as the mail bags go on direct to Headquarters and no one takes the trouble to send our letters back. There is one consolation, in another ten days their provisions will all be gone so they must return when, I hope, we shall all go back to Natal. All our jams, tinned things etc., are all gone and we live entirely on rations and in fact are quite grateful for a discovery we made that Enos Fruit Salt is a capital substitute for baking powder in making bread. Now

that the Fort is nearly finished there is little to occupy the men with and we all find it very monotonous. Every morning, we stand to our arms from 5am until daylight, which is not until 6.30 and you can understand how pleasant that is in these frosty mornings.

Our latest news of the General is that he is starting with a flying column this day for Ulundi, from which he is now only about 10 miles distant, but the country is difficult and dangerous so that he can only move slowly. A special messenger from Sir Garnet Wolseley arrived yesterday with a long telegram for Lord Chelmsford. We all fancy that peace will be made at any price. The King has already sent 200 oxen and some ivory as a peace offering but the guns do not come and they are to be the first signs that he really means not to fight.

Because of the Isandlwana disaster and the general mishandling of the campaign, Lord Chelmsford was relieved of his command and replaced by General Sir Garnet Wolseley, regarded as the best soldier of his day. Due to the length of time it had taken to reach South Africa and then the frustrations of physically taking command of the army in the field, Wolseley did not take over until Chelmsford achieved his victory at Ulundi. Curling continued:

I met [Captain] Fred Campbell of the 94th a few days ago. I suppose I knew him as a boy a long time ago. He wished to be remembered to you and Papa.

I passed through Escourt on the road from Maritzburg but not then knowing that Fred Birkett was living near there, did not enquire about him. I met a cousin of his in the Native Contingent: he is anything but a nice fellow. Emmy's friend's cousin, Captain [Bindon] Blood is with the Lower Column, a very long way from this.

What a block there is on promotion just now, only four steps since Jan 22, when poor Smith was killed.

I could not help thinking when we were burying him, how nearly I shared the same fate. He did not appear to be assegaied and most probably died from the effects of falling down the rocks. We found his horse dead a little above him and nineteen other white men who had all either fallen or been shot down while climbing the rocks. Your letters, when they come, are most cheerful and pleasant: what great travellers you have all become. Papa will never be satisfied with Ramsgate after this. I long to see the place again and shall be quite heartbroken if I get promoted to a battery out here or, what is worse, in Mauritius or St. Helena.

Nearly all the Captains in these batteries have been sent out for the war and return home as soon as it is over so it will simplify matters very much to promote me to one of their vacancies …We all think it very probable that the Battery will be ordered home as soon as the war is over and it quite possible that I may be promoted before and may come with it. Would it not be pleasant? We hear that the remainder of the Battery has been stopped at another fort, so it matters little which fort you remain in if you are stuck in one at all.

Fort Marshall was built and garrisoned on 18 June by two companies of 2/21st Regiment. Two troops of 17th Lancers were based there and patrolled the area. Captain F. Vibart commanded the two guns that had been sent out as replacements for those lost at Isandlwana. The Fort consisted of two joined pentagons, roughly 130 metres in length by 30 metres wide. The defences were little more than a shallow ditch with earth and stone battlements.

5 July 1879 Fort Marshall To Mama
We heard this morning of yesterday's battle. Forbes, the correspondent, got here at daylight having ridden all night through a dangerous country. He hopes to get to the end of the wire about 50 miles off this evening: anyhow, he is far ahead of all the other correspondents.

He is a great, strong, coarse-looking man, able to undergo any amount of fatigue and to put up with any amount of snubbing. These Specials are a terrible nuisance. They expect to be welcomed everywhere and in fact come whether you welcome them or not. One feels at the same time that it is dangerous to be uncivil to them. They are obliged to be pushing, unsnubbable men, no others would get on at all.

Archibald Forbes was the most influential war correspondent of his day. His highly descriptive and punchy prose, together with his determination to be first with the news, made him the natural successor to the great William Russell. Forbes was a superb horseman, having been trained as a trooper in the Royal Dragoons, and processed great stamina. His career lasted no more than ten years but in that time he changed the way wars were reported.

In the Zulu War he was very critical of Lord Chelmsford and hounded him long after the war was over. Having stood in the British square at Ulundi and watched the destruction of Cetshwayo's army, Forbes was anxious to send off his account with the first courier taking news of the victory to the telegraph at Landman's Drift. With the countryside full of scattered bands of Zulus, Chelmsford prudently thought it too dangerous to send a messenger.

Scornful of the General, Forbes blurted out: 'Then, sir, I will start myself at once'. Afterwards he admitted: 'I was sorry for myself the moment I had spoken'. In a generous act, Forbes took Melton Prior's latest sketch of the Ulundi battle as well as some staff messages.[4]

Leaving at dusk, Forbes carefully followed the wagon tracks, frequently stopping to hide from dark figures of Zulus he saw by the light of blazing kraals. Once he was clear of the area around Ulundi, Forbes made good progress, changing horses six times, including at Fort Marshall. At about 3p.m. the following day, an exhausted Forbes reached Landman's Drift having ridden 120 miles in 20 hours.

The telegraph had been extended to the Cape so news now reached London twenty-four hours later.

Having sent his report, Forbes then rode on to Durban, where he mailed his full story and Prior's sketches. Incredibly he had travelled 295 miles in just 55 hours. Forbes' report was the first to reach Britain and was read out in both Houses of Parliament. It bought him even greater fame, and his exploit came to be known as 'The Ride of Death', and there was even a media suggestion that he should receive the Victoria Cross. In the event, Lord Chelmsford even blocked Forbes's claim for a campaign medal, which was not the wisest act. Angered by this, Forbes conducted a campaign in print to have Chelmsford held accountable for the incompetent way the war had been conducted. In this, he was only partially successful for, although Chelmsford never again held a field command, he was showered with honours by his peers. An exhausted and disillusioned Archibald Forbes retired from reporting and concentrated his remaining twenty years on lecturing and writing books.[5]

6 July 1879 Fort Marshall To Mama

How pluckily the Zulus still fight: they are apparently unable to get large armies together now. From the 22,000 that attacked Colonel Wood at Kambula [sic] 100 miles from the Chief Kraal Ulundi, they dwindled down to 10,000 or even less that attacked yesterday near the Kraal itself. From the top of a mountain close to us, we saw Ulundi in flames but it was not till this morning that we heard of the fight that our people had.

Lord Chelmsford can now resign most peacefully and we all expect him to do so as soon as he can hand the command over to Sir Garnet Woolsy [sic]. He has not an easy job before him, I think. The country is getting blacker every day and there is now hardly a blade of grass in our line of communications; all has been burnt. Sir Garnet will have to get the Army back with its 10,000 men and 600 wagons and he is dealing with an enemy who apparently will not make peace but will fight to the end.

We have now done nearly all the harm in country that we can. All the open country has been overrun, the kraals burnt and the crops destroyed. We cannot get the cattle: they have been driven into an inaccessible country far out of reach.

I suppose we need not fear the Zulus attacking us in any considerable force unless they can get us at a disadvantage, but still it will be interesting to see the result.

Lord Chelmsford proceeded at a snail's pace towards Ulundi. After four weeks of slow progress, covering about 100 miles in four weeks the objective was reached. Chelmsford's Column formed a huge square on the plain at Ulundi. It took less than half an hour of concentrated Martini-Henry, Gatling and artillery fire to break the Zulu's spirit. Curling's battery was represented by just two guns under the command of Colonel Harness, who wrote of the battle:

The guns opened fire on the enemy at about two thousand yards or more, from all four sides, And the Zulus came on pluckily in small groups taking wonderful advantage of cover. But our fire was tremendous, as you can imagine, and after half an hour or so they regularly turned and bolted; then the lancers and other mounted men went out with a cheer from us and I believe did their work well, but Drury-Lowe told me their horses were a good deal pumped. The Zulus ran so fast they had a considerable distance to go before they got to the scattered retreat of the enemy. In the rear face of the square the enemy got to within forty yards. On my own side, the left face, they did not come within four hundred yards I should say, but my two seven-pounders made excellent shooting.[6]

With British pride restored and Chelmsford able to resign with some credit, the column withdrew to Fort Marshall, where it was broken up on 27 July. Most marched down to Durban, where they embarked for Britain, while the rest, including Curling's battery, were formed into two Flying Columns. Curling's column was commanded by Lieutenant Colonel Baker Creed Russell, 13th Hussars, one of Wolseley's 'Gang'. A veteran of the Indian Mutiny and the Ashanti War, Russell was regarded as a very able and energetic officer. He took his column, called the Baker Russell Column, and proceeded to the north-west in a sweep that searched for the fugitive

King Cetshwayo. Along the way, Curling was able to write a letter from Fort Cambridge, about 20 miles south of Hlobane:

5 August 1879 Fort Cambridge, Zululand To Mama
We have had a move since I last wrote and are in quite a different part of Zululand about 40 miles from my old station, Fort Marshall. We form part of a small column under Colonel Baker Russell, who seems to be a smart, go-ahead man, though of course he knows nothing about the style of fighting out here as yet.

We have been marching for the last three days and halted today to give the cattle a rest. Tomorrow, we move on again into a country where we have never been before, leaving a small fortified post here.

Zululand is now covered with little forts which are useful in preventing Zulus from returning to their kraals without our knowledge. When they come back and give up their arms, they will bring their cattle which will be a good security for their future behaviour. The Zulu King has still some 10,000 men who will follow him. They are all young men who own no cattle or wives and who have nothing to lose if they are beaten, so there is a good chance of our having another fight. Anyhow, another week will show whether the campaign is over or not. I am so glad to get out of the fort and thoroughly enjoy being on the move again. I dined with Fred Campbell last night: he was sent up with some troops to make the fort here a few days ago. I have not heard from you now for a long time: your last letter was written just after arriving at Ramsgate. The changes in the different Divisions have quite upset all postal arrangements and our letters are flying about all over the country.

Sir Garnet's protégés have completely taken charge of everything out here and the whole of the old staff have been shipped back to England. Many of them have been but a month or two out here.

Curling then takes a traditional army view on the question of flogging as a means of maintaining discipline in the field. He also adds a rather extreme theory of his own. During the period of the War, no less than 545 British soldiers were flogged: the highest number in one year for many years. The wrong doer was usually given twenty-five lashes for offences ranging from drunkenness and stealing to insubordination and desertion. A common offence was 'dereliction of duty', which covered those sentries who fell asleep when on guard duty, and merited fifty lashes. Once the increase in flogging became known in Britain, there was an outcry against this barbaric punishment, especially as it had been used on young recruits, and led to it being banned. He concluded:

> We shall have some terrible disaster some day caused by the newspapers and Members of Parliament trying to govern armies in the field. It will be quite impossible to keep up discipline now that flogging is done away with. However, it will soon be established again as men will now have occasionally to be shot and then what an outcry there will be.[7]

12 August 1879 Emlongana Mifuni Station, Zululand To Mama
We have been on the move almost continuously since I last wrote. Colonel Baker Russell, who commands this column, seems inclined to be far more energetic than the commanders we have been under before.

Finding that our guns cannot get over the country, he has turned us into cavalry and I returned last night from a three days patroll [sic] right through the most difficult part of Zululand. We heard that the Zulu King was hiding in a kraal about 50 miles off, so Baker Russell took out the whole of the cavalry, about 400 strong, to try and catch him.

We started at daybreak three days ago taking nothing with us but some preserved meat and biscuit in our haversacks and went right into the heart of Zululand. The country was covered with Zulus who ran up into the mountains as we advanced. If they had chosen, they could have cut us all off as, in crossing the mountains, we had to go through numerous places in single file leading our horses. However, they only fired at us once and nobody was hit. When we had gone about 30 miles, the horses were too done up to go on, so we reluctantly turned back. As it was, we had to leave about 50 horses behind us and many men came back on foot. We slept at night with nothing but our greatcoats on and our saddles for pillows and as we were in the saddle from daylight till dark for three days, were pretty done up when we returned last night. We can never drive the Zulus out of the mountains; at any rate, it will take years to do so and I have no wish to have to assist in doing it. I think Sir Garnet is too sensible to allow the war to drag on. If we had only been allowed to fight in the proper way, the war would have been over now. After the action at Ulundi we might have burnt most of the kraals and taken any number of cattle besides killing plenty of Zulus but we did nothing and reaped no benefit from our victory.

I shall not know what to do when I get home; it will take some time to get civilised. It is now nearly seven months since I have slept without my clothes and boots except a couple of weeks at Ladysmith when I was sick. There seems but little chance of our going home and still less of being promoted. I almost despair of seeing you again. There will be two vacancies very shortly in batteries out here and it will be so very convenient to promote me to one of them unless I can get some kind friend to put in a word for me.

The two guns taken from Isandlwana were found abandoned just six miles from Ulundi. They were taken to Durban and put on display in a shed at Pine Terrace, where they proved to be a big attraction with the public. The missing limber was found with them and, upon inspection, they were declared undamaged. The Zulus had made an unsuccessful attempt to fire them using rifle percussion caps. Colonel Harness was asked what he wanted done with the guns, which represented too many bad memories for him, so he said, 'Send them home – so they are going home. I thought it best to say so, although I have really not much feeling in the matter'.[8]

8 September 1879 Luneburg To Mama

Your letters are beginning to arrive with great regularity as the Post Office people have found out that we belong to Baker Russell Column. Unfortunately we heard this morning that the column is to be broken up and we start for Utrecht tomorrow morning.

When we arrive at Utrecht we shall either be ordered to Pretoria or Pietermaritzburg: we hope the latter but probably the Battery will be divided. Colonel Harness has gone down to Maritzburg on leave and hopes to get leave home at once. As soon as we are settled I think I shall put in for leave too, if I don't get some steps in the meantime. The Zulu War is now completely over and the natives are most friendly. The Border tribes are the only ones that give any trouble. We are now encamped close to the spot where Captain Moriarty' Company was destroyed and have found the skeletons of several men who were killed while trying to escape.

Curling refers to the attack at Intombe Drift on the morning of 12 March. A Company of the 80th (The Staffordshire Volunteers) Regiment had been sent out from Luneburg to bring in a convoy of supply wagons, which had been delayed by the muddy road and the swollen Intombe River. Unable to complete the crossing before nightfall, Captain Moriarty was compelled to form a laager on the northern bank, while a small section made camp on the south bank.

As the following dawn mist began to lift, a volley was fired into the slumbering camp and 900 charging warriors charged in amongst the unprepared soldiers. Moriarty managed to get off three shots before being stabbed to death. The slaughter was swift, but some soldiers managed to swim the narrow river and join their comrades on the north bank. Lieutenant Harward directed a covering fire until it was noticed that about 200 Zulus were crossing the river and attempting to encircle them. Pausing only to order Sergeant Anthony Booth to fall back on a farmhouse three miles to the rear, Harwood mounted his horse and galloped off to Luneburg to raise the alarm. He was followed by most of his men and a few escapees.

Booth was left with just eight men and a few escapees, who armed themselves. Calmly forming them into a square formation, Booth and his small band managed to keep the Zulus at a distance with volley fire as they slowly retreated. By the time they reached the deserted farmhouse, the Zulus had given up and returned to plunder the camp.

For his bravery and calmness, Booth was justly awarded the Victoria Cross. Lieutenant Harwood, on the other hand, was court martialled for abandoning his men under fire. Somehow, he managed to convince the court of his innocence and he was acquitted of the charge. Sir Garnet Wolseley was furious but could not change the Court's ruling. Instead, he let his feelings be known in a general order that was read out to every regiment. With his career and reputation in tatters, Harward had little option but to resign.

12 September 1879 Luneburg To Mama

There is a small tribe here living in some caves in a mountain that overlooks the road, who will not submit. They have continued to fire on everybody passing by and have prevented any small parties from moving about. The first day we came here we surrounded their caves and summoned them to surrender. Eight of them came out with their arms and gave themselves up. Unfortunately, some of our men were fired upon from another cave and our own niggers immediately assegaied the prisoners. The others then refused to come out. Large fires were lit at the mouth of the cave to smoke them out, but without avail.

We have been here three days and they will not give in so, as we move tomorrow and this nest of …(?) cannot be left here, the caves are to be blown up with gun-cotton. We are expecting to hear the explosion every minute. It seems cruel but must be done. The climate is getting as it always does just before the rains – very oppressive.

These recalcitrant natives were the remnants of Mbilini's band who, although small in numbers, were still able to disrupt military traffic passing along the Luneburg to Lynchburg Road. The blowing up of their caves finally ended all hostilities and the Zulu War was over.

With the War concluded, Curling fully expected to be sent home and to gain his captaincy. Once again, despite promotion, he was to be disappointed and destined to spend a further three frustrating months in the Transvaal, a country anxious to be rid of British occupation.

24 September 1879 Wesselstrom To Mama
I am quietly settled down in this little out of the way place and hope to remain here until I get orders to go home or to some place via England. You will find this village marked on the map as quite a large place but it only contains about six houses. It is, however, quite a large town for the Transvaal.

The rainy season has set in and it is poor for travelling and you cannot make certain of going even a few miles in a day. The remainder of the Battery has gone to Heidelburg en route for Pretoria but I hope not to be ordered to follow them but to remain here for the next two or three weeks at least.

Fortunately we are nearly all starving so until supplies are sent up, we cannot move. We hear that there are some young Subs on their way out to replace me and Fowler but I rather fear that they will not allow one of them to replace me in command of a detachment. The end of November ought to see me in England, at least I hope so. I should like very much to be with you and Papa in the South of France for a short time. How jolly it will be if we spend Christmas all together again this year. As Emmy says, if I don't look sharp, home will be so changed I shall not know it.

The next letter brings the first news of Curling's long awaited promotion, something which he receives with less than enthusiasm.

2 October 1879 Wesselstrom, Transvaal To Mama
Two of your long letters arrived yesterday: as usual they made a trip up to Pretoria where the headquarters of the Battery are, and so arrived a week later than they should have done. However, they brought the first news of my promotion. I ought to feel very glad but I don't feel so, as our meeting again seems a long way off. I should so have liked to have been with you for the wedding: they will all have so many fresh ties that I shall be quite out of it when I come home. Papa was very kind in taking so much trouble about my promotion. He was successful, too, as the very good fall I have got shows.

During Curling's service in South Africa, his brother and two sisters, were all married.

After some lobbying by his father, Curling was finally promoted to Captain.
8 November, 1879 Wesselstrom To Mama
I received a letter from you dated Oct.4th, three days ago, by far the quickest delivery we have ever had. There are three mails still missing and the last letter I got was dated September 8th, so you can see how badly managed our postal arrangements are.

I can hear nothing of my getting away. Colonel Law evidently intends to keep me as long as he can. I fear very much that I shall lose the battery to which I am promoted as a battery in active service must have all its officers with it. It is one comfort that I never could have got up for the march on Carbul [sic] through in time to earn another medal. I don't think I am strong enough for a long campaign in a hot climate, so it may turn out for the best that I have not been able to get away. We are all very weak now and sickly. I suppose it comes from the fatigues of the campaign that has just finished and from the bad food which is worse now than it has ever been. I have not tasted any fresh vegetables, not even potatoes, fresh milk or butter for six months and the bread we get is bad and made of Indian corn flower [sic]. My detachment consists of fifty men: ten of these are in hospital and one died a few days ago. Fever is the general complaint and it comes from having no protection from the intense heat of the sun.

If eventually they send me to join by way of England, I shall be able to see you all and, should the campaign have terminated, get leave until the last troopship leaves in April which will give plenty of time to make any arrangements. If, on the other hand, there is fighting still going on, I shall come in for another medal and eventually so much service ought to do me good.

There is nothing to tell you about this country. The local papers are full of rumours about the Boer fighting but I believe all these reports are only got up to keep the troops in the country as they spend no end of money. I am afraid my last letter was rather dismal but I was much depressed at being kept here doing nothing, when my (new) battery was fighting and everybody who had been a few months out here, going home.

Footnote. Curling did, finally, embark on the *Malabar* on 4 February and sailed for Bombay. From there he travelled north, through the Punjab and the Khyber Pass, until he reached the Afghan capital, Cabul. Here he took up his appointment as a Captain with C/3 Battery at the British cantonment.

The Third Afghan War did not end until the following September with General Roberts' epic 300 mile march from Cabul to lift the siege of Kandahar. Curling's battery stayed behind at Cabul, as the more portable Mountain Batteries were favoured and better suited to the rugged terrain. Curling remained at Cabul for six months before the British, both unable and reluctant to occupy both the capital and Kandahar, withdrew to hold the strategic Kurram Valley and the Khyber Pass on the North-West Frontier. Finally, Henry Curling returned home in early 1881, having served abroad without leave for three years.

The rest of his career was peaceful, uneventful and unspectacular. On 6 February 1885 he was promoted to major and given command of D/3 Battery at Aldershot and Exeter. It was regarded as an exceptionally smart field battery so that for some years it was selected as the instructional battery at Okehampton Camp. In 1895 Curling, now a lieutenant colonel, was made commanding officer of the Royal Artillery in Egypt. He was there at the time when Kitchener was appointed Sirdar and planned the invasion of the Sudan and the belated revenge for the killing of Gordon of Khartoum. Curling's fighting days were over. He was transferred to command the Garrison Artillery in Dover, just a short distance from his Ramsgate home. His final appointment, which took him to Pembroke Dock, saw him retire as a full colonel on 16 April 1902.

A lifelong bachelor, he lived out the rest of his life at the family home, Chylton Lodge in Ramsgate. Comfortably off, he retained his interest in his old corps which had been his home for over thirty years. He generously gave donations to his former battery and helped old comrades. In 1903, he followed both his father and brother by becoming a Justice of the Peace and frequently sat on the Ramsgate bench. Like his parents, he had developed a liking for the French Riviera and spent much of his time in Menton.

On New Year's Day, 1910, Henry Curling passed away at Chylton Lodge, aged sixty-three. After a service held at the Holy Trinity Church, he was buried at the Ramsgate Cemetery alongside his parents.[9]

One thing Curling would not do during his retirement was talk about his Zulu War experiences and it must have surprised many who read his obituary to learn that he had been an Isandlwana survivor. Indeed, his obituary in the local *East Kent Times* made only passing mention of his military career and none about his miraculous escape. Instead, it was left to an old comrade to write a fulsome obituary in the *Royal Artillery Leaflet*, to reveal Henry Curling's part in the greatest British military disaster.

Henry Curling was not a great military figure but, by virtue of his escape from the front line at Isandlwana, he was unique. The few survivors of the battle were either interviewed or recorded their experiences in articles and books. Curling, apart from his statement to the Court of Enquiry, chose to remain silent about Isandlwana for the rest of his life. Apart from his natural reticence, perhaps there were deeper psychological reasons for his reluctance to talk about this episode of his life.

Appendix 2

Family Tree of the Prince Imperial

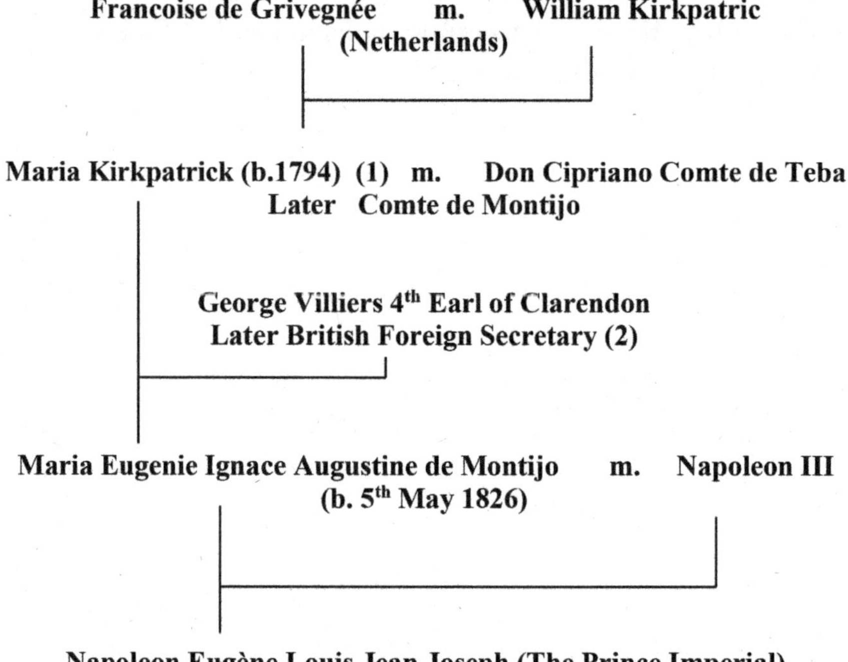

Appendix 3

Stress

The human condition of 'stress' affected many during the war, not least King Cetshwayo. A number of senior British officers underwent periods of severe depression, including Chelmsford in the aftermath of Isandlwana when he requested that he be replaced. Colonel Wood, in his memoirs, recalled the effect of eighteen months of campaigning on his men and even himself, which he described as stress from the difficult military situation, especially in the three-month period following the disaster at Isandlwana. Wood was unable to sleep for more than 2-3 hours at a time and participated in sentry rounds twice nightly, he attributed this to his self-proclaimed 'state of high anxiety'.[1] Colonel Glyn suffered a breakdown at Rorke's Drift but eventually recovered sufficiently to take a limited part in the second invasion of Zululand.[2] Colonel Hassard, Officer Commanding Royal Engineers, had such a severe nervous breakdown that he was replaced. Colonel Pearson, the defender of Eshowe, was invalided home suffering from mental and physical exhaustion.

Suicide amongst the troops was rare but not unknown. Defenders of Rorke's Drift also suffered, including Corporal Schiess and Private Jones VC, who later being of unsound mind, shot himself in the mouth. Sergeant Stratton, of the 2/24th, killed himself during the march into Zululand. At Eshowe, Private Knee of the 99th Regiment was a patient in the hospital but drowned himself in a nearby shallow stream. An unnamed private of the 99th regiment was in the hospital tents at Fort Pearson when, on 13 March, he suddenly dragged himself out of his sick-bed and threw himself into the Thukela river. In August 1881 ex-Trooper D'Arcy VC of the FLH went to stay with friends on the Eastern Cape. His friends found him tense and depressed and on the morning of 7 August his room was found to be empty and his bed not slept in. Despite a search over the following days, no trace of him was found until 28 December when the skeleton of a man was found in the hills nearby. The remains were thought to have been those of D'Arcy, who had wandered off alone and died of exposure. Such was the poor understanding and lack of recognition of a real medical disorder that, in the 1870s, palpitations, irritability of the heart and debility were the recognized medical conditions that accounted for the seemingly irrational psychological behaviour of affected soldiers while on campaign. In writing about his experiences during the war, Captain W. C. F. Molyneux, ADC to Chelmsford, commented on the effects of combat stress that gripped many soldiers.[3]

Fleet Surgeon Norbury noted that the circumstances associated with the lingering siege at Eshowe produced a greatly increased incidence of anxiety among many of the defenders. He described this as a 'depression of spirits' which, if combined with sickness or hospitalisation would compound the effects of the condition to the extent that recovery from any sickness would be made more difficult. Upon entering the besieged garrison at Eshowe, Molyneux remarked that: 'Coast fever and typhoid had claimed many victims, while rough fare, watchfulness and anxiety had all set their mark on all'.[4]

The number of British soldiers invalided during 1879 was much higher than expected, due to hard campaigning. Seventy soldiers were invalided specifically for a diagnosis of palpitations, caused by stress on the heart, compared to none in 1878 and 1880. Rheumatism and debility accounted for another 318 servicemen returning to Great Britain compared to 9 in 1878 and 51 in 1880. By the end of the war, soldiers who were deemed to be mentally unsound were, usually and quietly, moved back to Durban where they were held until they could be returned to England. This procedure led to a curious incident.

By the end of September 1879, the last detachments of the British Army had left Zululand with their baggage. Curiously, one event put the finishing touch to the war. Lieutenant General Sir William Butler wrote that just before one crowded transport was due to sail for England, the captain received an order to delay sailing; six soldiers found to be insane during the course of the war (including Rorke's Drift defender Private Wall) were about to be embarked under escort for consignment to a home lunatic asylum.

The captain, nervous at losing high tide, waited impatiently. A boat containing the six additional passengers arrived. On the transport a mass of men of different units, many already demobilised, lined the sides, having a last look at Durban. The lunatics, still in their uniforms, scrambled up the ladder and immediately vanished into the crowd to the consternation of the escort and the ship's captain.

The shore escort wanted to depart before the ship sailed and rapidly gave such descriptive details as they could remember before rowing back to shore. On board, the ship's officers held an emergency conference with the military. For fear of starting a general panic, news of the occurrence was kept a close secret. A select group of observers was enrolled, from men known to the officers or wearing decorations, and they were sworn to secrecy and detailed to watch different portions of the ship. All the way to Cape Town the observations continued. Any man sitting in isolation or in the throes of seasickness found himself under suspicion. At frequent intervals a passenger would be tapped on the shoulder and led to an inspection by a panel consisting of the ship's doctor, captain and an army officer. By the time the ship reached Cape Town there were twenty-six men in detention. Accordingly, an urgent request was sent from Cape Town for someone to come from Natal who could positively identify the lunatics. An asylum orderly was hastily despatched to the Cape only to discover that none of the men detained were the missing lunatics. On the contrary, six of the men detained had been engaged in the search for the lunatics and had been the most conscientious in reporting others as madmen. The lunatics were never found.[5]

Appendix 4

A Selection of Mr Punch's Unabridged Comments About the War, From the 1879 Punch Compendium

TELL THAT TO THE MARINES, 22 February

We want sober, steady, strong and seasoned men, to supply a grievous gap left by defeat and disaster in our line of Southern African defence. The Marines – 2,000 of the best infantry and 800 of the best artillery in the English service, are ready and willing to volunteer for this ugly and urgent duty.

'*Per mare, per Terram*' is the motto of the Corps, the most unflinching, unwavering, unconquerable, incorruptible and unfavoured body of men in the British Army.

'You are wanted at the front,' Tell that to the Marines, and in the front you will find them.

'You are likely to be outnumbered and outmatched,' Tell that to the Marines, and they will turn a deaf ear, or if they hear, they won't believe you.

We all know the 'Sodgers' – their rank and file steady, sturdy, true to their duty, and faithful to their flag and their officers under all circumstances, and against all provocations: their officers good men and true, gallant soldiers, poor, for the most part, unfashionable, unpetted, and uncomplaining, and known to the Swelldom of the Service as "empty bottles", well-explained as "good fellows that have done their duty, and are ready to do it again." Here are evidently the men, all of John Bull's armed sons, to tackle the Zulu, and face the odds and hardships of a wild country and a dangerous service. You have only to 'Tell that to the Marines' and if the Marines, don't tell that to Cetewayo and his warriors in very unmistakable language.

IMPERIALISM IN EXCELSIS, 1 March 1879

Defy mankind from Russia to Peru
And from Afghanistan to Zulu.

STRANGE OFFICIAL MISTAKE IN GEOGRAPHY, 8 March 1879

To have placed Chelmsford in Africa.
PHRASE BOOK FOR THE USE OF GENERAL OFFICERS.
(With Mr Punch's compliments to Lord Chelmsford)

On learning that an army has been cut to pieces – Dear Me! You don't say!
On losing the baggage train of a Division – Awkward – Very.
On receiving an officer who has ridden for his life twenty miles through an enemy's country, carrying despatches – Very Kind of you indeed.
On accepting an offer to head a foreign hope – I'm afraid you are giving yourself a great deal of trouble.
On seeing a Regimental Camp in flames – Odd! Isn't it?
On receiving a pair of Regimental Colours, recovered, after a desperate struggle, – I'm afraid you must have found them rather heavy.
On learning that a regiment is 'missing' – Fellows should take more care – really!
On finding a position turned – I call this quite too provoking!
On receiving the news that the troops under his command have been out-generalled and cut to pieces – Now, who is responsible for this?
On riding up to three score of Englishmen who have defended themselves for thirteen hours from the night assaults of thousands of victorious and bloodthirsty savages, and who have thus saved an army if not a Colony, from destruction – 'Thank you all very much for your gallant defence'!

ARMS FOR THE ENEMY, 22 March 1879

Some indignation has been somewhat unduly created by statements which appeared in a daily newspaper, stating that a firm in Whitechapel, and another at Manchester, are manufacturing arms for shipment to the Zulus. But the aid thus afforded to a savage enemy may be not by any means so bad as it seems. Dealers can have no interest in sending CETEWAYO and his soldiers any better firearms than the worst manufactured for exportation at Birmingham. The worse, the cheaper, therefore the more profitable for the vendors. Parties engaged in selling the Zulus rifles so bad as to be sure to burst in their hands, also sell the Zulus, and are driving a trade which is the reverse of unpatriotic, however unscrupulous. *Punch* therefore hesitates to say that the fellows ought to be hanged.

CIVIL AND MILITARY, 5 April 1879

Lord Chelmsford, before entering on the Zulu Campaign, published a handy little pamphlet for the information of his officers and men, in which he gave rules for conducting hostilities in Africa. From the desponding and doleful tone of some of his recent despatches, his lordship's retirement from his command seems not an impossible contingency. It would be a pity if his Lordship should carry out this intention till he has appended an additional chapter to his instructive and (when followed) no doubt useful brochure; something to this effect.

How to ensure a defeat, and how to behave under it.

Having carefully perused and mastered the above rules for successfully engaging the Zulus, all that now remains is to deliberately march into their teeth.

Knowing that a strongly fortified camp is the key and nucleus of defence against this vigilant and active enemy, the commanding officer should quietly move off with the bulk of his force, leaving the tents unentrenched, and the waggons unparked 'in laager'. He may, at the same time, send verbal orders that the camp is to be defended.

If the enemy presents himself, he cannot do wrong, to follow him up. It will be time enough when the enemy proves himself a Will-o'-the Wisp, whose object has been to mislead and draw away the opposing force, to treat him accordingly.

While advancing, he had better not weaken his force by detaching scouting or reconnaissance parties, and should turn a deaf ear to all such disquieting reports that firing is going on in the direction of the camp left behind him.

There will be no harm if, in order to show the responsibility of his position, he, later in the day, order one of his Staff to go to the top of a hill with a telescope, and look towards the camp. He will, of course, be satisfied by the assurance of the Staff officer 'that he thinks it's all right'.

If late in the evening he sees reasons to suspect that the enemy have been playing him a trick, as savages will, his best course will probably be to fall back on the camp, and should he find the camp destroyed, the stores plundered, and its defenders slaughtered to a man, it will be his duty to put up with this extremely disagreeable state of things with all the equanimity he can command.

Now is the time for extreme caution. Should there be reason to conclude that the enemy is moving off, and that he must be encumbered with spoil, the best plan will be to let him pass unmolested.

On the other hand, should he come across a handful of men who have held a position of the utmost importance against overwhelming odds for a long winter's night, he may safely 'thank them very much'.

After this, he should lose no time in instituting a strict Official Enquiry how the mischief came about. Should it be proved by 'supplementary testimony' (furnished by officers of his personal staff) that the Commander-in-Chief is not responsible, and that somebody else has been to blame, all the better for the Commander-in-Chief, and all the worse for somebody else.

Having brought matters to this point, he will stand aside and wait for events.

Should the Colonists chafe, and the indignant British lion growl, he may suggest that an officer of rank should be sent out immediately to assist him, and, if need be, to take his place. He may at the same time remember that for a very long time he has not been at all well. Lastly, should the growl of the British lion get so loud as to be annoying, if he feels that more responsibility is being thrown upon him than he can bear, there will be nothing for it but to pack up his cocked hat and writing-desk and come home!

AWAITING LORD CHELMSFORD – Victoria Cross, 19 April 1879

CETEWAYO AND KETCH.
The Zulu monarch's name. by its lett'ring to speak
As if 'twere a proper name, Latin or Greek,
And pronounced CE-TE-WAY-O, is not the right way,
We are told that Ketchwayo is what we should say.

KETCHWAYO's accounted a barbarous wretch,
And his name also puts us in mind of JACK KETCH.
In one thing King KETCHWAYO and KETCH agree,
They were both little babies once, even as we.

Ay, and both of those babies their nurses, perchance,
In their arms were accustomed to dandle and dance,
And hush them, and rock them, and lullaby sing
And cry 'Ketchy-Ketchy' to each little thing.

UPSIDE DOWN, 26 April 1879

Le Monde talks of 'Sir Bartle Frere' Perhaps it is only a neat way of expressing Le Monde's opinion that the distinguished High Commissioner's name should be turned topsy-turvy, the better to correspond to his policy.

BRITISH MISSION TO THE HEATHEN.
Old Style – HENRY MARTYN
New Style – MARTINI HENRY.

SONS OF NEPTUNE AND MARS, 14 June 1879

On Wednesday last week a battalion of Royal Marines, amidst hurrahs, embarked at Portsmouth for Zululand. The permission given the Royal Marines to join the Army in the campaign against CETEWAYO is regarded as a recognition, though a tardy one, of the value of the services ever wont to be rendered at need by that gallant and effective, but hitherto somewhat snubbed and sat-upon force. It is, however, only a partial tribute of honour to whom honour is due. The Marines, to whom this concession has at length been made, are limited to Artillery and Light Infantry. They include no cavalry. Why will government still obstinately persist in ignoring the Horse Marines?

QUEER SITE FOR A CHURCH, 21 June 1879

By all means raise a memorial to the brave who fell at Isandlwana; but would not a preferable place for it be inside St. Paul's? Or if the monument must needs be a church, had it not better stand in some neighbourhood where it would have a chance of being occasionally occupied by a congregation? Have we gone the right way to convert the Zulus by invading their territory? Are they likely ever to frequent a sacred edifice erected on a battlefield which Christian and heathen have made memorable by mutual slaughter? The only place of worship to build with propriety over interred carnage would be a Temple of Mars.

ADVICE TO BRITISH OFFICERS, 9 August 1879

Mind how you obey the word of command to skedaddle. No officer can be court-martialled for disobedience to orders by which he gets killed.

WHAT WILL BE DONE WITH HIM? 27 September 1879

Can anyone say? –
Will he be sent to the Tower?
Will rooms be taken for him at Claridges?
Will he be banished to Cyprus?
Will he join the circle at Hughenden Manor?
Will he be mobbed some Sunday soon at the Zulu-logical Gardens?
Will he be released on parole, and enjoy the privilege of gazing at his own
    effigy at Madame Tussaud's?

Will he be carried captive in the Lord Mayor's Procession on the Ninth of November next (as in the Roman triumphs of old) and afterward have to stand the fire of Lord Beaconsfield's rhetoric in the Guildhall?

Will he be produced as the latest African novelty at the opening meeting of the Royal Geographical Society?

Will he be allowed to lecture and exhibit himself and his kraal at St. James Hall?

Will the Aquarium eventually get hold of him?

Will he be the Lion of the next London Season?

Will he appear at Exeter Hall?

Will people at last learn to spell and pronounce his name correctly?

Won't he be photographed?

THIS WILL BE DONE WITH HIM.

He will be photographed in several Cartes – each utterly unlike the other – in his fat and lean states, with and without his crown and in and out of his court cow-tails.

He will be taken as the trade-mark for a new 'South African Relish'.

He will appear as the principal figure in more than one highly imaginary group in more than one of the Illustrated pictures.

His biography will form a substantial part of the padding to the current numbers of several shilling magazines.

For nearly three weeks his name will loom large in the 'Extra-Parliamentary utterances' of all the less responsible members of the Ministry.

He will be missing, like the Cabul massacre, from Lord Beaconsfield's first rural oration.

For a month his swarthy physiognomy will appear and disappear in a dissolving view, at the Royal Polytechnic Institution.

He will enlist the sympathies of many thousands of well-meaning people, who will take the deepest interest in him for nearly a month.

He will appear in effigy at Madam Tussaud's and continue as an addition to that most perennial of exhibitions until his wax is required for a newer novelty and a more startling sensation.

And then he will be forgotten!

CHESS PROBLEM SOLVED AT CAPE TOWN, 18 October 1879

Zulu King-Castled.

DEMAND FOR ARMY DOCTORS, 25 October 1879

WANTED, for employment as Medical Officers in the British Army, an adequate number of thoroughly well-educated physicians and surgeons, willing, on occasion, to expose their lives to the utmost danger in active service, without any expectation of receiving the Victoria Cross, or being otherwise distinguished or rewarded. They must have no objection to put up with indignity or neglect, be content with an amount of pay not exceeding a sufficiency for their daily maintenance, and be prepared on their discharge to depend for their subsistence upon such private practice as they may hope to pick up by beginning the world again late in life. As the want of competent Army physicians and surgeons is just now very urgent, the supply being far from equal to the demands, immediate applications are confidently expected at the War Office.

Appendix 5

Medals etc.

ISANDLWANA, 22 January 1879

(Sotondosa's Drift, near Rorke's Drift.)

VICTORIA CROSS
Private S. Wassall, 80th Regt.
Lieutenant N. J. A. Coghill, 1/24th Regt. Posthumously awarded in 1907.
Lieutenant T. Melvill, 1/24th Regt. Posthumously awarded in 1907.

RORKE'S DRIFT 22 and 23 January 1879

VICTORIA CROSS
Lieutenant J. R. M. Chard, Royal Engineers
Lieutenant G. Bromhead, 2/24th Regt.
Surgeon J. H. Reynolds, Army Medical Department
Acting Assistant Commissary J. L. Dalton, Commissary Department
Corporal F. C. Schiess, Natal Native Contingent
Corporal W. W. Allen, 2/24th Regt.
Private F. Hitch, 2/24th Regt.
Private A. H. Hook, 2/24th Regt.
Private J. Williams, 2/24th Regt.
Private R. Jones, 2/24th Regt.
Private W. Jones, 2/24th Regt.

DISTINGUISHED CONDUCT MEDAL
Colour Sergeant F. Bourne, 2/24th Regt.
Corporal M. McMahon, Army Medical Corps (withdrawn for theft and
    desertion)
Second Corporal F. Attwood, Army Service Corps

Wheeler J. Cantwell, Royal Artillery
Private W. Roy, 1/24th Regt.

NTOMBE RIVER, 12 March 1879

VICTORIA CROSS
Sergeant A. C. Booth, 80th Regt.

HLOBANE MOUNTAIN, 28 March 1879

VICTORIA CROSS
Brevet Lieutenant Colonel R. H. Buller, 60th Rifles
Major W. K. Leet 1/13th Regt. [Major Leet applied directly to a friend
  in the War Office for the V.C. and uniquely received it. He is variously
  referred to as Leet or Knox-Leet.]
Lieutenant H. Lysons, 90th Regt.
Lieutenant E. S. Browne, 1/24th Regt.
Private E. Fowler, 90th Regt.

DISTINGUISHED CONDUCT MEDAL
Corporal W. D. Vinnicombe, Frontier Light Horse
Trooper R. Brown, Frontier Light Horse
Private J. Power, 1/24th Regt.
Bugler A. Walkinshaw, 90th Light Infantry

KHAMBULA, 29 March 1879

DISTINGUISHED CONDUCT MEDAL
Troop Sergeant Major Learda, Natal Native Horse
Acting Sergeant E. Quigley, 1/13th Regt.
Private. A. Page, 1/13th Regt.

WHITE MFOLOZI RIVER, 3 July 1879

VICTORIA CROSS
Captain Lord W. L. de la P. Beresford, 9th Lancers
Sergeant C. D. D'Arcy, Frontier Light Horse
Sergeant E. O'Toole, Frontier Light Horse

DISTINGUISHED CONDUCT MEDAL
Troop Sergeant Major S. Kambula, Natal Native Horse

ULUNDI, 4 July 1879

DISTINGUISHED CONDUCT MEDAL
Colour Sergeant J. Phillips, 58th Regt.
Gunner W. Moorhead, Royal Artillery.

The Anomaly of Victoria Crosses not Awarded

Lieutenant Harford, Sihayo's Homestead. Following the engagement, Chelmsford offered Lieutenant Harford a decoration for his bravery. Being the archetypical gentleman he was, Harford politely declined out of courtesy to Lord Chelmsford. The matter was never raised again, and Harford bitterly regretted his moment of politeness for the remainder of his long service. *Harford*, Payne, David and Emma. 2008 Ultimatum Tree Ltd.

Captain Duck, Veterinary Corps. Part of Chelmsford's personal escort, he was recommended for the VC at Hlobane for bravery at the Devil's Pass but the request was refused on the grounds that he should not have been there. *Forgotten Battles of the Zulu War*, Greaves, Adrian. 2012, Pen & Sword.

Trooper Barker, Natal Carbineers. Recommended by Major General Sir Evelyn Wood for surrendering his horse to his adjutant, Lieutenant Higginson, while fleeing Isandlwana. Wood's recommendation was rejected by the War Office in London on the grounds that too many Victoria Crosses had already been issued.

No decorations were issued for the actions at Gingindlovu or Nyezane, though Sergeant Jenkins of the Cape Mounted Rifles (CMR) was personally thanked by Chelmsford for his bravery in leading a charge against the Zulus at Nyezane. He was given an immediate field promotion to Lieutenant, a rare and more valuable reward as it included an enhanced pension.

The Royal Red Cross (The RRC, known as the nurses' VC) was first issued to nurses who took part in the South Africa campaign. The decoration was instigated at the request of Queen Victoria as a result of the bravery of the twelve nurses who took part in the Anglo-Zulu War. The citation is for:

> The zeal and devotion in providing for and nursing sick and wounded sailors, soldiers and others with the Army in the field, on board ships, or in hospitals.

Six Royal Red Crosses each were awarded to the nurses of the Stafford House and the Army Hospital Corps. For the intriguing history of resistance by the military to a decoration being awarded to women, see *Sister Janet*, Stossel, Katie RCN. 2006, Pen & Sword.

The Welshness of the 24th Regiment

Students of the Anglo-Zulu war will be familiar with the role of the 24th Regiment in South Africa. Since the 1964 film *ZULU*, myths promulgated the 'Welshness' of the Regiment during its time in South Africa until more recent empirical research effectively proved the Regiment's link to the UK was with Warwickshire – not Wales. Indeed, during the 1879 war the 24th was the Warwickshire Regiment and remained so for two years following the war. Even when the regiment returned from South Africa there was no connection or contact with Brecon. A brief review of the Regiment's actual post-war postings evidences this.

1st Battalion

The 1st Battalion saw continuous service in various Mediterranean garrisons after 1867, then moved to South Africa on 4 February 1875. As soon as tidings of the disaster at Isandlwana reached England, recruits were urgently drafted from eighteen different regiments to re-form the lost 1st Battalion at Aldershot. On 1 March 1879, a draft of 520 non-commissioned officers and men embarked on the *Clyde* at Woolwich for South Africa. Just six months later, on 27 August, this newly constituted battalion embarked for the return to England on the *Egypt*, arriving at Portsmouth on 2 October and moving to New Barracks at Gosport. Men drafted from regiments in England into the reconstituted 1st Battalion after Isandlwana were then permitted to return to their original regiments. Over time, 709 men took the option and were replaced with 358 new recruits.

On 26 November 1880 the battalion was moved by train to Colchester. In 1885 it was posted to Ireland before being posted to Aldershot in 1889.

2nd Battalion

The 2nd Battalion had been based at Aldershot before moving to Dover in August 1875 and to Chatham in 1877. On 1 February the battalion left Chatham by two special trains for Portsmouth where it embarked upon HM Troopship *Himalaya* for South Africa and, after three months of training, participated in the Sandilli Rebellion.

On 12 February 1880, following the Anglo-Zulu war, the 2nd Battalion embarked in the SS *Ontario* to take up its posting to Gibraltar, going into quarters in Casemate Barracks. On 12 August 1880 the battalion embarked for Bombay on the *Orantes*, arriving on 2 September. The battalion remained at Secunderabad from 1880 to February 1884, then was in Burma until 1892.

Meanwhile, on 1 July 1881, the regiment was ordered to be discontinued, its two battalions then stationed respectively at Colchester and Secunderabad, to become The South Wales Borderers. Until then neither battalion appears to have had any connection with Brecon or Wales. For confirmation, see *Records of the 24th Regiment*, Paton, Glennie & Symons, 1892. As a serving officer with the Regiment in Berlin (1961-4) no mention was ever made of the Anglo-Zulu war – until 1964 when the film *ZULU* was released. Then, overnight, and to our surprise, we had a new history.

Medical Matters in the Anglo-Zulu War

AZWHS Journal No 33. Dr Andres Traverse

Under the sub-tropical conditions of colonial warfare in Zululand, army, naval and civilian surgeons were constantly challenged by the often-insurmountable numbers of sickness cases among the troops, in addition to the associated workload. Adaptation to the circumstances and ceaseless effort was necessary for all medical and hospital personnel, in order to provide an acceptable level of care. At the same time, these men were not immune to battlefield risks and disease. In describing his personal experiences during combat in 1879, Dr Andrew Duncan, a civil surgeon, befittingly described the responsibilities and perils of medical officers under fire:

> Albeit the non-combatants in the army are honoured with but a slender modicum of glory, they very often come in for a lion's share of the danger. Bullets cannot discriminate between the fiercest of enemies and the messenger of balm and healing, and will tear through the middle of a gonfalon blazoned with the Geneva cross as readily as through a regimental flag. The surgeon non-combatant though he requires a courage of a higher order than his fighting associate; he has to perform the most difficult and delicate of operations under fire, and has to preserve his coolness all the time. As a rule he shrinks from no self-sacrifice; he works with quiet brave perseverance through the long watches of the night, while others are taking their repose; and in the heat of combat is generally like to that of the gallant Reynolds at Rorke's Drift.

Woolfryes summarised the difficult conditions and circumstances encountered by his staff in the coastal belt of Zululand and Natal, stating that:

> The duties throughout the campaign were severe and unremitting, especially those of the Medical Officers of the 1st Division ...owing to protracted

occupation of entrenched camps on the Coast line between the Tugela &
Inyezane rivers – a district proverbially unhealthy from its marsh mists, etc &
indifferent water supply – suffered from exceptional sickness & mortality, the
result of the conditions above with fatigue & exposure superadded.

The tragic deaths of Surgeon Major Shepherd and Civilian Surgeon Cobbin
are well documented in accounts of the Anglo-Zulu War. However, the loss
of other medical staff has not been given the same attention and is therefore
less well known. These include Acting Surgeon Brice, attached to the NNC
and killed at Isandlwana, and Civil Surgeons A. A. Woods and G. H Garland,
who both died from disease during the campaign. Surgeon Major Allcock
was invalided back to England a month before the invasion of Zululand;
Surgeon Major W. J. Ingham and Surgeon Major W. E. Dudley were both
sent home on sick leave in May and June respectively. The non-combatant
role of the men of the Army Hospital Corps (AHC) changed in light of the
constant danger of Zulu attacks on the convoys of wounded after Isandlwana.
The issued ceremonial sword bayonet was all but useless in defence, so the
men were each armed with a revolver as a very necessary precaution. The
corps, too, suffered its fair share of losses during the campaign, particularly
at Isandlwana where Lieutenant of Orderlies Arthur William Hall and ten
enlisted men died in action. By the end of hostilities, another corps officer
and nine men had died of disease, seven of which served in the coastal area
of Zululand. A further twenty-nine members of the corps were invalided
back to England.

The case of Staff Surgeon Longfield, HMS *Tenedos*, serving with
Chelmsford's relief column and critically wounded at the Battle of
Gingindlovu on 2 April 1879 is interestingly significant. His experiences
both as a medical officer and patient throughout the following three months
gave him the unique opportunity to assess the merits and shortcomings of
the complete system of medical services provided for the sick and wounded
of Pearson's Column. This did indeed reflect the overall organisation and
level of care rendered by the medical services during the entire campaign
up to that point in time.

At the height of the Battle at Gingindlovu, while attending to a wounded
private of the 99th Regiment, Longfield was severely wounded in the

right arm by a large spherical ball. This had entered the arm immediately below his deltoid muscle causing a comminuted fracture of the humerus. The naval surgeon was quickly removed by Staff Surgeon Shields. Upon examining his colleague on 10 April, Norbury's assessment of the wound was guarded, as he thought Longfield might lose his right arm. By the end of the month, a discharge was noted through the soft tissue wound, which seemed to be healing, with Norbury contemplating a surgical procedure to repair the broken bone. A month later pieces of dead bone had worked their way through the skin which made the removal of fragments easier. By the beginning of June, Longfield felt that good progress was at last being made and that a new splint seemed to stabilise the arm sufficiently for further optimal healing. Now a patient, Longfield's experiences were reflective of the deficiencies and inefficiencies plaguing the medical services. In a report to his superiors, he wrote:

When I came to my turn to be dressed, I found to my astonishment that no splints save ordinary wooden ones had been brought, four of these had consequently to be applied, though owing to the height to which the fracture extended they afforded little or no support. From the 2nd to the 7th I lay under a tent in the laager at Gingindlovu, the conditions of which had become almost pestilential.

At my earnest request shortly before my removal thence the four splints were taken off and a hastily improvised angular one, composed of two strips of dial tied together with a piece of cord substituted for them. This subsequently from its want of rigidity proved more of a curse than a blessing.

On the morning of the 7th I was placed in an Ashantee cot and carried about a mile to a crowded entrenchment, where I was left to endure the heat of a broiling sun all day as best I might, the arm then being greatly swollen and in a highly inflamed state with much sympathetic constitutional disturbance. At sunset I was lifted in the cot on to some straw in a springless wagon in company of an officer of the 57th Regt who was suffering from a fracture of the fibula.

The following morning at 2.00am I was roused out of a sleep induced by a strong subcutaneous injection of morphia by the wagon being jolted downhill at a good pace causing me most undesirable torture. At length the driver succeeded in arresting his refractory oxen and we proceeded more quickly. No care or attention on his part could mitigate the horrors of that terrible journey which lasted from 2.00am to 9.00pm broken by one short spell to give the oxen a rest and which for miles led straight across country. As darkness fell and there was no possibility of selecting our road our sufferings were proportionately increased until at last from the long continued pain my senses appeared to become blunted the ends of the bones could grind together without an effort on my part to prevent my doing so. I may say that I was informed that the ambulance would have jolted me even more severely owing to the disselboom having been broken at any rate the experiment was never tried.

It is with much regret that I have been testimony to the utter inefficiency of the whole arrangements for the sick and transport of the wounded of this column and to the apathy and indifference with which effort is met which has for its object its amelioration of the sad state of affairs. Had we been flying before a victorious enemy, or had time been pressing, there might have been some little excuse for the treatment we received: but such was not the case. The Zulus were broken and fled in all directions and a garrison was left in the vicinity of Gingindlovu. There was nothing therefore to prevent our being allowed to remain till some measures had been taken to provide proper transport for at least the most severely wounded. The day before we started no rations were supplied to the sick nor were they on the day of their coming in and how the poor fellows fared who prosecuted their journey to the Base Hospital at Herwen will be apparent from the following extracts from a letter which I have received from the officer who shared the wagon down with me.

'If you are at all comfortable where you are, don't attempt to come to this place. The food is bad what little there is and there is a most hellish row kicked up day and night. I think it was very lucky that you stayed at Tugela. I assure you that the journey was enough to kill any man in fact it did kill one, he was found dead in the wagon in the morning.'

Arrived here, [Fort Tenedos] appliances of all descriptions were found to be as scarce as they were at Gingindlovu. The Field Hospitals at Forts Pearson and Tenedos could not supply between them an ounce of carbolic acid, and I had to wait several days before this was sent to me thro' a private source in Durban. I was no stranger however to such shortcomings as these, after an experience of two and a half months in charge of what goes by the name of a Field Hospital, an experience which taught me that urgent demands for Medicines and Appliances would in nine cases out of ten be treated with supreme indifference and that Forms and Returns were considered of far more importance than the wants and requirements of the patients who came under my charge. I can safely affirm that this great camp at the present moment does not contain one ounce of castor oil nor a grain of acetate of lead [Dysentery and diarrhoea] being everywhere prevalent and I hear complaints of Medical Officers of every branch that it is quite impossible for them to treat their sick for the simple reason that there is nothing whatever to treat them with. This as I have said before is nothing new.

By 12 June, Norbury reported that his colleague Longfield had been transferred to the base hospital at Durban to convalesce and that the wounds were healing well, with a more certain prognosis long term. The staff surgeon would soon be invalided back to England after he was granted a pension certificate.

Surgeon Blair-Brown fell victim to disease and contracted the prevailing fever at Helpmekaar. He was sent to Ladysmith to recuperate, after which he stayed to administer the base hospital. The continued losses of able medical officers and AHC personnel constituted a severe blow to an already overstretched medical service, which was difficult to remedy.

In this arduous environment, and especially in the line of fire, military and civilian surgeons were expected to wear the cloak of Aesculapius and carry the mantle of Mars in performing their duties. This became obvious to all when among other feats performed by the Army Medical Department (AMD), medical officers were awarded the Victoria Cross. At Rorke's Drift, Surgeon James Henry Reynolds deservedly earned himself the esteemed distinction. Another recipient of the medal, Surgeon Major Edmund Baron Hartley, was recognised for his bravery at Morosi's Mountain in June 1879 while serving with the Cape Mounted Rifles. Separate from the Zulu conflict, a simultaneous sideshow developed in South Africa known as the Basuto War. Hartley demonstrated his act of courage:

> In attending the wounded under fire, at the unsuccessful attack on Morosi's Mountain in Basutoland, on 5th June 1879, and for having proceeded into the open ground, under a heavy fire and carried in his arms, from an exposed position, Corporal A. Jones of the Cape Mounted Riflemen, who was wounded. While conducting him to a place of safety the Corporal was again wounded. The Surgeon Major then returned under the severe fire of the enemy in order to dress the wounds of other men of the storming party.

In lobbying the War Office for recognition, respect, adequate pay, benefits and parity in rank with line officers, medical staff would at last be able to justify their claims publicly in clearly demonstrating their importance. Furthermore, at the Battle of Kambula, the exemplary conduct of the surgeons and members of the AHC, under adverse and challenging conditions, was also noted and furthered the cases of both the AMD and Naval Medical Department. The performance of the medical officers and civil surgeons was praised by Woolfryes in his reports. Civil Surgeons Jolly and Connolly risked their lives during the retreat from Hlobane; their bravery described aptly by Woolfryes:

> They were last in the retreat back to the camp when pursued by many thousand Zulus and they frequently dismounted and assisted the wounded and helpless men at their imminent risk.

The next day, the Zulus, fresh from a great victory at Hlobane, launched an aggressive and relentless attack on Wood's defensive position. The medical services were further tested and all involved performed well:

> Civil Surgeon Jolly and two orderlies, AHC, was with the garrison in the fort during the attack and rendered valuable aid to the wounded there. Surgeon Major O'Reilly, Surgeons A. L. Brown and Thornton, Civil Surgeon Connolly, and Hospital Dresser Armitage remained at the field hospital in the camp. The field hospital from its position was exposed to a severe crossfire, most of which fortunately passed over head, but several of the hospital tents were struck by Zulu bullets. Surgeon Major O'Reilly reports, Surgeons A. L. Brown and Thornton and Civil Surgeon Connolly laboured hard during the whole engagement attending to numerous wounded, by whom our resources were severely taxed. An amputation of the upper arm was performed by Surgeons Brown and Thornton in a very exposed part of the camp during the hottest part of the fight. Colonel Wood in his despatch after the battle says, 'The wounded were cared for most promptly by Surgeons O'Reilly, A. L. Brown and staff generally under fire'.

At the Battle of Ulundi, the field hospital located inside the square was situated closest to the heaviest fighting, with all the medical and support staff performing admirably in giving aid to 101 wounded men. The Natal native stretcher bearers were kept busy, and they too suffered casualties, though only a few deaths were actually recorded in the records and literature.

The attitude of the AMD towards the use of civil surgeons and civil practitioners was mixed, certainly not complimentary in the early part of the campaign. However, despite the criticisms, the civilian medical volunteers performed well in general, particularly at Hlobane and Kambula. Civil Surgeon Lewis Reynolds too demonstrated the value of his colleagues, and was even asked to report on the proficiency of the new medical arrangements compared to the old regimental system. Those civilian surgeons unfamiliar with military medicine protocol and the need for improvisation soon learned to adapt. In performing their duties, Woolfryes gave credit to the medical officers and civil surgeons in his report:

> I feel it incumbent upon me to state that the duties were performed such zealously and efficiently by the officers, AMD and the Civil Surgeons in many cases to the detriment of their health which broke down from over-work.

The contribution of the Navy's medical officers throughout the campaign cannot be understated. By acting in a well organised and self-reliant manner, their conduct and support of the AMD reflected well on the Navy. However, in his official reports, Woolfryes omitted pertinent facts regarding the vital role played by his naval colleagues both in the zone of active conflict and in the care of hospitalised army personnel.

Given that Chelmsford's army was waging war on natives whose principal weapon was a stabbing spear, it might sound surprising that the vast majority of wounds presenting for treatment were in fact bullet wounds. Assegai wounds were found to be less common due to the very deadly nature of hand-to-hand combat. At the British camp at Kambula, Surgeon Major O'Reilly attended to only five wounded survivors from Hlobane.

At the beginning of the campaign the Zulus possessed chiefly old inaccurate Tower flintlock and percussion muskets, while quite a few prominent members of the tribe possessed modern rifles. After Isandlwana, the cache of captured Martini Henry's bolstered the Zulu firepower, with potentially devastating consequences for the British. The quality of the ammunition, which included spherical balls mostly hammered and irregularly shaped from pieces of lead, used for the varied types of antiquated firearms, caused a variety of bullet wounds. The generally poor understanding of the use of modern firearms by the Zulus arguably benefited the British in combat, particularly in view of the large number in possession, especially immediately after Isandlwana. The effect of each type of bullet depended on the shape of the projectile and range of discharge. While the Martinis were very much deadly at long range, the muskets were mostly fired at ranges less than optimal to cause significant damage. With less effective fire, most hits on the British troops caused mostly superficial wounds, requiring simple treatment with uncomplicated recovery. However, the Martini Henry bullets tore at the flesh and smashed bones. The unfamiliar use of the firearm resulted in often inaccurate fire which helped prevent higher casualties among the British in the post-Isandlwana period. Nevertheless, despite the poor marksmanship of the Zulus, many shots could not fail to make their mark amongst the massed ranks of redcoats, particularly at Ulundi, where Chelmsford's square was exposed in the open. The field hospital located inside the defensive position was situated closest to the heaviest fighting, with all the medical and support staff performing admirably giving aid to the wounded. At Rorke's Drift, Kambula and Gingindlovu, most of Chelmsford's men hit by Zulu gunfire sustained wounds mainly to the head, neck, chest and arms due to the protection available in the defensive positions.

The theory of germ-based disease in mainstream medicine had been gaining momentum in the 1870s, to the extent that Listerism and the use of carbolic acid for antisepsis had effectively reduced the incidence of infections in wounds. During the Anglo-Zulu war, the use of carbolic acid was deemed a necessity by the medical officers. While complete antiseptic treatment of wounds was impossible on campaign, Surgeon Major Charles Cuffe, serving with Wood's Flying Column, reported that the chemical was very effective for the purpose intended. By understanding the importance of antisepsis, Surgeon Blair Brown, a pragmatic medical officer, also advocated personal cleanliness and thorough instrument washing. He also favoured the new elastic ligature or bandage technique as a tourniquet taught by Professor Esmarch. The standard yet old-fashioned method involved the use of the belt, buckle and pad type of tourniquet which was more uncomfortable for the patient.

As a proponent for the benefits of fresh air in surgical treatment, Blair-Brown was particular in treating severe gunshot wounds in a well-pitched marquee with adequate ventilation. He felt that stuffy enclosures such as huts, which were often the only facility available for surgery and patient recovery, were sources of contamination and subsequent infection. He also preferred to use simple techniques in performing surgical tasks, as he felt that simple oiled silk sutures, drainage tubes made from dark vulcanised India rubber and borax were basically all that was usually necessary. His technique for surgical closure of wounds was usually uncomplicated, with minimal interference during the critical healing process which allowed for optimal results. Furthermore, Blair-Brown believed that AMD personnel understood the treatment of war wounds better than their civilian counterparts. He commented on the nearly overwhelming weight of his responsibilities following the Isandlwana disaster and the loss of his senior colleague, stating that a total of 646 medically treated wounded regular and colonial troops were assigned to his care at Helpmekaar. It is almost certain that this group included both sick and wounded, as his figure exceeds the total official number of wounded for the entire campaign.

Surgical procedures performed during the Anglo-Zulu War were mostly successful, unless patients died from loss of blood and shock during the operation. However, surviving the post-surgical healing period would be the challenge. Before the advent of antibiotics, secondary infection would take the lives of many patients. Gangrene and painful erysipelas or cellulitis worked to kill the chances of wound healing and while every precaution was taken to prevent these complications, they were difficult to treat. For the ligation of damaged large blood vessels, silver wire was popular, though catgut would later reach prominence as the quality improved.

Today, the use of general anaesthetics is commonplace in surgery. In the 1870s, nitrous oxide, ether and chloroform were all available to surgeons. This marked a leap for medical advancement which was not entirely embraced enthusiastically by all medical officers in the British army. While the use of safer anaesthetics, namely nitrous oxide and ether, required bulky equipment, chloroform was easy to transport and administer. Although some medical officers felt that pain was an integral part of any surgical treatment, chloroform was extensively used during the Anglo-Zulu War to facilitate surgical procedures, especially amputations and removal of bullets and bone fragments. Surgeon Major J. H. Porter strongly advocated the use of the anaesthetic, calling it:

> One of the greatest blessings and should be carefully treasured by the army
> surgeon and no waste allowed …every drop is worth its weight in gold.

Immediate or latent shock and loss of blood pressure was a recognised complication of severe wounds and surgery due to haemorrhaging or blood loss. The signs and symptoms were well understood, though effective treatment was in general nothing more than a cookbook approach and involved administrating consolation or encouragement, cordials, beef tea and wine or brandy.

The medicines available for Fleet Surgeon Norbury during the siege at Eshowe included vital opioids, opiates, aloes, diuretics, purgatives and linen for bandages. Norbury also turned to natural products to augment his diminishing supplies of medicines. He used parts of the bark of the waterboom tree readily available close to the fort at Eshowe. He managed to extract tannic acid from this product which worked well as an astringent, though the Zulus used the medicine as a purgative. Ironically, the surrounding area was in fact very rich in natural medicines, which have always been highly regarded by the Zulus for their healing powers. The Dlinza Forest is located three miles from the besieged garrison and arguably, through no fault of his own, Norbury missed a great opportunity to capitalise on the availability of such *materia medica*.

According to official records, it can be determined that a total of 191 medical officers and civilian counterparts served in South Africa in 1879. Army medical department medical officers serving with the regular forces, including those holding command or administration posts, totalled eighty-four. Twenty-one of these did not arrive in Natal until after the victory at Ulundi. There were forty-nine civil surgeons on contract with the AMD to serve with Chelmsford, and a further fifteen civil practitioners were recruited. Eighteen medical officers and civil surgeons served with the colonial forces, of which nine did not participate in the Anglo-Zulu war, though they were engaged with units involved in separate conflicts. The Stafford House South African Aid Committee sent two medical personnel, and the Naval Medical Service contributed a total of twenty-three medical officers in various capacities. Of the latter, nine naval surgeons served directly with the regular forces, though officially their primary responsibility lay with the health and welfare of the men belonging to the Naval Landing Brigade. The loss of fifteen medical personnel by the end of May 1879 by attrition, due to deaths, disability, wounds and resignations upon expiration of contracts, were an inconvenience which severely dented the efficiency of the medical services. In addition to these losses, some succumbed to the prevailing sickness and were, therefore, temporarily disabled. At the height of efficiency of the medical services, the total effective strength of the AMD, supported by other departments and volunteers, likely never exceeded 130 medically trained staff.

On campaign in South Africa, pragmatism and resourcefulness were expected from all medical officers in the face of arduous circumstances and continuous demands placed on their shoulders. Surgeon General Woolfryes never wavered in his tasks and commitment to an efficient medical service. Notable contributions by the surgeons, nurses and supporting bodies, were made to the advancement of contemporary medicine. The establishment of the profession as an important service to the British army and navy was a reflection of the quality of the men and women involved. Surgeon J. H. Reynolds and Surgeon Major Hartley were rewarded for their valour, while other colleagues were noticed for their bravery in the face of the enemy. By demonstrating the use of perceived sound principles in promoting a high standard of medical care and applying themselves to the advancement of their profession, further notable contributions were made. In aiding the recovery of sick and wounded, Surgeons Major Blair-Brown and Shepherd, Fleet Surgeon Norbury and Civil Surgeon Stoker, amongst others all played significant roles. At times during the war, good medicine and life-saving measures were achieved for the wrong reasons, given that contemporary thinking and lack of microbiological knowledge was waiting for the next step forward.

Native Medicine and Treatment of Zulus

Treatment of the sick and wounded by the AMD did not restrict itself to British soldiers, colonials and native troops. Several accounts describe the care administered to wounded Zulu prisoners by the medical officers and civilian surgeons. Given the animosity towards the Zulus as an enemy, particularly following the Isandlwana catastrophe, one might be surprised to learn that medical officers and their civilian colleagues often demonstrated a high level of care and professionalism concerning their sick and wounded prisoners.

After the Battle of Gingindlovu, sixteen severely wounded Zulus were taken on an unavoidably rough ride to Fort Tenedos. Upon arrival, they were left practically unattended in two wagons and given little food for three days. Concerned medical officers finally arranged for proper accommodation and care for these thirsty and emaciated men, all suffering from severe and infected wounds due to the neglect. One Zulu required immediate amputation for multiple Gatling gun bullet wounds and died from shock soon after the procedure. Of the remaining fifteen, all received proper medical treatment for a variety of injuries, including three fractured thigh bones and flesh wounds.

Even as wounded prisoners under the care of British medical officers, the Zulus preferred to use their own therapies rather than accept conventional surgical techniques. In caring for gunshot wounds and other injuries, Zulus often carried their wounded comrades to the highest elevation in the area for treatment. The wounds would be exposed to the sun for a week or two and carefully washed several times a day. Witnesses noted remarkably rapid healing in the majority of cases. One such intrigued observer of this practice, Dr George Stoker, believed that the optimal healing of wounds was made possible by the theory that unusually pure air was found at higher altitudes. Working in South Africa as part of the Stafford House South Africa Aid Committee contingent, Stoker's medical contribution during the Balkan wars of 1876 and 1877-78 had not impressed his superior, who questioned the surgeon's surgical abilities. During the AZW his duties partly involved the surgical care of wounded Zulus requiring treatment for gunshot wounds and burns. Based on the practice of exposing wounds to fresh air, Stoker developed new techniques at the Oxygen Hospital in London and later successfully applied his knowledge during the Second Boer and First World Wars. He is best remembered for his pioneer work in developing a successful method of healing sores, burns and other diseases using therapy involving mixtures of oxygen combined with ozone. Today, this very effective mode of treatment has advanced – to the extent that it is commonplace in medicine and dentistry.

The grasslands, woodlands and high elevations of Zululand are rich in indigenous plants which have always played a pivotal role in traditional native medicine. Almost every plant has a medicinal use. The traditional healer, in most if not all native tribes, was the witch doctor, who would make up remedies in various forms and perform procedures to treat wounds and sickness. Generally, the typical ailments among the native troops serving under the British were intermittent fever, diarrhoea and dysentery. It was common for natives and Zulus to eat meat from dying and diseased cattle which was often not properly cooked and therefore, caused much of the preventable sickness.

Natural medicines made from herbs and roots of trees and plants, were available for malaria, dysentery, diarrhoea, coughs, colds, influenza, pain, intestinal worms and rheumatism. The root, stem and leaves of the common fern would be crushed and boiled to be consumed to deal with intestinal worms. Other disorders of the bowels were treated with enemas, using a cow horn to pass copious amounts of fluids, preferably salty water, into the large intestine. This would be retained for as long as possible, even if the patient had to stand upside down. After expelling the contents, the process would be repeated a number of times to wash out any toxins. The belief in witchcraft was strong, and charms were often worn around the neck or tied to an afflicted part of the body. Another common practice in the treatment of disease was the process of cupping or scarification. This involved pinching a small fold of skin close to the problem, nicking the area with a sharp object and rubbing gunpowder or powdered roots into the fresh wound. At the same time, cattle would be sacrificed as part of the ritual of healing.

The use of traditional medicines derived from local plants could have greatly benefited the white soldiers. The besieged garrison at Eshowe lay within walking distance of a rich natural medicinal source, the Dlinza Forest. Fleet Surgeon Norbury experimented with some plant medicines but was likely unaware of the availability of numerous local herbs, bulbs, aloes, trees and planted ground cover which would have augmented his meagre medical supplies.

Reports regarding the ill-treatment of wounded Zulus filtered back to England, to the extent that the perception of blood thirsty vengeance for the defeat at Isandlwana would even extend to retribution against wounded and vulnerable Zulus. It is true that in the aftermath at Rorke's Drift, British troops spared no stragglers and wounded Zulus, particularly in view of the massacre at Isandlwana and the brutal slaying of several defenders in and around the hospital. Records regarding the medical treatment administered to the large number of wounded Zulu warriors after the battle are non-existent. Given the fact that this event has been thoroughly examined by writers, this suggests that medical care was definitely not administered by the vindictive British at Rorke's Drift. Captain Cardew acting as Deputy Adjutant and Quartermaster General (DAQMG) to Major General John Crealock and the 1st Division remarked on the bravery of the Zulu warriors and the undeserved brutal treatment of the wounded. He recounted an incident where:

> After one of the battles he himself heard the order given by one general 'Let Loose the Murderers', which meant to order out the native allies to kill the prisoners and all the wounded, and the killing was not confined to the Native allies, but the European soldiers, and even the officers took part in it.

The issue regarding the treatment of wounded Zulus captured by Chelmsford's troops was soon raised in the House of Commons. Unsubstantiated insinuations of cruelty towards Zulus wounded by British soldiers, including members of the AMD, were addressed by the Government. It reassured any doubters that the medical officers of the AMD always upheld the highest professional standards expected of them in caring for all wounded equally, regardless of their colour. Surgeon Major Cuffe, in writing to *The Times* newspaper with his comments concerning these issues, stated that the wounded Zulus cared for at the hospital in Utrecht were treated alongside Chelmsford's native invalids and administered proper care and attention. The prisoners made frequent remarks regarding the kindness shown, which, they admitted, would not have been reciprocated had British wounded fallen into the hands of the Zulus.

Generally, those fortunate Zulus that were given medical aid were reportedly well cared for. After Ulundi, some were given medical aid on the battlefield, while the severely wounded, where possible, were transported to Utrecht for treatment. Sister Janet Wells, stationed at the Utrecht Base

Hospital, came into contact with many wounded Zulus as patients and wrote of the treatment rendered to these men, for whom she developed a high respect. She noted that some Zulus refused major surgical treatment such as amputations where necessary, rendering the outcome very poor; but were nevertheless not denied the care required. Captain W. C. F. Molyneux witnessed an incident where an act of compassion by the British troops was noticed by Zulu messengers sent back to Ulundi during Cetshwayo's attempt to peacefully end hostilities without another slaughter in early June 1879. In his mind, this did enhance public relations. He wrote:

> These messengers, must have been reassured by one curious sight. That day an old Zulu woman, in the last stage of decrepitude, had been found in a deserted kraal; some men hearing moans proceeding from a bundle that looked like a chrysalis, had in the kindness of their hearts brought the nuisance into the camp. She had been wrapped up tightly in a fresh hide, raw side inwards, put out in the sun to harden (so that the skin might protect her from the dogs), and then deserted. Our men had cut a peephole for the naked skeleton, and were feeding her with green mealies, which is all she would eat; but her great joy was snuff made out of Cavendish tobacco. Our fellows did what they could for her till she died …and then gave her a decent burial.

Further acts of compassion were reported, including that of Lieutenant Colonel Lonsdale Hale, Royal Engineers, who demonstrated an interest in the welfare of Zulus who had lost all following the wholesale burning of their kraals in and around the Umlalazi Plains. During the evacuation of troops from Port Durnford in late August 1879, Hale organised a substantial distribution of mealies and mealie-meal to the near-starving natives.

Of Chelmsford's black irregular troops, Woolfryes reported that the records pertaining to sickness statistics among these men were not consistent with the high morbidity and sickness-related death rates when compared to those of the regulars and colonial volunteers. The surgeon general was of the opinion that these men preferred returning to their homes to be treated by their witch doctors, where the natives expected a higher success rate. Of a total recorded strength of 5,436 native irregulars, in addition to approximately 320 combat deaths, 766 men were admitted to hospital for a variety of sicknesses. Most of these were unclassified, whereas only thirty-nine required care for wounds sustained in action. Blair-Brown's treatment statistics for the men under his care at Helpmekaar and Ladysmith included eighty-four mounted Basutos. Accurate records available regarding the treatment of the sick and wounded black soldiers are limited and do not truly reflect the extent of the suffering experienced in these units.

Combat Stress, Sickness and Treatment

In the mid- to late-nineteenth century, insanity, melancholia, neurosis, nostalgia and exhaustion all described the effects related to combat stress or battle fatigue and anxiety. Such was the poor understanding and lack of recognition of a real medical disorder that in the 1870s, palpitations, irritability of the heart and debility were the recognised medical conditions that accounted for the seemingly irrational psychological behaviour of affected soldiers while on campaign. In writing about his experiences during the Anglo-Zulu War, Captain W. C. F. Molyneux, ADC to Chelmsford, commented on the effects of combat stress which gripped many soldiers:

> No one can account for the madness which seizes upon bodies of men at times. It is no use saying it is only the young soldiers that are thus affected; old ones may be less liable, but they are not impervious to it.

The human response to combat stress has not changed in the time since the Anglo-Zulu War. Some men crack while others do not. It is debatable whether the limits of resistance are determined by character, heredity, upbringing, ideology or simple biochemistry. True anxiety disorders can develop after exposure to a terrifying event in which grave physical harm has occurred or was threatened. Wounds to the mind left soldiers open to imputations of malingering, allegations of cowardice and even charges of desertion. However, understanding stress disorders and interpreting the response to combat has made great strides since the nineteenth century.

The prevalence of the effects of campaign experiences increase over time in soldiers subjected to both intense combat and non-combat stress. Today, we attribute many of the signs and symptoms to a condition known as Post Traumatic Stress Disorder (PTSD) which, in a chronic state, can last for many years. This debilitating anxiety disorder should not be confused with combat stress reactions, which is generally short term. In other words, as a psychiatric disorder, PTSD is different from depression, anxiety or fear in the face of battle. Soldiers in the nineteenth century, both officers and men, were not expected, and did their best not to, feel anxiety or display fear in the midst of combat. Medical officers attributed this to the stolid disposition of the average soldier, who showed no imagination or curiosity as to the future and even recollection of past stirring events. Generally, soldiers simply learned to accept the effect of a traumatic experience and to get on with their lives the best they could. This attitude was also rooted in the nineteenth century view of life and death among the poor, who represented the vast majority of enlisted men and quite simply accepted their station or class in society. There was little or no prospect of certainty, in an age of low life expectancy, to the extent that suffering in this group was not unexpected.

However, mental illness could not be considered in the restricted realm of degenerates with weak constitutions, when no one could account for the fact that officers were found to suffer disproportionately from stress disorders and were much more likely to be invalided home. In the war of nerves during the AZW, there are numerous accounts of inexperienced and often exhausted new recruits gripped by fear and behaving irrationally both in combat and on duty. In most circumstances, cooler heads prevailed with strong leadership from the officers. Rorke's Drift survivors were not immune from the long-term effects of the epic fight for survival, though most of those affected simply learned to live with the experiences and had normal lives thereafter. For years afterwards Private Robert Jones VC appeared to be tormented by flashbacks resulting from his experiences in defending the hospital at Rorke's drift, during which he received assegai wounds. The post traumatic effects may have been the cause of his recurring headaches and his suicide, which was officially determined as: 'Shot himself in the mouth being of unsound mind'. Other defenders, such as Corporal Ferdinand Scheiss and Private William Cooper, who died in unfortunate circumstances were probably suffering from depression not related to battle stress. Fleet Surgeon Norbury noted that the circumstances associated with the lingering siege at Eshowe produced a greatly increased incidence of anxiety among many of the defenders. He described this as a 'depression of spirits' which, if combined with sickness or hospitalisation, would compound the effects of the condition to the extent that recovery from any sickness would be made more difficult.

Upon entering the besieged garrison at Eshowe, Molyneux remarked that: 'Coast fever and typhoid had claimed many victims, while rough fare, watchfulness and anxiety had all set their mark on all'.

These men were generally considered to be debilitated, suffering from anaemia and somewhat affected by irritability of the heart if displaying such symptoms. Without doubt, fighting the Zulus was, for many soldiers, a terrifying experience, the prospect of which caused greater anxiety in most individuals as the campaign lingered.

Many medical officers believed that debility, palpitations or irritable heart also occurred among non-combat troops who laboured with heavy packs during long marches. The straps of the webbing were thought to place too much pressure on the chest which gradually restricted blood flow to the heart. Colonel Wood, in his memoirs, recalled the effect of eighteen months campaigning on his men and even himself, which he described as stress from the difficult military situation, especially in the three-month period following the disaster at Isandlwana. Wood was unable to sleep for more than 2-3 hours at a time and participated in sentry rounds twice nightly. Wood attributed this to his self-proclaimed 'state of high anxiety'.

A real attempt to establish stress disorders in the British army began twenty years after the AZW with the work of Dr Anthony Bowlby, civil surgeon during the Second Boer War. That campaign lasted three years and involved ten times the number of British troops compared to the war against the Zulus. With more time and a greater number of casualties, a proper analytical approach to assessment and understanding of sickness in the British army was possible. By the end of the nineteenth century, the terms palpitation, irritability of the heart and debility, had given way to 'disordered action of the heart' (DAH), and rheumatism. Bowlby failed to diagnose the actual presence of true mental disorders since he was too focused on DAH. Contemporary thinking once again attributed this condition to the effect of exertion on a soldier's chest by tight and restrictive webbing, which had been modified in the 1870s to deal with that particular issue. Clearly, the effects of the new webbing design and later alterations changed very little. However, he described many symptoms which are identical to many associated with today's understanding of PTSD.

He described headaches, neck pain and discomfort in the back and limbs all associated with general feebleness of the muscular system and paralysis. Many of the afflicted soldiers were sent to the hospital as cases of rheumatism. During the Second Boer War 3,631 servicemen were hospitalised with a diagnosis of DAH, with 41 per cent invalided back home. A further 24,460 troops were admitted for rheumatic fever or rheumatism, with 4,305 men sent home. However, a systematic investigation of war pension files at the Royal Hospital Chelsea revealed that most of these rheumatism-related pensioned veterans showed no objective signs of the disease within one year of discharge. This was remarkable as the unexpected, if not speedy, recovery from a condition with a poor prognosis, often resulting in death from heart failure, continued to perplex the medical establishment. Also, of a further 20,767 men hospitalised for debility in the period 1899-1902, many later appeared to have no demonstrable signs of organic disease of a somatic origin.

Accepting these records and the findings by Bowlby and his colleagues, it is possible to form a statistical impression of the extent of stress-related disorders on the British army campaigning against the Zulus. The number of British soldiers invalided during 1879 was much higher than expected due to hard campaigning. Seventy soldiers were invalided specifically for a diagnosis of palpitations caused by stress on the heart, compared to none in 1878 and 1880. Rheumatism and debility accounted for another 318 servicemen returning to Great Britain, compared to 9 in 1878 and 51 in 1880. Later, a retrospective analysis of the incidence of mental diseases from 1886-1908 by Lieutenant Colonel A. G. Kay showed an association between increased incidence and war. The rates of both admission and discharges rose significantly between 1899–1902; the most prevalent forms were depressive and delusional disorders. With regularity, DAH had become a convenient diagnosis during the Second Boer War.

In Queen Victoria's army, treatment of stress disorders, which were clearly either undiagnosed or misdiagnosed, consisted of rest and morale reviving efforts for most men. Acutely affected soldiers could expect no help financially or medically if discharged without a proper diagnosis. Even seeking advice from a doctor in civilian life, might land someone in a lunatic asylum. During a campaign, the emphasis on rest and the provision of comforts in the form of tobacco, healthy beverages, brandy, good food and reading materials, was deemed paramount to restoring one's mental constitution. At Eshowe, Molyneux stated that upon greeting members of the garrison:

> The universal cry was want of tobacco, tea leaves and coffee grounds being carefully preserved, dried and smoked; otherwise they were not in actual want.

In the majority of cases where combat stress and other non-specific disorders had taken their toll, the availability of quality comforts quite likely eased the tormented mind. Since improving and maintaining optimal health and morale was key to preventing these problems, Colonel Wood demonstrated his leadership qualities further during the second invasion of Zululand by ensuring that that his men were fed well. His Flying Column was treated as much as possible to fresh bread from field ovens on a daily basis, to the extent that he simply ignored written concerns from the Commissariat expressing alarm at the overdrawing of rations. Wood's eventual response was uncompromising, since he considered that his men had captured enough cattle to settle any trade with the Department.

Since the mid-nineteenth century, wars have been associated with a syndrome characterised by unexplainable symptoms. While psychiatric casualties were scarcely acknowledged and still less treated, a debility syndrome with or without somatic characteristics was accepted by the military medical establishment as a plausible diagnosis during the AZW. The terminology associated with this affliction has changed over time and today, with advances in medical science, the same disorder is arguably recognised as a neuropsychiatric syndrome. Few reliable psychiatric casualty statistics are available for wars fought in the nineteenth century and given the inconsistent nature of diagnosis, at best, any figures remain estimates.

Footnote: Major Ronald Ross of the Royal Army Medical Corps spent most of his working life trying to solve the 'great problem' of how malaria affected soldiers. He knew that soldiers throughout the British Empire were dying in unacceptable numbers from fever and, being astute, he also knew that whoever solved the problem would reap the rewards. He sought to resolve the problem in Europe, through Africa to India but finally found the solution by looking through a microscope, eventually receiving the Nobel Prize in 1920.

Appendix 8

Sister Janet's Obituary

The Times, Saturday June 10, 1911

The death took place on Tuesday last at Wood View, Purley, of Mrs. George King (Sister Janet, Royal Red Cross and Imperial Cross of Russia).

Janet Helen King was the daughter of Prof. Benjamin King, ARAM., and was born in London. When she was but 18 years of age, deeply impressed by the accounts of the suffering of those fighting in the struggle between Servian Independence and Turkish supremacy, and impelled by a high sense of duty, she entered the Protestant Deaconess's Institution to be trained for nursing the sick and wounded in war. Quickly becoming proficient, she was selected as one of a party of nine sent out by that institution to assist in nursing the sick and wounded engaged in the war between Russia and Turkey in 1877-78. The party proceeded to Bucharest under orders to the Russian National Red Cross Society, and were there directed to join the army of the Tsarevitch, which was operating on the Lom. They travelled by railway as far as Fratesti thence in rough carts to Semnitza and crossing the Danube by the bridge of boats to Sistova, where they waited for an escort to Vardin. Sistova was at the time of their arrival not only crowded with wounded from Plevna, but was being ravaged by typhus, so that the sisters found plenty of work to do while they were detained there. The escort having been provided, the sisters continued their journey in rough carts, suffering on the way from much privation from the bitter cold.

At Vardin they found their services sorely needed, and throughout the winter months they worked from early morning until late at night. Sister Janet was placed in charge of 200 patients who lay in huts scattered among the hills. More than once as she passed from hut to hut on her daily mission she was attacked by the wild dogs, and twice she was attacked by Bashi-

Bazook patients. Communication across the Danube was stopped, coarse black bread was the only diet, and there was no news from home. When the army of Suleiman Pasha was driven back on Rustchuk the sisters were sent there, experiencing another terrible journey. Half of them were down with typhus, and Sister Janet was so severely tried in nursing her companions that on the capitulation of Rustchuk she returned to England, having been decorated for her services with the Imperial Order of the Red Cross of Russia.

Sister Janet was appointed Superintendent of the hospital at Newcastle-on-Tyne, and was selected by the Stafford House Committee for service with Surgeon General Ross in the Zulu War. At Utrecht, 3,200 sick and wounded passed through her hands, many of her patients being Zulus. Sir Garnet Wolseley, when he visited the hospital at Utrecht, personally thanked Sister Janet for her work, and on the conclusion of the war she was awarded the South Africa medal and received from Queen Victoria the decoration of the Royal Red Cross for 'the special devotion and competency displayed in nursing duties with her majesty's troops'.

Sister Janet married Mr George King in 1882.

The funeral service takes place today at St. Mark's, Purley at half past 2.

(Similar obituaries appeared in most regional newspapers, across the depth and breadth of the United Kingdom).

The 'Part Time' Zulu Army

By 1879 it was believed across Natal that everything about Zulu society was based around its military structure, forgetting that the Zulus relied on its warriors meeting with arms only once a year for just two weeks' national service; it was not a regular, armed army. As soon as young Zulu men attained the age of about 16 years, known as *inkwebane*, they were formed into fledgling companies or *amaviyo*, which after a year's probation would be placed in a regular *ibutho* or regiment. This first year bonded the young warriors and symbolised the transition from boyhood to manhood. The new *inkwebane* might either belong to another regiment with which the young one was incorporated, or it might be newly formed. As a rule, several regiments of different ages were combined at the same *ikhanda* or barracks so that the young soldiers might have the benefit of the experience of their seniors, and on the latter dying out, might take their place and maintain the name and prestige of the *ikhanda*. In this manner loyal corps were formed, occasionally some thousands strong, and their duties required them to undertake a form of national service, to be trained in a number of social duties, including general policing, farming crops and guarding the king's cattle, but also, when called upon, to join their allocated regiment as a fighting warrior.

The Zulu army was soundly structured and consisted of twelve such corps, each with one or more regiments with its own *ikhanda*. These corps necessarily contained men of all ages, some being married, others unmarried, some being old men scarcely able to walk and others boys. Five of these corps consisted of a single regiment, while the remaining corps was composed of several regiments. Each corps or regiment possessed its own military *ikhanda* and was controlled by one commander, one second-in-command and several junior commanders who controlled the flanks in action. The uniform of the Zulu army was clearly laid down and was different in each corps. The great distinction was between the married and unmarried regiments. The former were obliged to shave the crown of the head and to wear a ring made of hemp and coated with a hardened paste of gum and grease; they also carried shields with predominately white colouring, whereas the unmarried regiments wore their hair naturally and had coloured shields.

By the time of the Zulu War, the total number of regiments in the Zulu army amounted to thirty-four, of whom eighteen were married and sixteen unmarried. Seven of the former were composed of men over sixty years of age, so that for practical purposes there were only twenty-seven Zulu regiments fit to take the field, amounting to some 44,000 warriors. By 1878 Lord Chelmsford's intelligence confirmed that King Cetshwayo had in excess of 40,000 warriors at his disposal: 17,000 between twenty and thirty years of age; 14,500 between thirty and forty; 5,900 between forty and fifty; and 4,500 between fifty and sixty.

The *ibutho* in residence at Ulundi was the uThulwana. These were the men who looked after the king, and their work was rarely of a military nature; they maintained the nearby military *amakhanda*, the royal homesteads, and engaged in planting, reaping and fulfilling the king's wishes. Each *amakhanda* was cared for by a skeleton staff and was only occupied when the King called up its *ibutho*. There were twenty-seven *amakhanda* scattered about the Kingdom. Thirteen of them were located in the region of the Mahlabatini Plain, near Cetshwayo's residence at Ulundi. Ulundi itself was a huge complex of some 1,200 huts whose garrison was more-or-less permanently in residence.

Until 1878, the machine of military service in Zululand was, in effect, an integral part of everyday life in the kingdom, although, unlike the British army of the time, the part-time Zulu army was neither professional nor well trained. The only military training Zulu warriors received took place during their initial induction into their age-set regiment; in all matters they relied on instructions from their *indunas* who, in turn, demanded absolute obedience from their warriors. Tactical drill was unknown to the Zulu army, though they could perform a number of essential movements with some accuracy, such as forming a circle of companies or regiments. Their skirmishing skills were extremely good, and in the coming war would be performed under heavy fire with the utmost determination. The officers had specific duties and responsibilities according to their rank, and discipline was most rigidly enforced. Commodore Sullivan, writing in August 1878, gave an accurate account of the discipline of the Zulu army. He stated that the regiments were so well disciplined that: 'The men never fell out of the ranks on the march under any pretext; they marched at the double, and were said to keep up from 50 to 60 miles daily, carrying their own provisions.'

Each year's *umKhosi* or 'First Fruits' ceremony at Ulundi was traditionally held for the king to review his assembled regiments and herds of cattle. It was also the occasion for young men who had attained the age of about 16 years, known as *inkwebane*, to be formed into companies or *amaviyo*, which after a year's probation was placed in a regular *ibutho* or regiment. This first year also symbolised the transition from boyhood to manhood as a warrior. The new *inkwebane* might either belong to another regiment with which the young one was incorporated, or it might be newly formed. As a rule, several regiments of different ages were combined at the same *ikhanda* or barracks so that the young soldiers might have the benefit of the experience of their seniors, and on the latter dying out, might take their place and maintain the name and prestige of the *ikhanda*. In this manner loyal corps were formed, occasionally some thousands strong.

Due to the British invasion unfurling and war clearly on the horizon, certain additional and important pre-war ceremonies took place on arriving at Ulundi. Various medicines and potions were administered to the gathering warriors to enhance their fighting capacity and render them immune from British firepower. On the third day after their assembly at the king's homestead, the medicine men sprinkled the warriors with magical muti or medicine, and after all necessary formalities were completed the warriors commenced their long march of some seventy miles towards the British border with Natal. The march was initially led by a corps specially nominated by the king, followed by the remainder of the army along the *umsila*, the path beaten down through the grass by the advance corps. The advancing Zulu army would have been similar to a British division advancing in line of brigade columns, each brigade in mass, each regiment in close column. The line of provision-bearers moved on the flank. The intervals between the head of columns varied, according to circumstances, from several miles to within sight of each other, and with constant communication being kept up by runners. The march continued in this order, but the baggage and provision-bearers fell in at the rear of the column on the second day and the cattle composing the commissariat were driven between them and the rearmost regiment until the force approached the advancing British force. When the latter were within striking distance the whole army formed an *umkumbi*, or gathering, for the purpose of enabling the Commander-in-Chief to address the men and to give his final orders for attack.

Chelmsford made an arrogant error in choosing his invasion date to coincide with the annual *umKhosi* assembly of Cetshwayo's regiments at Ulundi. Had he invaded Zululand a week earlier or later, the massed regiments would have been back in their villages, widely scattered across Zululand – and most unlikely to re-assemble en-mass at Ulundi in time to oppose Chelmsford's invasion. Likewise, this 'fear' of a Zulu invasion of Natal was not as singular or to the point as it seemed. Beneath Frere and Chelmsford's veneer of their apparently laudable crusade to protect Natalians lay more subtle practical and commercial causes, including the subjugation of the Zulu people in order to facilitate the British policy of Confederation in South Africa. This was itself a smokescreen to support European commercial interests, both in Natal and the diamond fields, who needed access to the Zulu workforce. Almost as important, Frere considered the suppression of Zulu militancy was vital to protect the growing number of Boers, British subjects since the 1877 British annexation of the Transvaal, settling in Zululand. At the same time such suppression would, theoretically, confirm Britain's military invincibility to any potential adversary. It would also ensure the vainglorious Frere and Chelmsford honourable places in history.

Notes

Chapter 1

1. Lieutenant RA. (See Appendix 1 for Curling's letters home.)
2. *Cetywayo and his White Neighbours*, Haggard, Henry Rider.
3. Confirmed by *Cetshwayo's Dutchman*, Vign, Cornelius. (Vign was a young Dutchman who, during the war, was the only white man to be accepted by King Cetshwayo to live in the Zulu camp, which enabled him to observe the war from the Zulu perspective).
4. *Historical Records of the 24th Regiment, from its Formation in 1689*, Col. George Paton; Col. Glennie etc. Curiously, there was a fully equipped company of the 1st Battalion that appear to have been completely forgotten during the war. Patton wrote: *On 17th August, 1878, Captain Harrison and Lieutenants Spring and Roche, with B Company 1st Battalion 24th, consisting of four sergeants, five corporals, two drummers, and seventy-four privates, marched from King William's Town to the mouth of St. John's, or Ununvarboo, River, in Pondoland, where a settlement had been purchased from the Pondo chief, N'quaci. The British flag was hoisted there for the first time by Lieutenant General the Honble. T. A. Thesiger, C.B., on the 24th August, 1878, and an earthwork, to which the name of Fort Harrison was given, was thrown up by the detachment. B (later H) company remained at St. John's River mouth throughout the period of the subsequent Zulu War.* Because they were stationed just across the river from Natal they were not entitled to the South Africa campaign medal. Forgotten indeed. They may well have had a dull time – very different from that of their unfortunate colleagues. After the war the fort was dismantled.
5. Crealock Journal.
6. *Crossing the Buffalo.*
7. *ILN.*
8. When hostilities ended, the captured King Cetshwayo was taken off from Port Durnford by surfboat and into exile.
9. *Reminiscences of the Zulu War*, Maxwell, J., University of Cape Town, 1979.
10. Keens of London supplied mustard to the troops.
11. *ILN.*
12. *Lord Chelmsford and the Zulu War*, The Hon. French, Unwin Brothers, 1939.
13. *Journal from December 21st 1878 to February 29th 1880*, Hutton, Howard. 28 March 1879.

Chapter 2

1. *AZWHS*, Journal 7.
2. The salacious details of Eugénie's mother's lifestyle are fully reported in David Duff's book. *Eugénie and Napoleon III.* See Appendix 2 for the family tree of the prince.
3. *AZWHS* Journal 7.
4. Ibid.

5. Ibid.

6. As a clinical psychologist, I believe that Louis was destined from birth to become a neurotic extrovert. At first sight, this might indicate him to be a gregarious, flamboyant risk-taker keen to impress. He may well have appeared to everyone as such, but in psychological terms he had serious and destructive psychological problems. Before I proceed, I will define my terms. The eminent psychologist, Adler, originally defined neuroticism as the need to offset inner insecurity by displaying unusual behaviour. To a modern psychologist, a neurotic is one who coerces his environment – in order to gain control of events or people, or to be the centre of attention – a definition that clearly extends that of Adler. This need is usually based on childhood insecurity and subsequent neurotic behaviour and is the adult attempt to redress such inner, even subconscious, insecurity. This deficiency neatly ties in with a modern interpretation of extrovertism. An extrovert is one who 'shows out' behaviour in order to make up for under-arousal, usually as a child. Children who are controlled or repressed, frequently because they have suffered the controlling influence of the parental 'learning curve' need, in teens and onwards, to express themselves to make up this deficiency. It is common for adventurers and 'high-flyers' to come from strict families and many are the first born. Subsequent siblings are more relaxed as their parents settle into parenthood.

7. *AZWHS*, Journal 7, June 2000.

8. *The Washing of the Spears*, Morris, Donald.

9. Given that the climate was very hot and personal hygiene was haphazard, it is likely that the prince was suffering Dhobi Itch; a painful and debilitating condition of the upper legs and backside, especially unpleasant for the cavalry on long hot campaigns. This could have seriously restricted his movement, especially when mounting his horse, and may have cost him his life.

10. *The Washing of the Spears.*

11. The custom of a Zulu warrior was that if he killed an enemy he was permitted to slit the victim's stomach to allow its soul to escape. This was first seen at the Battle of Isandlwana, with severe mutilation of corpses that would shock the Victorian public and further reinforce their 'civilised' ideology.

12. The National Army Museum, Surgeon Major F. B Scott, Army Medical Staff (6807-386-11-6312/180).

13. *In Zululand with the British Throughout the War of 1879*, Norris-Newman, Charles, W.H. Allen, London, 1880.

14. *The Washing of the Spears.*

15. *The Washing of the Spears.*

16. *The Illustrated London News*, 5 July, 1879.

17. Ibid.

18. Ibid.

19. *The London Times*, 23 August 1879.

20. Ibid.

21. Ibid.

Chapter 3

1. Chelmsford's *Zululand Campaign.*

2. *Redcoats and Zulus*, personal account from a grandson of Zibhebhu. Near the banks of the stream the grass itself had been carefully plaited, leaving only a small opening

through which the British could enter, then trip the horses. Had Buller's men ridden just a few more yards, they would have been surrounded.

3. *Campaigns of a War Correspondent*, London, 1912. Personal account to the author from Mr Paul Cebekhulu, a grandson of Zibhebhu kaMaphitha, Black Mfolozi district, January 1997.

4. *Campaigning in South Africa and Egypt*, Melton Prior, London, 1896, Maj. Gen. W. C. F. Molyneux. Contrary to popular belief, there was no evidence that Trooper Raubenheim was tortured. His body was found mutilated on 4 July where he had fallen. The grass had been trampled where Zulus had gathered around the body to cut off certain body parts. There are no authenticated examples of torture employed by the Zulus during the Anglo Zulu War although, at Isandlwana, post death mutilations included the disarticulation by the Zulus of dead soldiers' jawbones for trophies, complete with beards. Facial hair was relatively unknown to the warriors and the luxurious beards worn by the soldiers fascinated them. Despite the soldiers' deep-seated fears that these mutilations were carried out before death, and therefore amounted to torture, there is no evidence that this was in fact the case. Interestingly, post Isandlwana, the practice of shaving became widespread throughout the army. Soldiers accepted the necessity of dying for their country but were reluctant to be disarticulated after death on the battlefield. Author's *Mail on Sunday* article, February 2006.

5. *The Graphic.*

6. Ibid.

7. Anstruther papers, NAM.

8. Chelmsford's report, British Parliamentary Papers, C. 2482.

9. Ibid.

Chapter 4

1. *Colenso Papers*, Folio 26, 25 July 1879, Bishop John William Colenso.

2. *Campaigns of a War Correspondent*, Prior, Melton. London, 1912.

3. Ibid.

4. *In Zululand with the British*, Norris-Newman, Charles, W. H. Allen, 1880.

5. British Parliamentary Papers, c 2482, Chelmsford.

6. *Campaigns of a War Correspondent*. Unfortunately, several of Prior's known pre-Ulundi sketches were not published. They were amongst the portfolio of sketches he lost during the Battle of Ulundi which have never come to light.

7. c 2482.

8. Drury-Lowe, official report.

9. *The Red Soldier*, 1977, reporting for the *Cape Argus* 'The Battle of Ulundi'.

10. *The Graphic*, 20 September 1879.

Chapter 5

1. *Parliamentary Papers*, W. E. Gladstone, London, 1879.

2. *AZWHS*, Journal 2, Dr Alan Spicer RAMC.

3. *The SA Journal of Sir Garnet Wolseley 1879-80*, entry for 21 August 1879.

4. *Anstruther Papers*, NAM.

5. From the genus *caecilian* (legless amphibians). Caecilians closely resemble burrowing snakes, but do not have external scales. They range in size from inches to several feet, with diameters up to an inch or two. Caecilians are carnivorous creatures, eating insects,

insect larvae, and worms in the wild. Some caecilians are oviparous (egg-layers), some viviparous (livebearers), and a few are ovoviviparous (the eggs hatch inside the mother where the young live in her until maturity). Many land-bound caecilians live their life burrowed underground. There are no known species in Europe, North America, Australia, or Antarctica.

6. *South African Journal,* Wolseley, 12 July 1879.
7. *AZWHS,* Journal 3.
8. *Crossing the Buffalo.*
9. Wolseley's Journal, 19 July 1879.
10. *Anstruther Papers,* NAM.
11. c 2482.

Chapter 6

1. *Colenso Papers,* 25 July 1879.
2. *Anstruther Papers,* NAM.
3. *Harford.*
4. *Papers of Lt. H. A. Amyatt-Burney,* NAM, London. Also, patience has its reward for Major Marter. Later in the campaign, he was to gain recognition and promotion to Brevet Lieutenant Colonel for leading the patrol that captured the Zulu king, Cetshwayo.
5. An *ILN* correspondent.
6. *Anstruther Papers,* NAM.
7. WO 32/7709. Also, ibid.
8. *AZWHS,* Journal 2. See also Appendix 3.
9. The *Further Correspondence* relates to personal letters in the *Blue Books* which Frere believed, until his dying day, vindicated him.
10. *The Zulu Kings,* Roberts, 1974. Also, the collection of George Chadwick letters.
11. Ibid.
12. Ibid.

Chapter 7

1. Wolseley Papers, 20 November 1879.

Chapter 8

1. *The Scramble for Africa,* Packenham, T., Abacus, 1991. Quoting Sir Garnet Wolseley to Sir Michael Hicks Beach, October 1879.
2. *War and Peace in South Africa – The Writings of P. Anstruther and E. Essex,* Butterfield, 1986 for a full account.
3. Ibid.
4. *The Scramble for Africa.*
5. Official accounts of eyewitnesses at Bronkhorstspruit, PRO WO 32/7825.

Chapter 9

1. *Reluctant Rebellion,* Marks, S., Oxford, 1970.
2. *The Rise and Fall of the Zulu Nation.* Laband, John, 1997.
3. Ibid.

4. *The Last Zulu King*, Binns, C. T., Longmans, London, 1963. For confirmation and an overview of a number of conspiracy theories relating to the king's death, see *The Natal Witness* articles printed in June 1886.

5. Anti-slavery papers *Colenso to Chesson 19 February 1884*. The Zulus called him Sobantu 'Father of the People' and the last honest white man. Bishop Colenso died in 1883 of an unidentified illness. Harriet Colenso rejected the belief that it was poison. 'So many and so minute are the precautions on this point which habitually surround a Zulu king. His clothes, his food, his very sticks all have their own carefully chosen guardians ... all this was habitual etiquette'.

6. *The Medical Times*, 1879.

7. *Destruction of the Zulu Kingdom*, Guy, Jeff, Longmans, 1979.

Chapter 10

1. See CO 879/25 Havelock to Granville, 15 March 1886 – quoted in *The Destruction of the Zulu Kingdom*, by Prof. Guy, J. Longmans, Bristol, 1979.

2. *Cetshwayo and his White Neighbours*, Haggard, H. Rider. London, 1882 and Gibson's *Story of the Zulus* Gibson, J. Y., Longmans, London, 1911 for agreement with this theory.

Chapter 11

1. *Colonial Office Papers*, Wolseley 879/16, 204. No. 151.

2. *The South African Journal of Sir Garnet Wolseley*, Preston, A., Cape Town, 1973.

3. Ibid. However, *The Illustrated London News* of 18 October 1879 wrote: 'In the entire history of Natal as a British province, no Zulu invasion has ever been attempted or threatened; no colonist or settler has ever yet been molested or annoyed by any of the Zulus. And the Lieutenant General of Natal, who should know best, has invariably denied that there was any danger of a Zulu attack on that side'.

4. *Zulu Kings and their Armies*, Sutherland, Jonathan and Carwell, Diane.

5. Paper by a Mr Brownlee – Secretary for Native Affairs in the Cape Colony

6. *The Zulu War: Islandhlwana and Rorke's Drift*, Furneaux, Rupert, J. B. Lippincott, 1963.

7. *Cetshwayo's Dutchman*: Journal of Vijn Cornelius, *Zulu Kings and their Armies*, Sutherland, Jonathan and Carwell, Diane.

8. *Zulu Battle Piece: Isandhlwana*, Coupland, Sir Reginald, Tom Donovan Publishing Ltd, 1948.

9. *The South African Journal of Sir Garnet Wolseley*, Preston, A., Cape Town, 1973.

10. Ibid.

11. Ibid. John Dunn, a local trader and known as a white Zulu chief, had befriended King Cetshwayo prior to the war. He became an influential advisor to King Cetshwayo, who appointed him to the rank of chief and gave him title to land bordering the Tugela River. Dunn then changed sides for the duration of the war, reverting to the Zulus post-war.

12. British Parliamentary Papers, C. 2482.

13. Colonial Office Papers, 879/16, 204. No. 49.

14. Colonial Office Papers, 879/16, 204. No. 123.

15. Colonial Office Papers, 879/17, 215. No. 151

16. *A Review of The South African Campaign of 1879*, Greaves and Knight, Debinair Publishing, 2000. Also, the Zulu War had a hidden and lethal sting in the tail; the war had convinced the watching Boer politicians and generals that the British army was not invincible. Encouraged by widespread discontent against British interests throughout

the Transvaal, the Boer community made secret preparations to resist further British influence. Only six months later in 1881 they commenced military action against the British at Majuba; it was a conflict that brought early disasters to the British and which developed into an even bloodier campaign, the two Boer Wars.
17. For a full account of the changes, see *Shaka's Children: A History of the Zulu People*, Taylor, S.
18. *Zulu Victory*, Lock and Quantrill. These cairns were carefully excavated and repaired by the official archaeological team from Glasgow University during 2000. (Author present).

Appendix 1
1. *The Curling Letters of the Zulu War*, Greaves and Best, Pen and Sword, 2001.
2. *Invasion of Zululand*, Clark, Sonia.
3. Ibid.
4. *Campaigns of a War Correspondent*, Prior, Melton.
5. Ibid.
6. *AZWHS*, December 1999.
7. *The Curling Letters of the Zulu War.*
8. *Invasion of Zululand.*
9. *East Kent Times*, 2 January 1910. Curling's grave is situated on the outer right side of Ramsgate Cemetery.

Appendix 3
1. Account recorded by Evelyn Wood, in *From Midshipman to Field Marshal*, London 1907.
2. Ibid.
3. Ibid.
4. *Journals of the AZWHS*. For further information, see *AZWHS Journal, June 1998*. Articles by Dr Andy Traverse. Also, see *Surgical Experiences in the Zulu War*, Surgeon Blair-Brown.
5. *AZWHS Journal*, 'Medical Services and Military Medicine during the Anglo-Zulu war of 1879' by Dr Andres Traverse.

Bibliography

Anglo Zulu War Historical Society Journals 1 – 57

Ashe, W. and Edgell, E., *The Story of the Zulu Campaign*, Sampson Low, 1880

Atkinson, C. T., *The South Wales Borderers 24th Foot 1689-1937*, Cambridge, 1937

Bryant, A. T., *The Zulu People*, Shuter & Shooter, 1949

Bulpin, T. V., *Shaka's Country*, Howard Timms, Capetown, 1952

Chadwick, George, *The Zulu War of 1879*, The Natal Educational Activities Association, undated

Clarke, Sonia, *Invasion of Zululand*, Brenthurst, South Africa, 1979

Clements, W., *The Glamour and Tragedy of the Zulu War*, Bodley Head, 1936

Colenso, Francis, *History of the Zulu War and its Origins*, Chapman and Hall Ltd, London, 1880

Colenso, John William, *Colenso Papers*, 25 July 1879

Cope, Richard, *The Ploughshare of War*, University of Natal Press, 1999

Coupland, R., *Isandhlwana: Zulu Battle Piece*, Collins, 1948

Creswicke, Louis, *The Zulu War*, E. C. Jack, Edinburgh, 1900

Cunynghame, Sir A., *My Command in South Africa*, Macmillan, 1879

Droogleever, R., *The Road to Isandhlwana*, Greenhill Books, 1979

Emery, F., *The Red Soldier*, London, 1977

Etherington, Norman, *Anglo Zulu Relations 1856–1878 – New Perspectives*, University of Natal Press, 1981

French, The Hon. Gerald, *Lord Chelmsford and the Zulu War*, Unwin, 1939

Glover, M., *Rorke's Drift*, Wordsworth Military Library, 1997

Gon, P., *The Road to Isandlwana*, London, 1979

Grant, James, *British Battles on Land and Sea*, Cassell, 1898

Greaves, Adrian and Best, Brian, *The Curling Letters of the Zulu War*, Pen & Sword, 2001

Greaves, Adrian, *Fields of Battle – Isandlwana*, Cassell, 2001

Greaves, Adrian, *Rorke's Drift*, Cassell, 2002

Guy, J. J., 'A Note on Firearms in the Zulu Kingdom with Special Reference to the Anglo-Zulu War, 1879', *Journal of African History*, Volume 12, Issue 4, 1971, pp.557–70

Guy, J. J., *The Destruction of the Zulu Kingdom*, J. Longmans, 1979

Hamilton-Browne, *A Lost Legionary in South Africa*, Werner Laurie, London, 1890

Hope, Robert, *The Zulu War and the 80th Regiment of Foot*, Churnet Valley Books, 1997

Laband, John and Thompson, Paul Singer with Sheila Henderson, *The Buffalo Border*, University of Natal, 1983

Laband, John, *Lord Chelmsford's Zululand Campaign*, Alan Sutton Publishing, 1996

Laband, John, *Rope of Sand*, Jonathan Ball, Johannesburg, 1995

Leach, Graham, *The Afrikaners*, Mandarin, 1989

Lord Chelmsford's Zululand Campaign, Army Records Society Vol. 10, 1994

Lloyd, Lt., *On Active Service*, Chapman and Hall, 1890

Meintjes, Johannes, *The Voortrekkers*, Corgi, 1973

Milton, John, *The Edges of War – A History of Frontier Wars 1702-1878*, Juta and Co., Cape Town, 1983

Montague, W. E., *Campaigning in South Africa*, Blackwood, 1880

Morris, Sir Frederick, and Arthur, Sir George, *The Life of Lord Wolseley*, London, 1924

Morris, Donald, *The Washing of the Spears*, Simon and Shuster, New York, 1965 (First Edition)

Mossop, George, *Running the Gauntlet*, Nelson, 1937

Newman-Norris, Charles, *In Zululand with the British Throughout the War of 1879*, W. H. Allen, London, 1880

O'Connor, Damian P., *The Zulu and the Raj – The Life of Sir Bartle Frere*, Able Publishing, 2002

Payne, Emma and Payne, David, *The Harford Diaries*, Ultimatum Tree, 2008

Preston, A., *The South African Journal of Sir Garnet Wolseley*, Cape Town, 1973

Prior, Melton, *Campaigns of a War Correspondent*, London, 1912

Reyburn, Lindsay, *The 1879 Zulu War Diaries of RSM F. W. Cheffins*, Private Printing, Pretoria 2001

Reynolds, Charles, *A Civil Surgeon*, Diary entry dated 27 January 1879, Private Publication, 2003

Ritter, E., *Shaka Zulu*, Penguin, 1955

Smith-Dorrien, H., *Memories of Forty-Eight Years Service*, Murray, 1925

Stalker, John, *The Natal Carbineers 1855-1911*, Davis and Son, 1912

Temple, B., *A Treatise on the British Martini-Henry*, Greenhill Books, 1983

Van der Post, L., *The Heart of the Hunter*, Penguin, 1923

War Office, *Précis of Information*, 1879

Whitehouse, Howard (Ed.), *A Widow-Making War: Life and Death of a British Officer in Zululand*, Paddy Griffith Associates, 1995

Wilmot, A., *The Zulu War*, London, 1880

Wood, Sir Evelyn, *Midshipman to Field Marshal*, Vol. 2, Methuen, 1906

Worsfold, W., *Sir Bartle Frere: A Footnote to the History of the British Empire*, London, 1923

Index